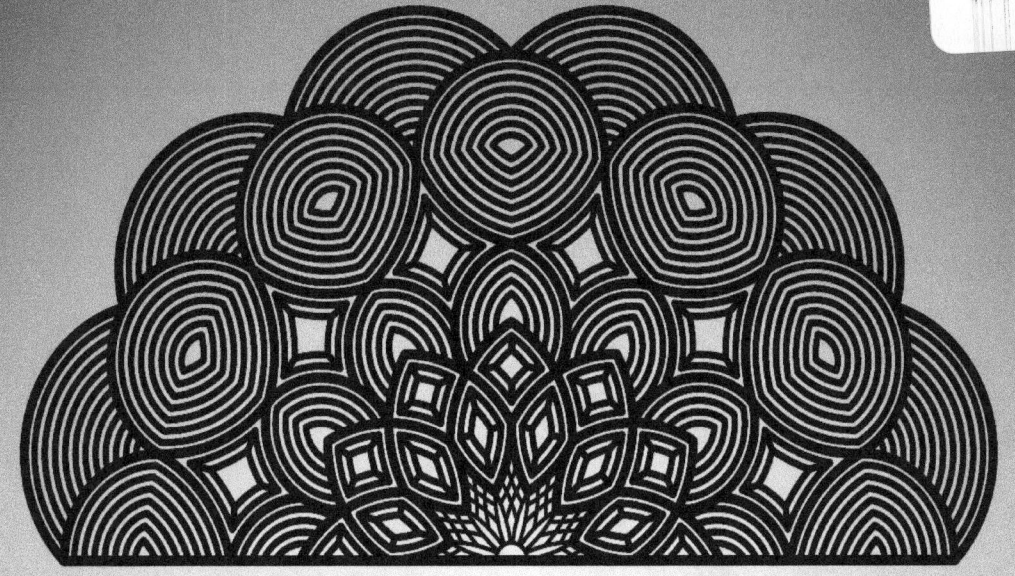

The Dime -A- Design Mandala Coloring Book

A Collection of 100 Distinctively Unique Mandalas and Sacred Geometry Coloring Pages For Adults of Every Skill Level!

By: Kaleb Williams

Copyright © 2019 Kaleb Williams- All Rights Reserved

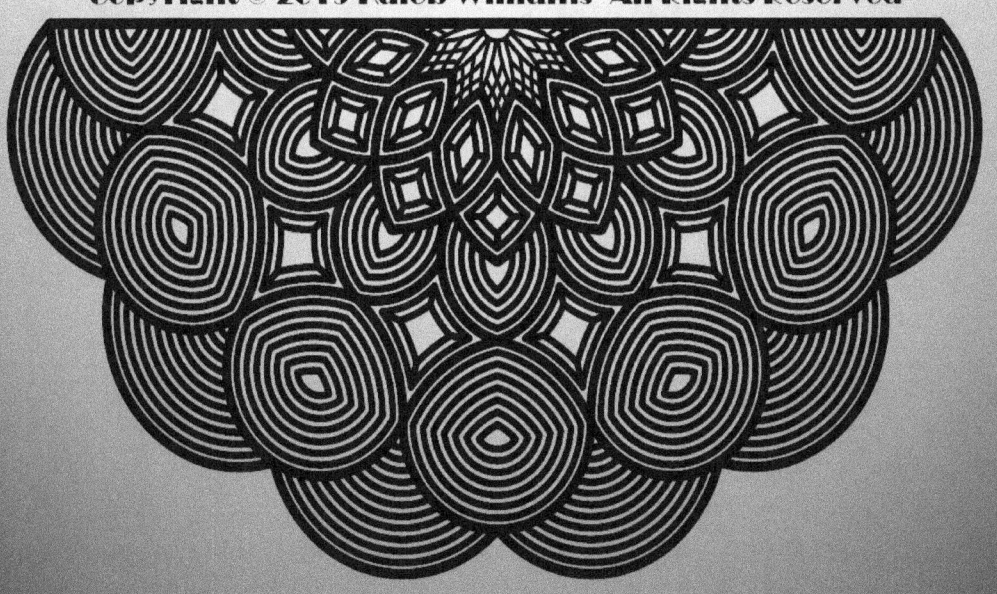

Copyright © 2019 Kaleb Williams.

All rights reserved. Copy and redistribution of this book is strictly prohibited with out the written permission of the author.

Distributed by: kindle direct publishing

Contact on:

Instagram: @kalebskreationz

Facebook: Kaleb's Geometry

Shout out to my beyond extraordinary wife, Lacie Williams, and to the rest of my loving family and friends who have been so supportive of me though out all of this. I thank you guys so much. I wouldn't be here without the support of you all!!!

And Thank you for your support by purchasing this coloring book!!!!! It means the world!!! Please share your finished pages with me on social media. I'd Love to see them!

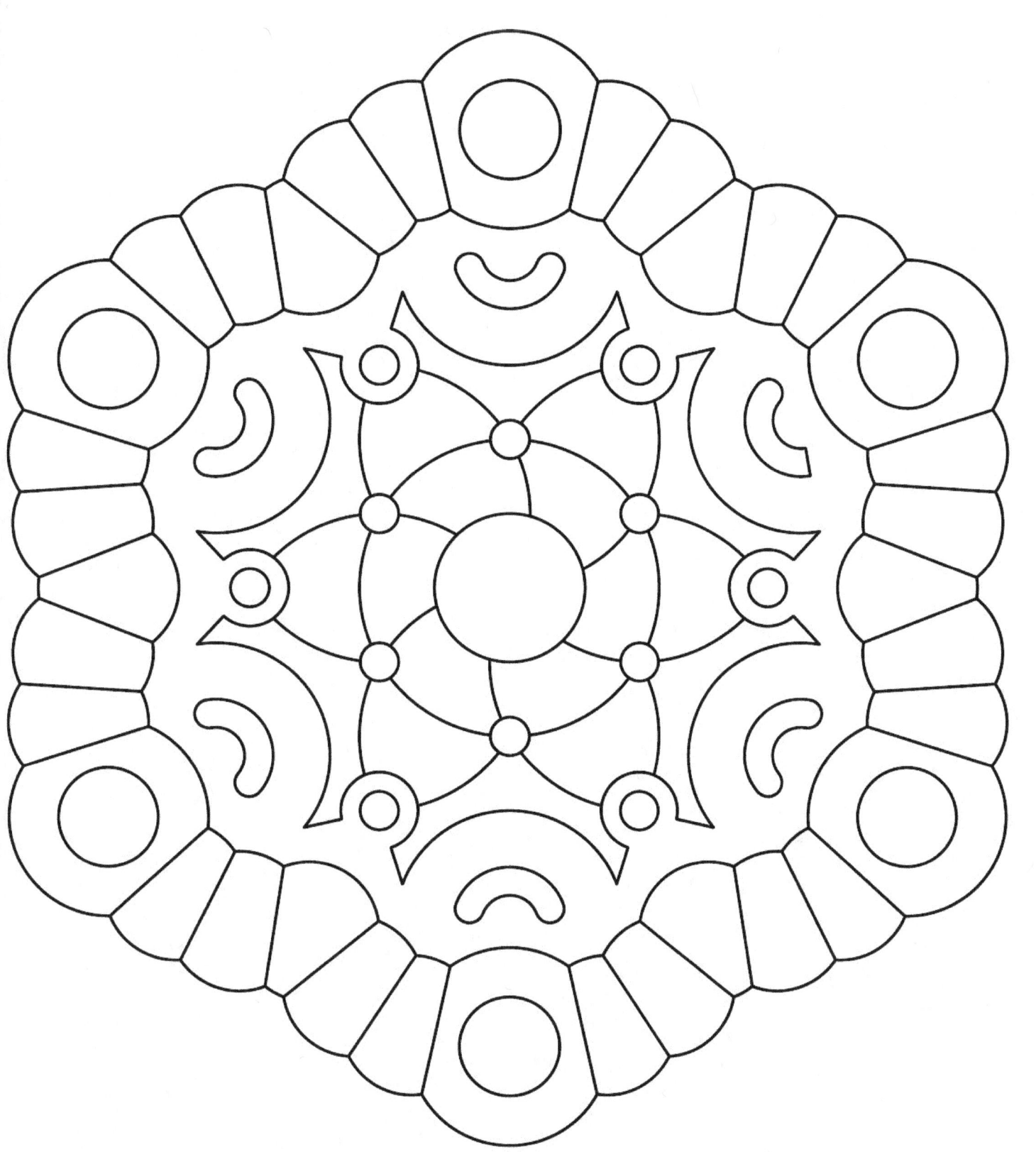

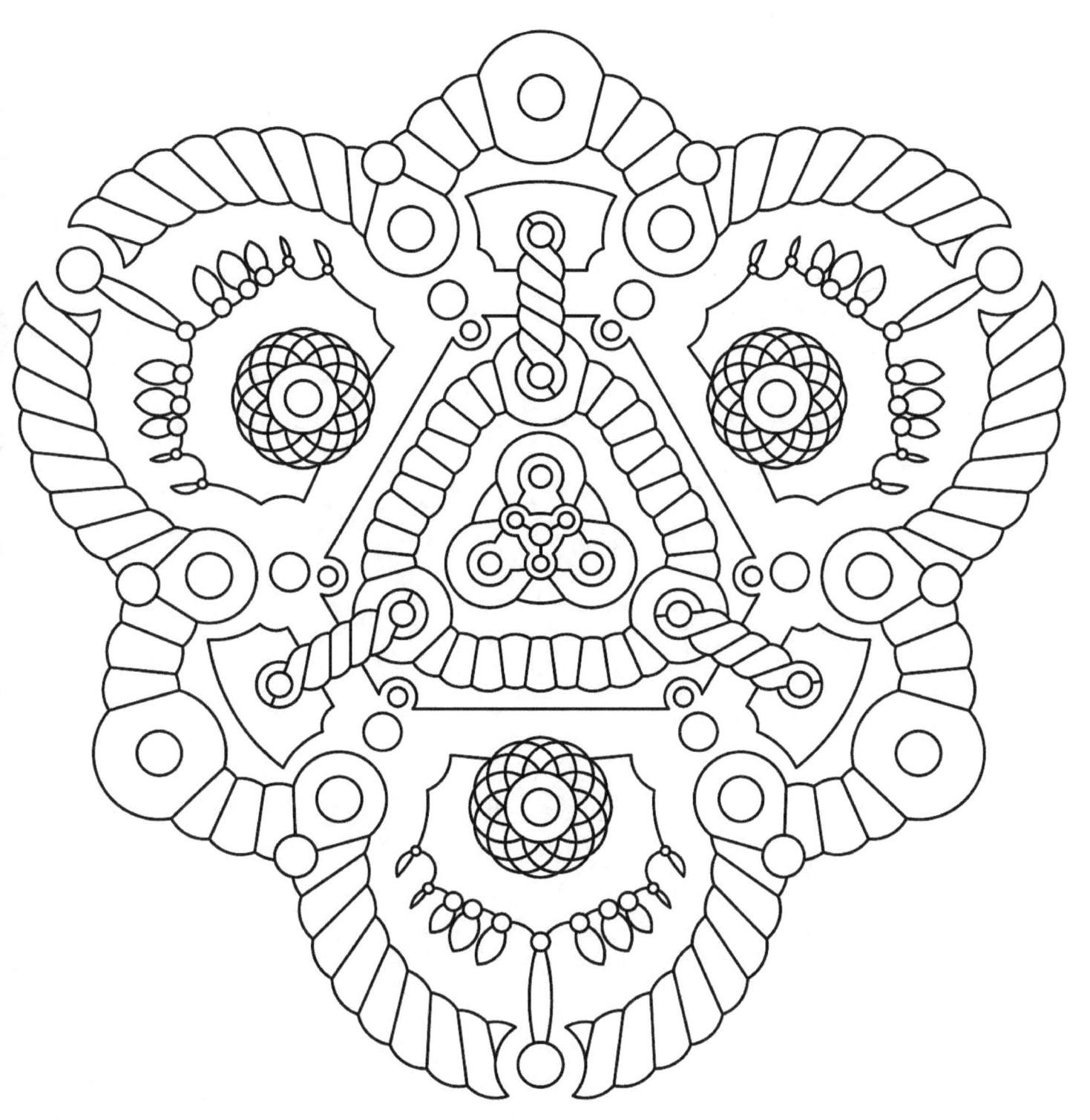

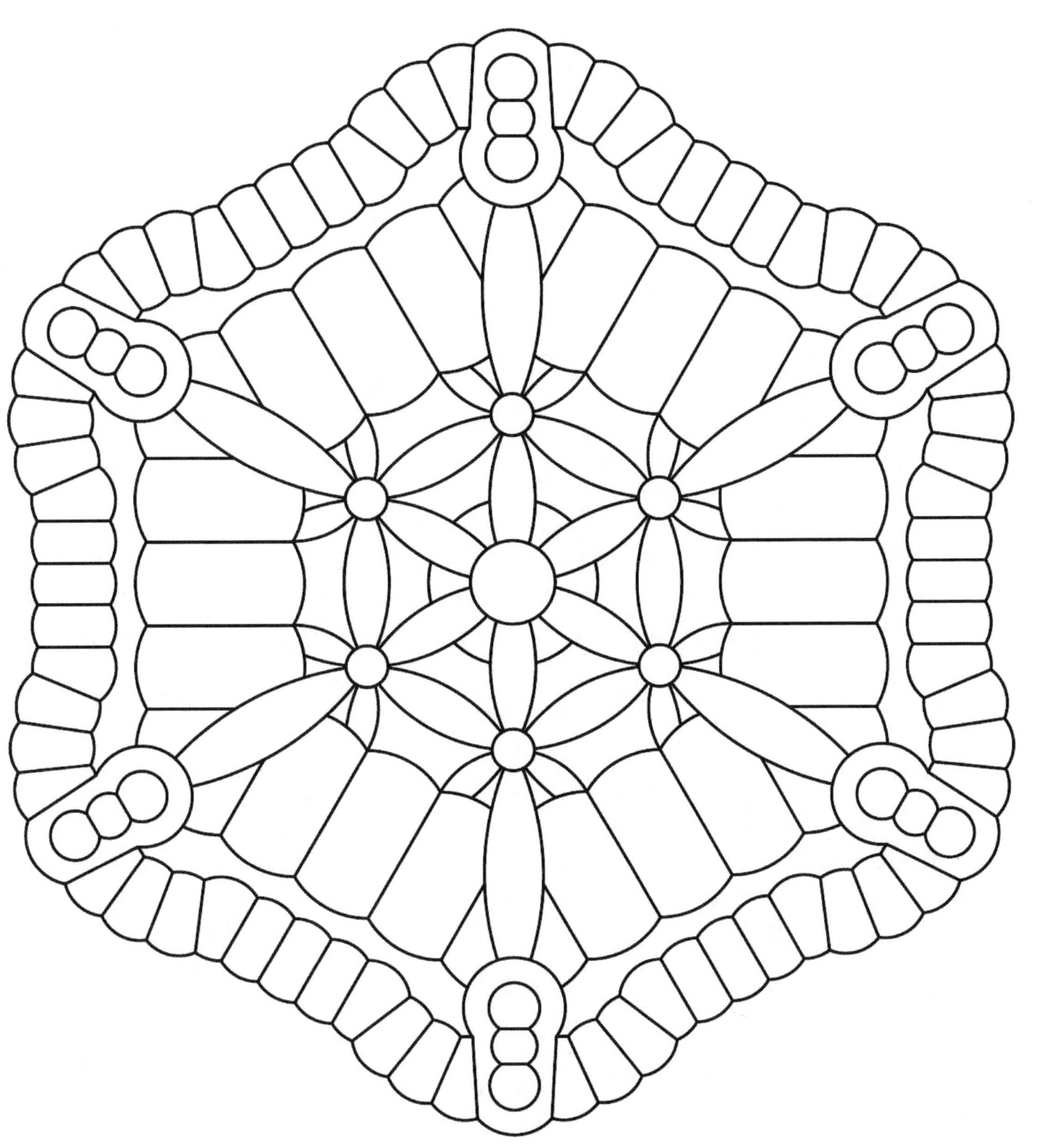

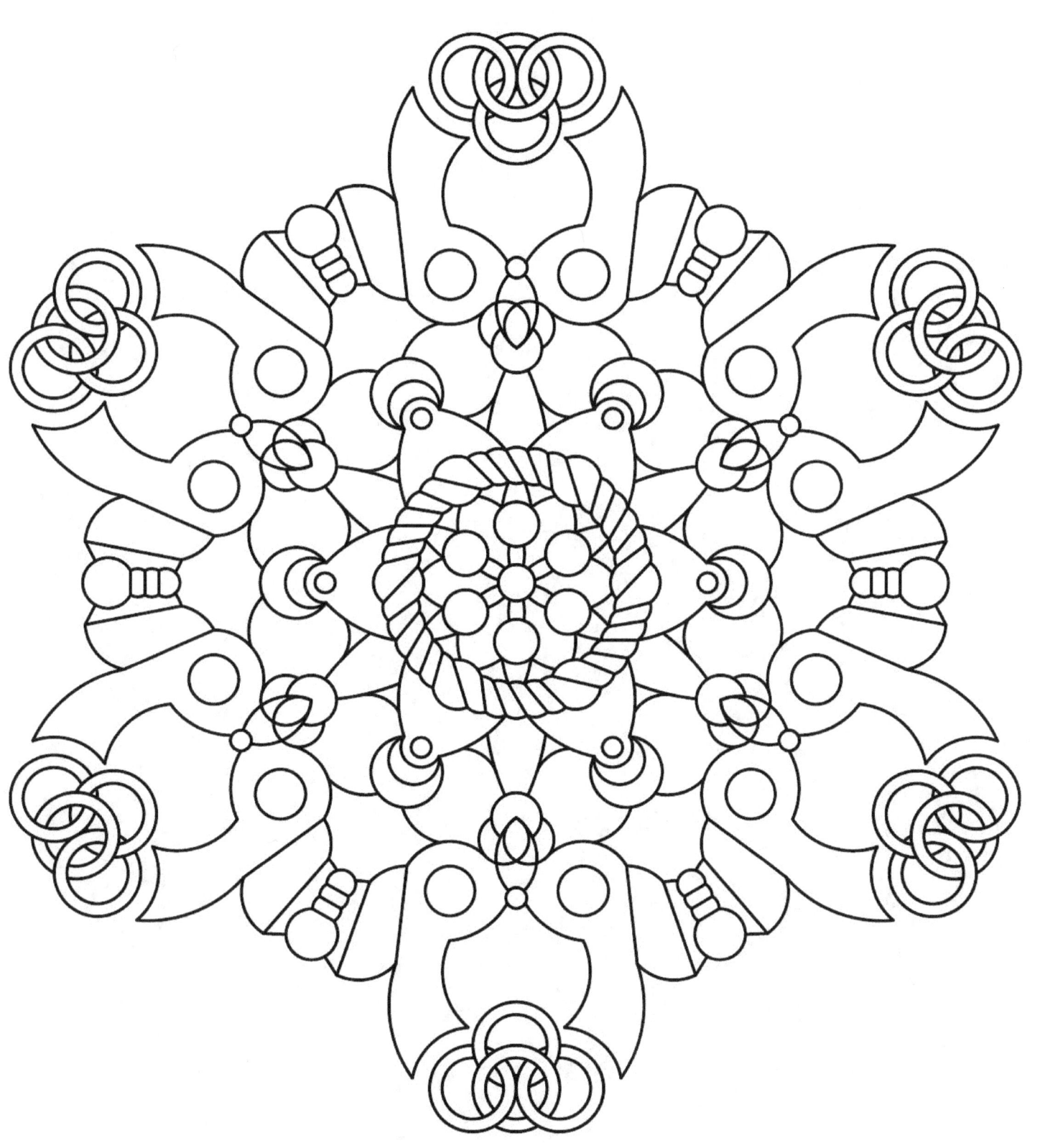

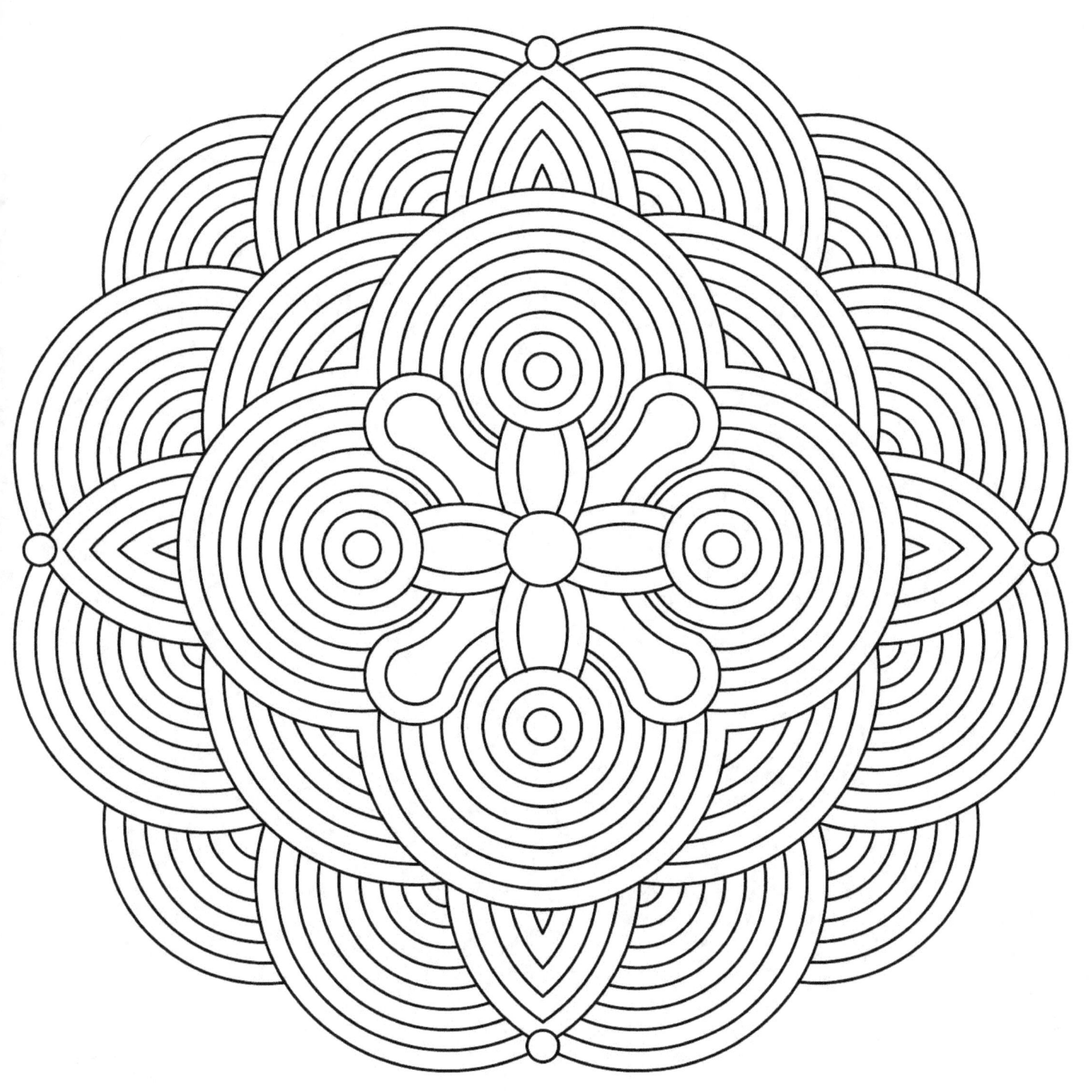

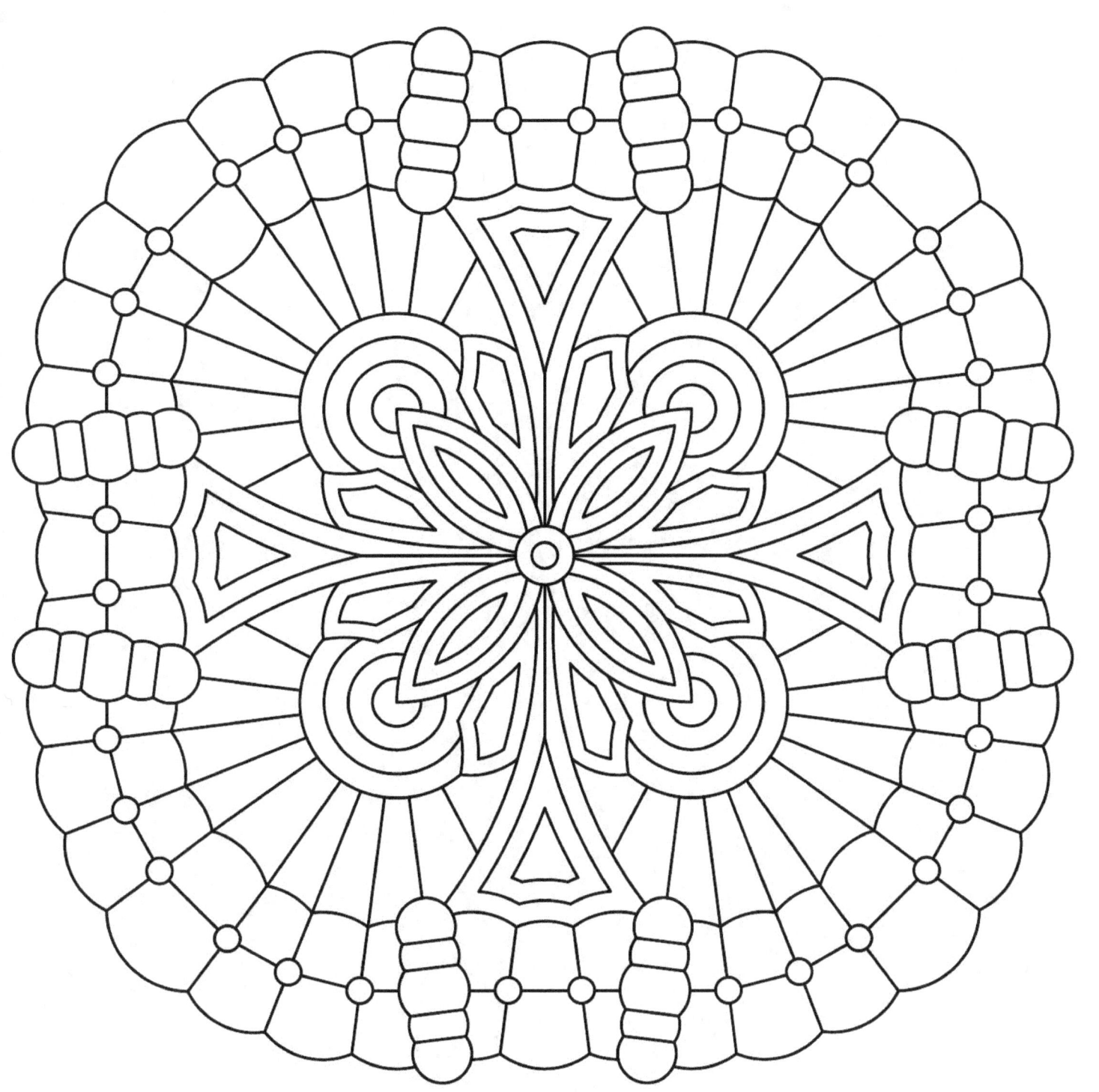

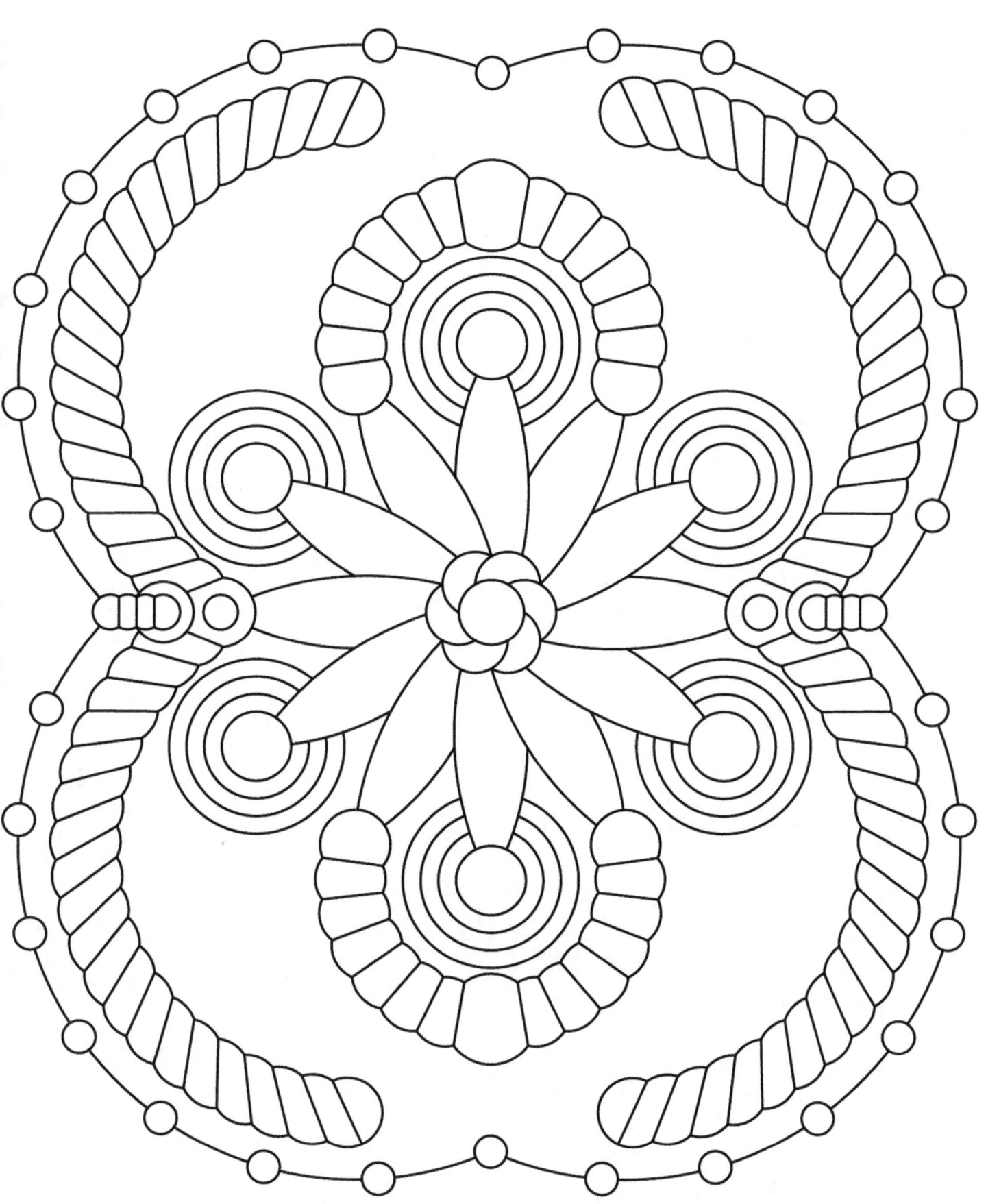

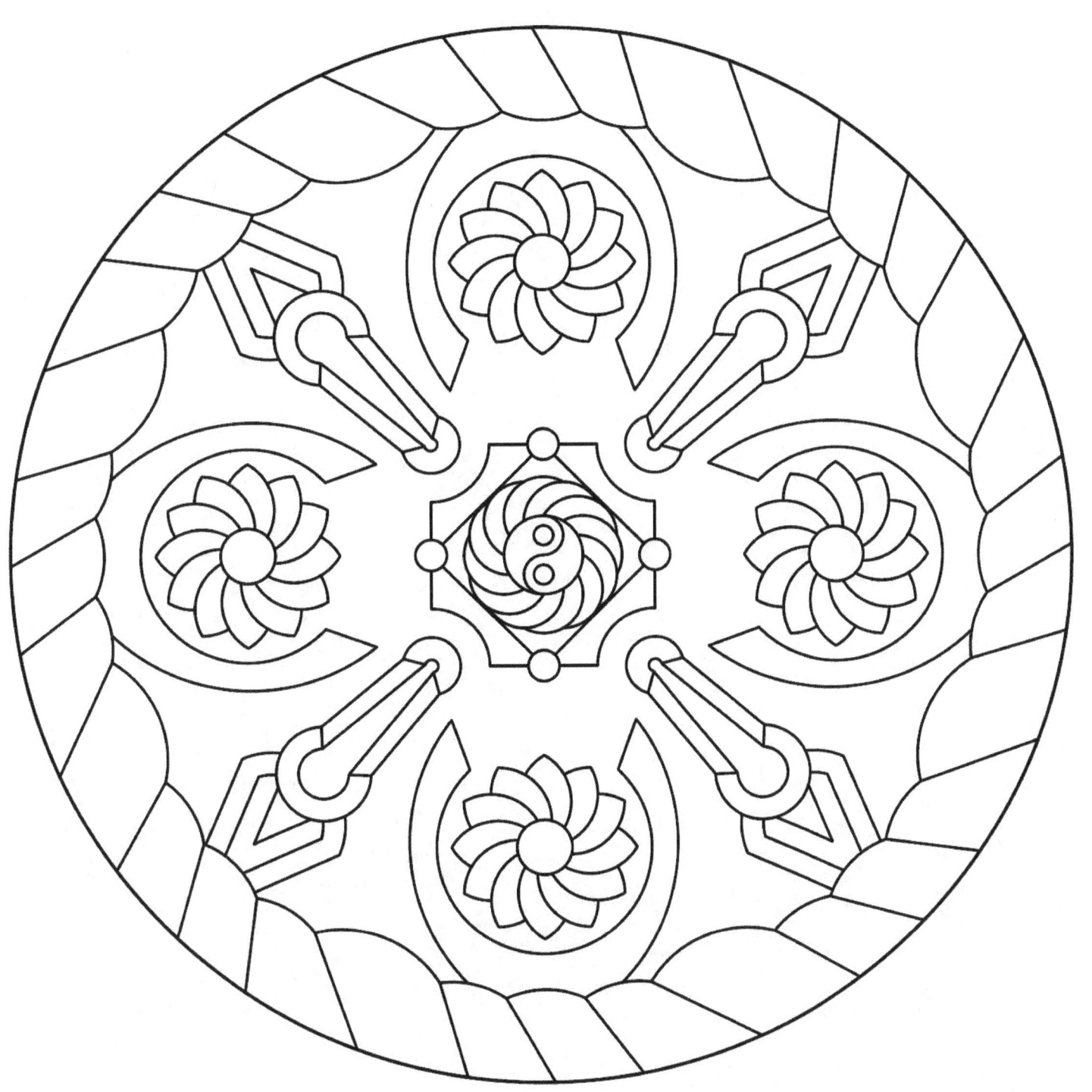

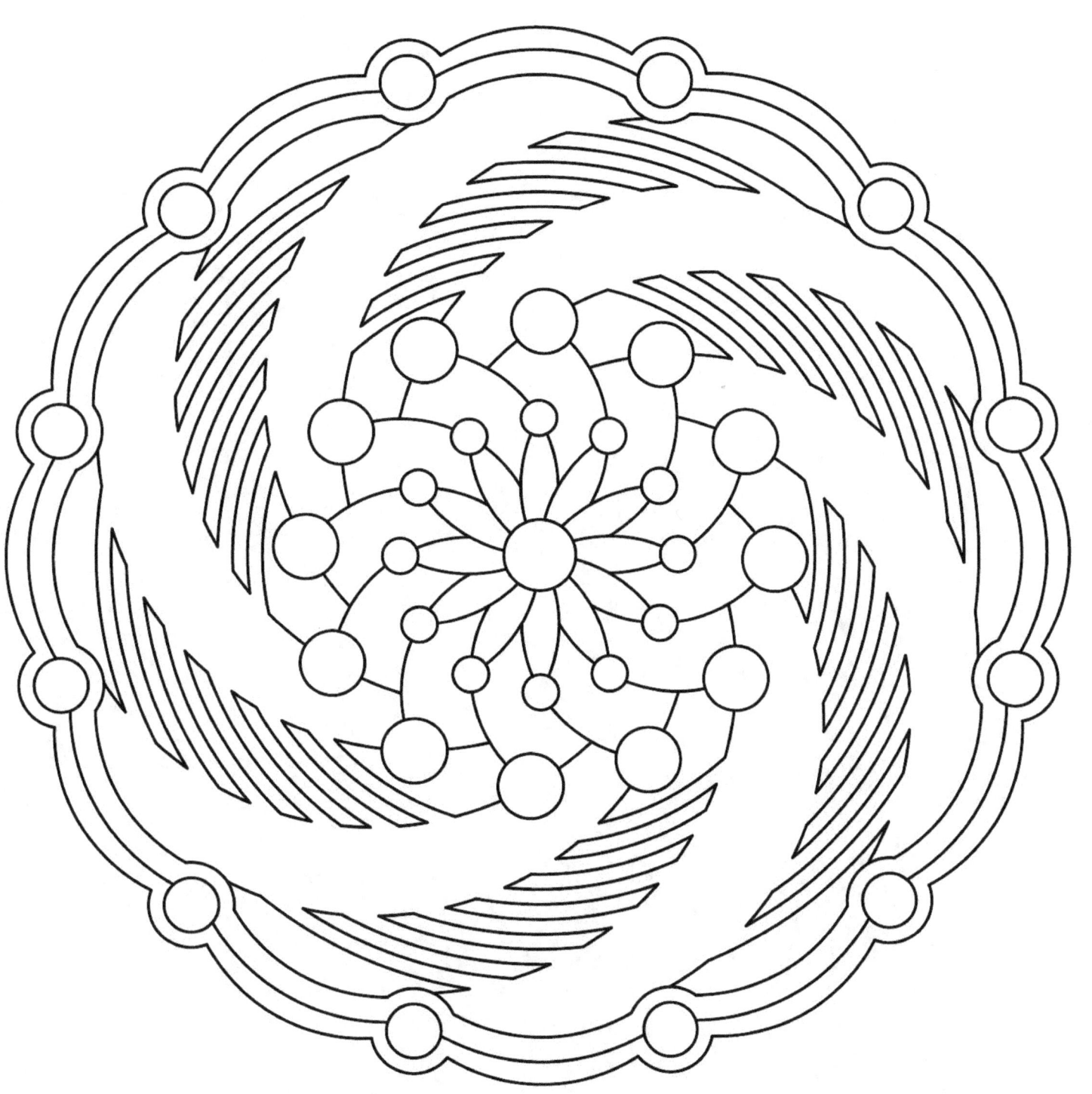

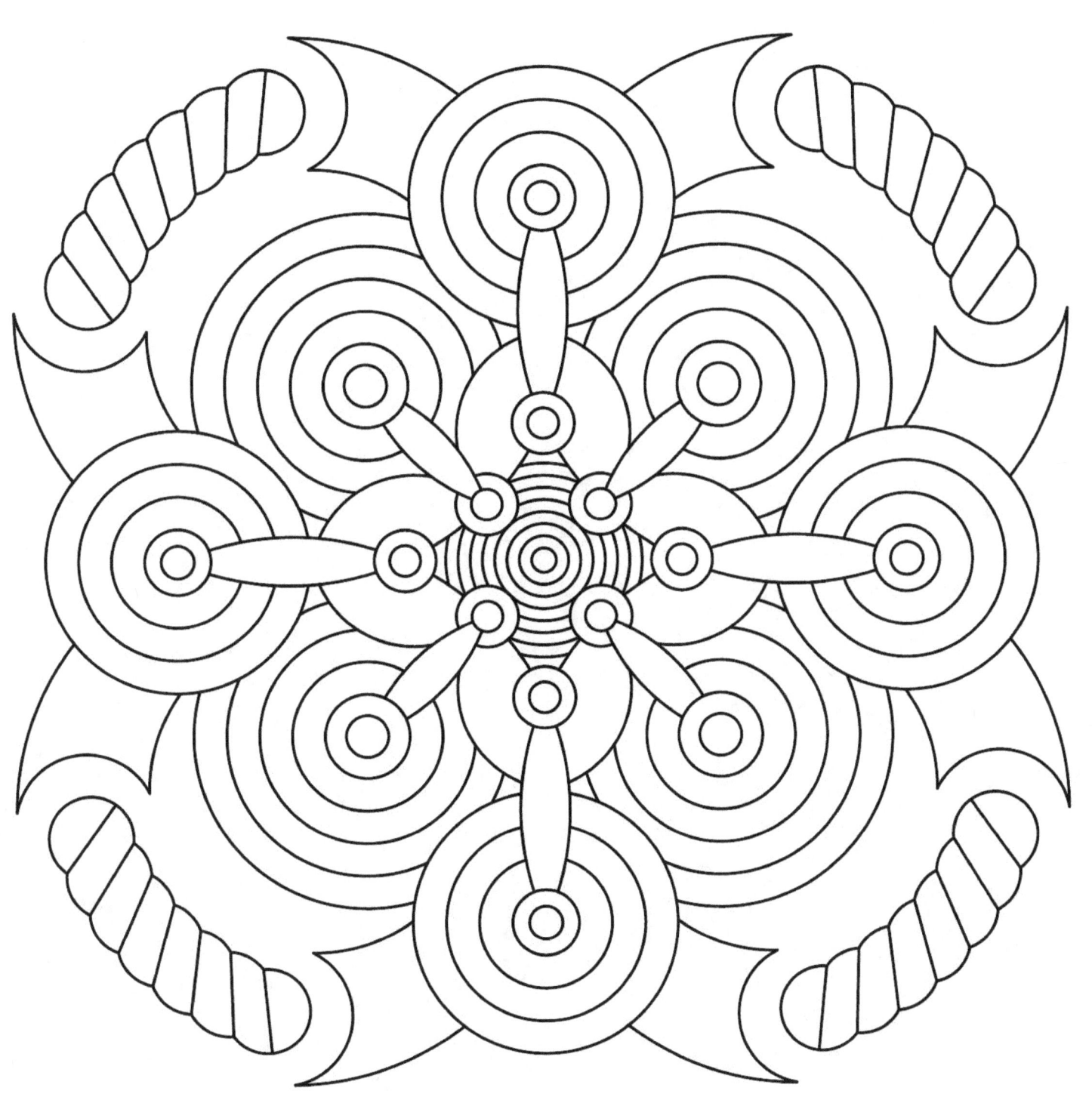

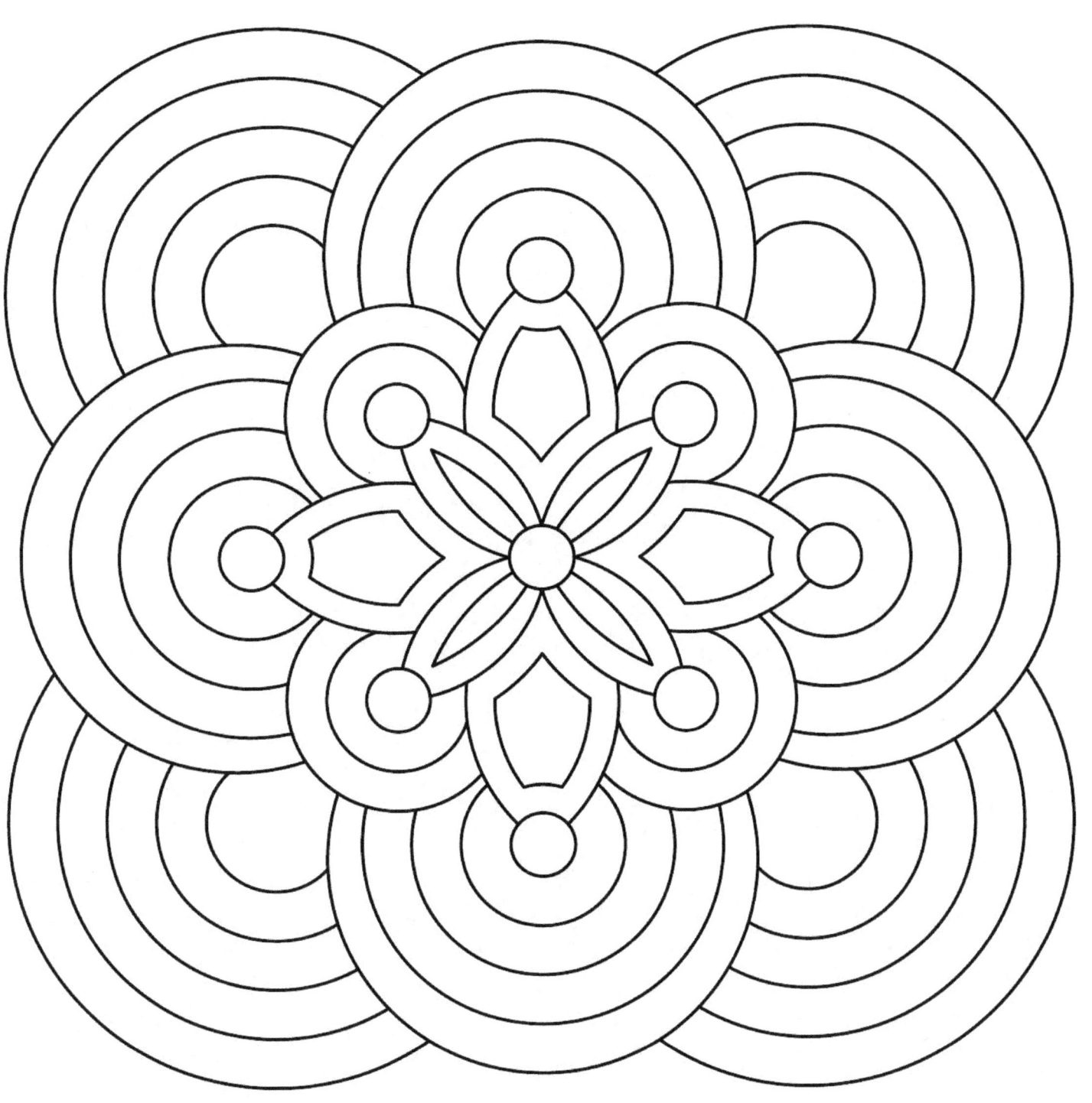

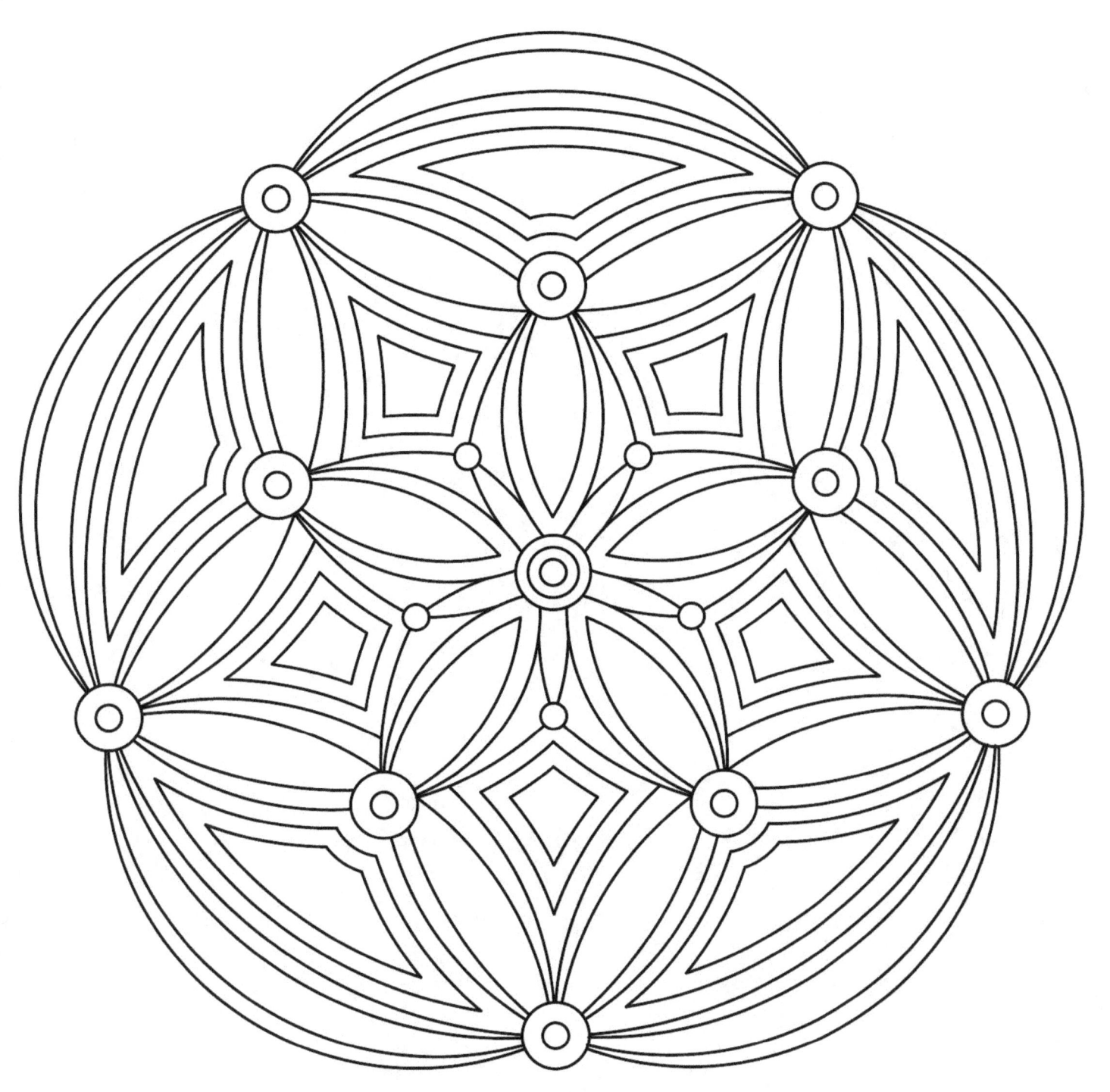

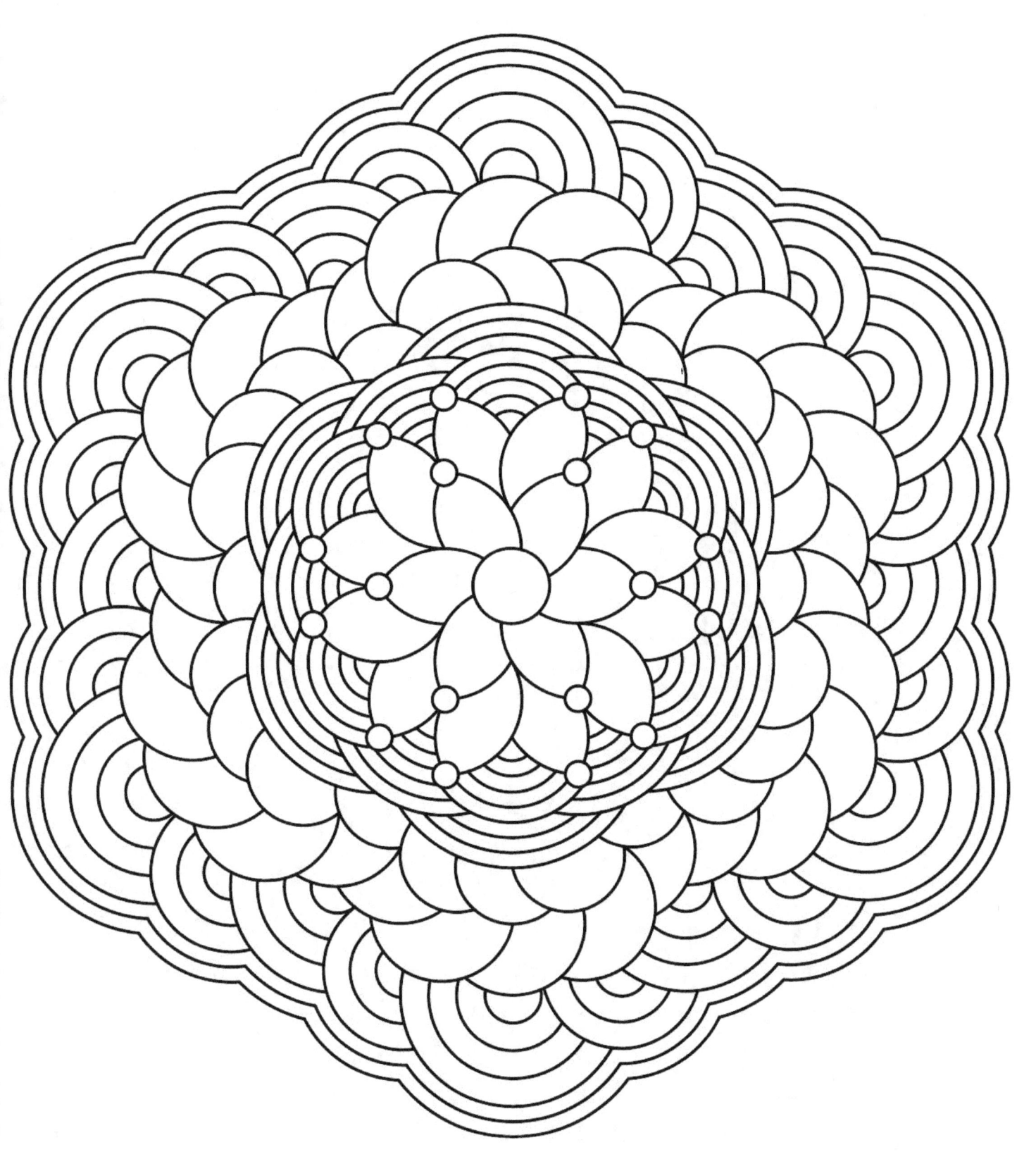

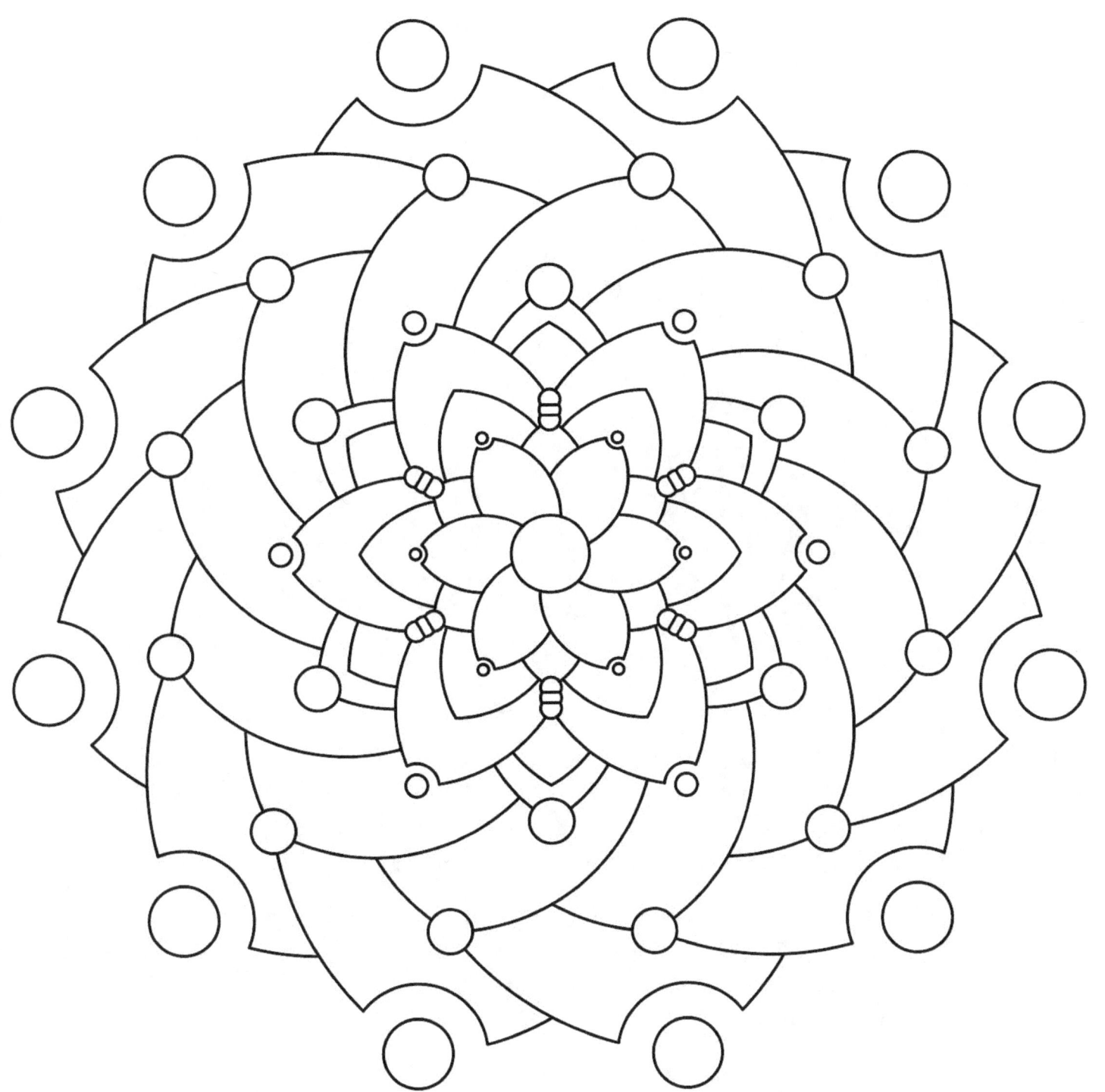

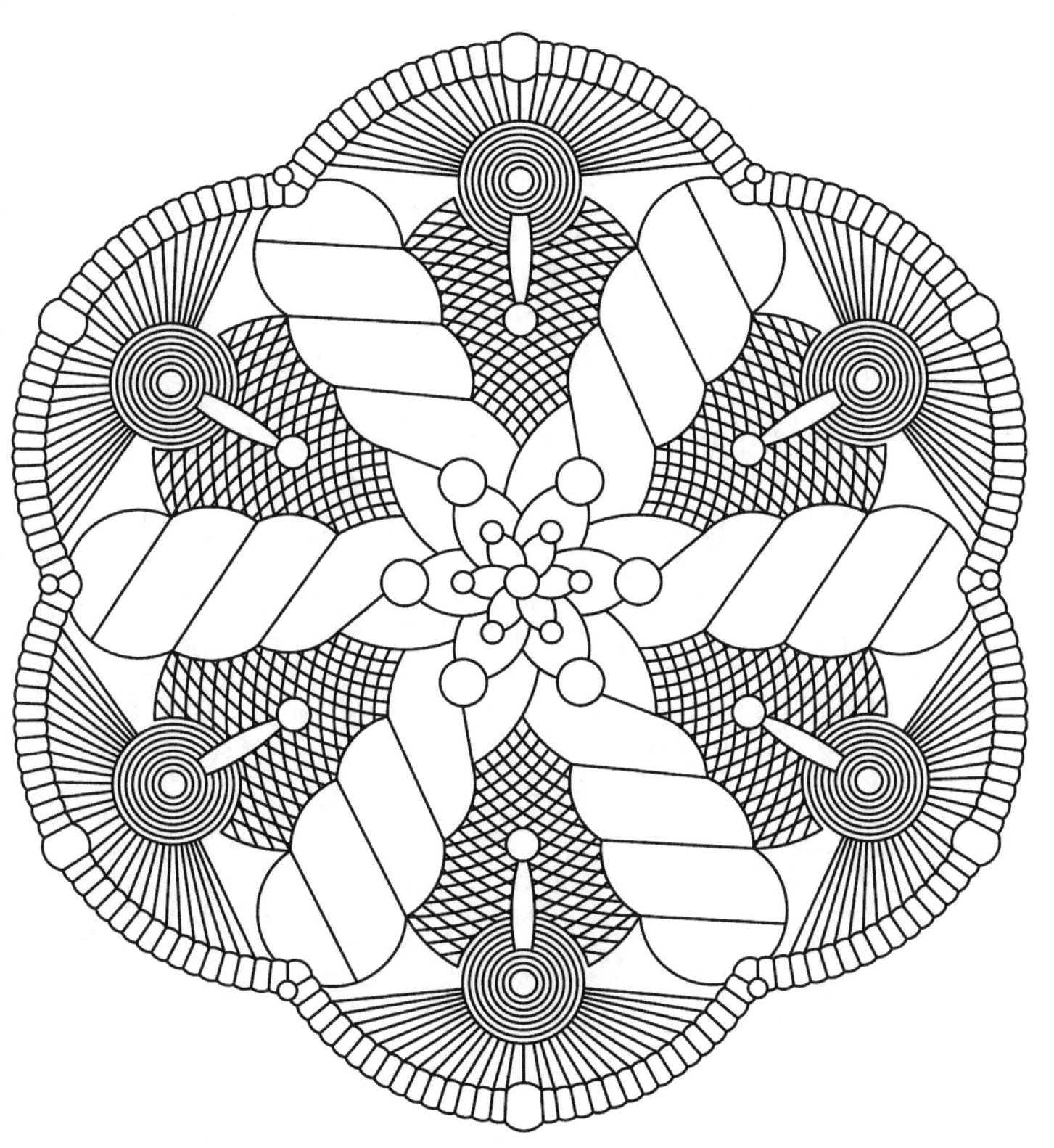

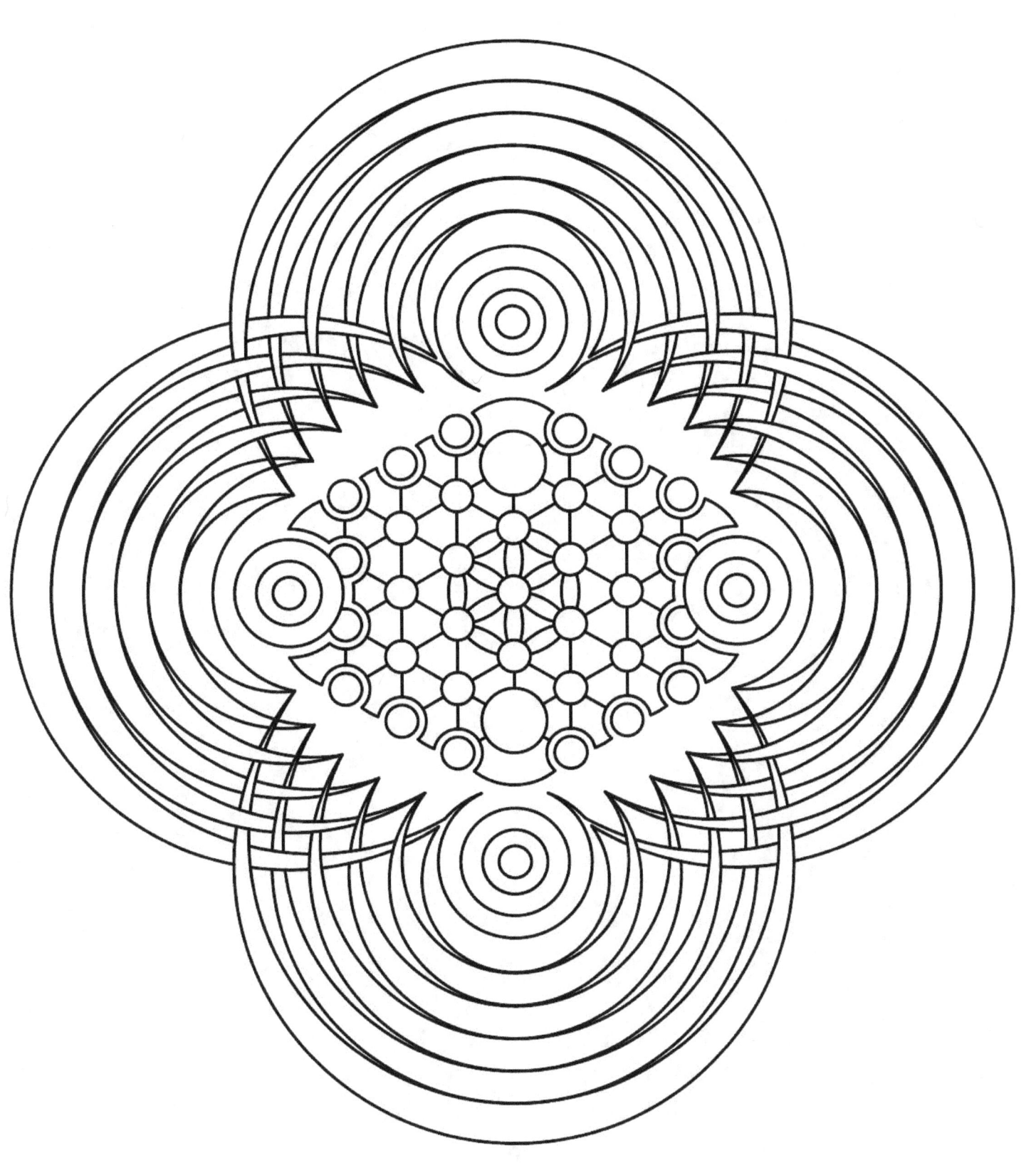

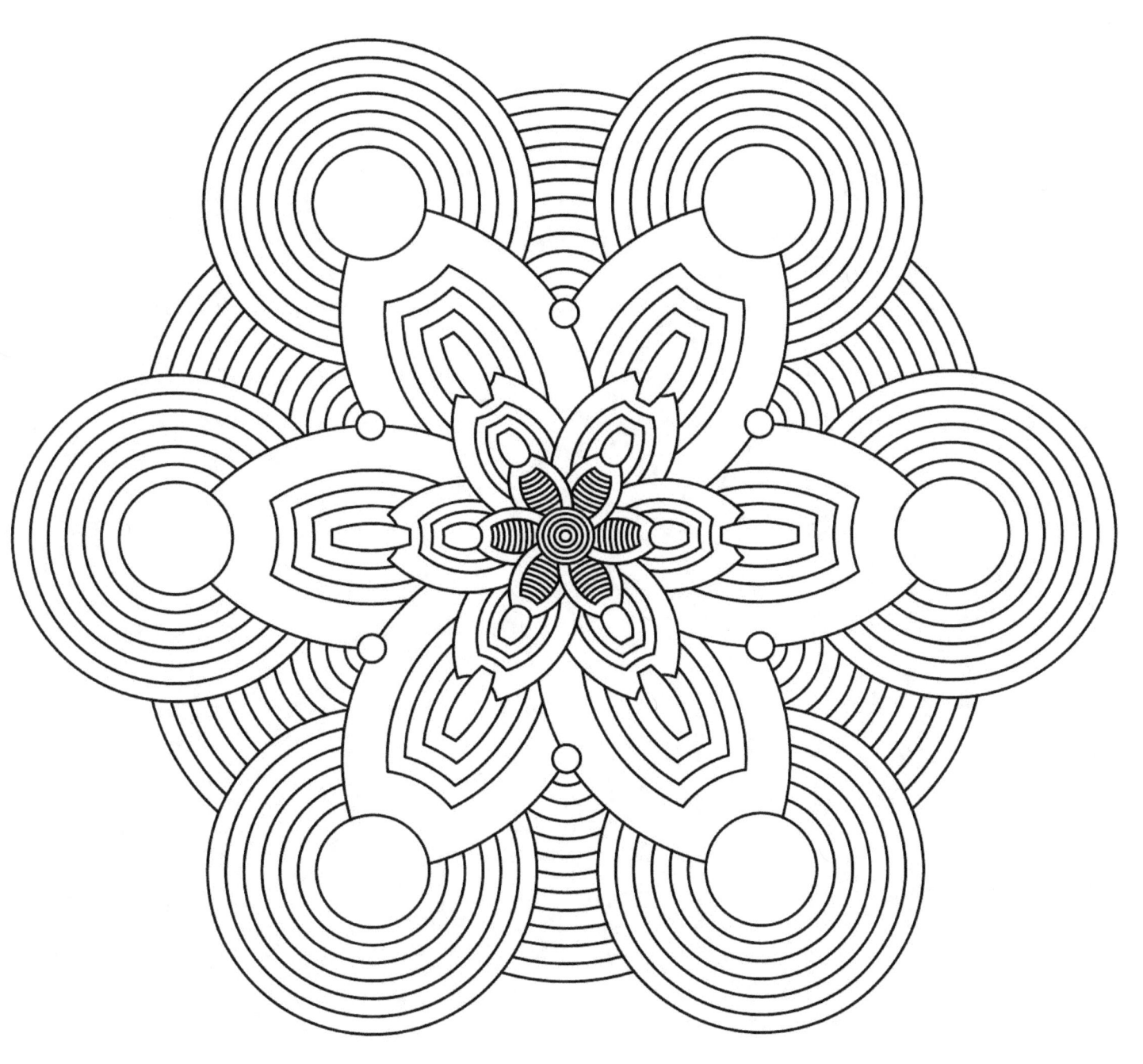

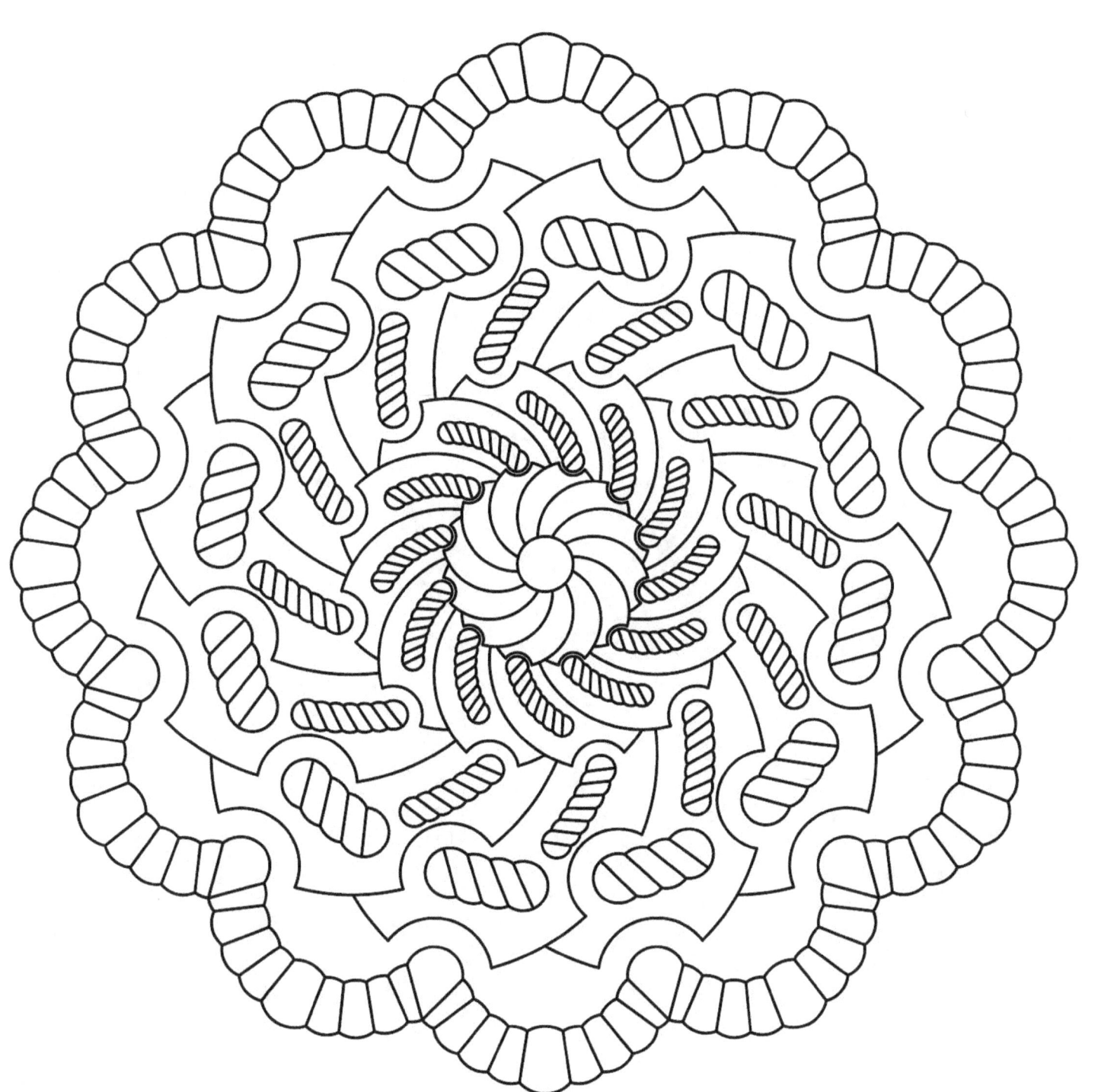

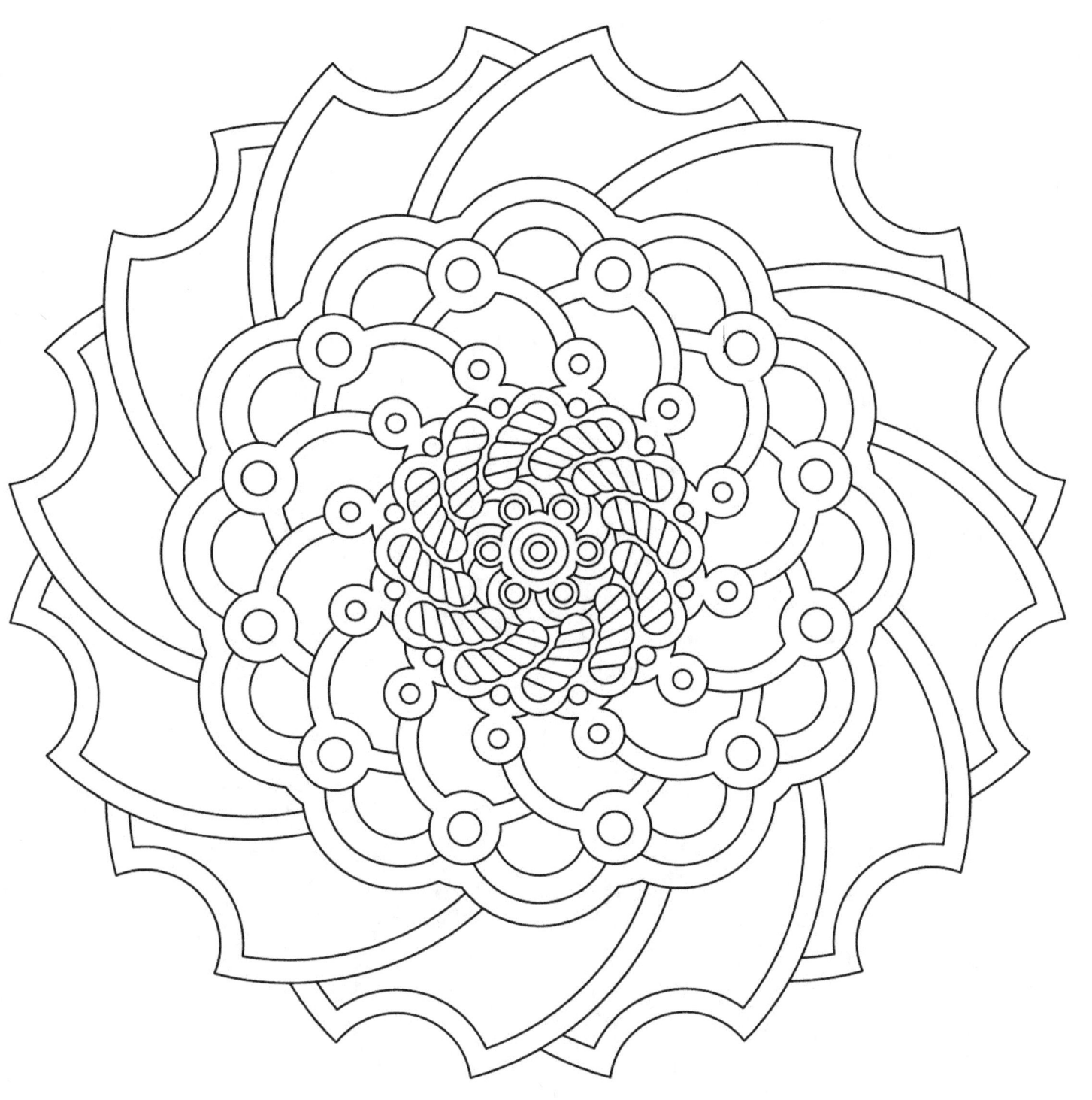

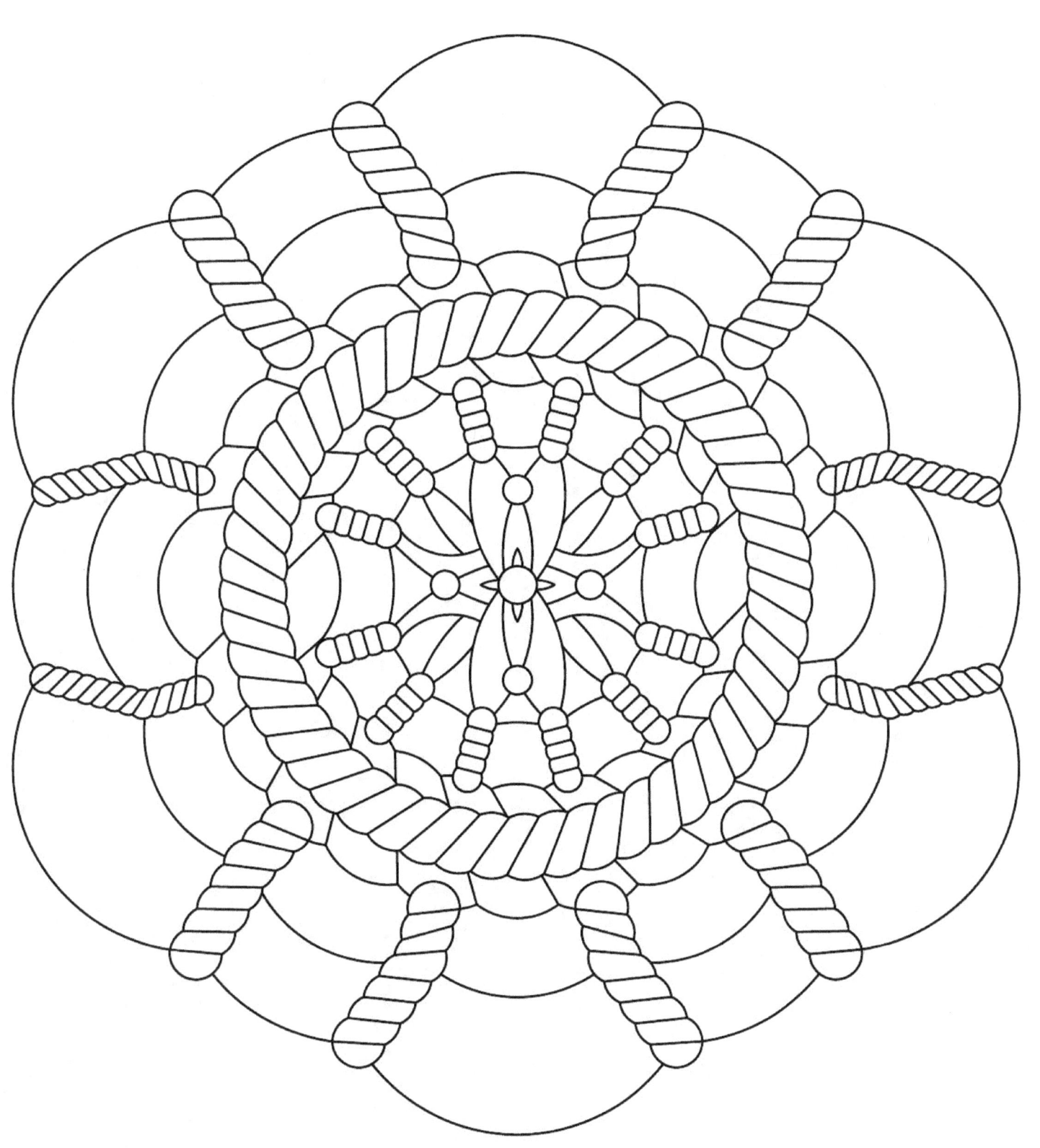

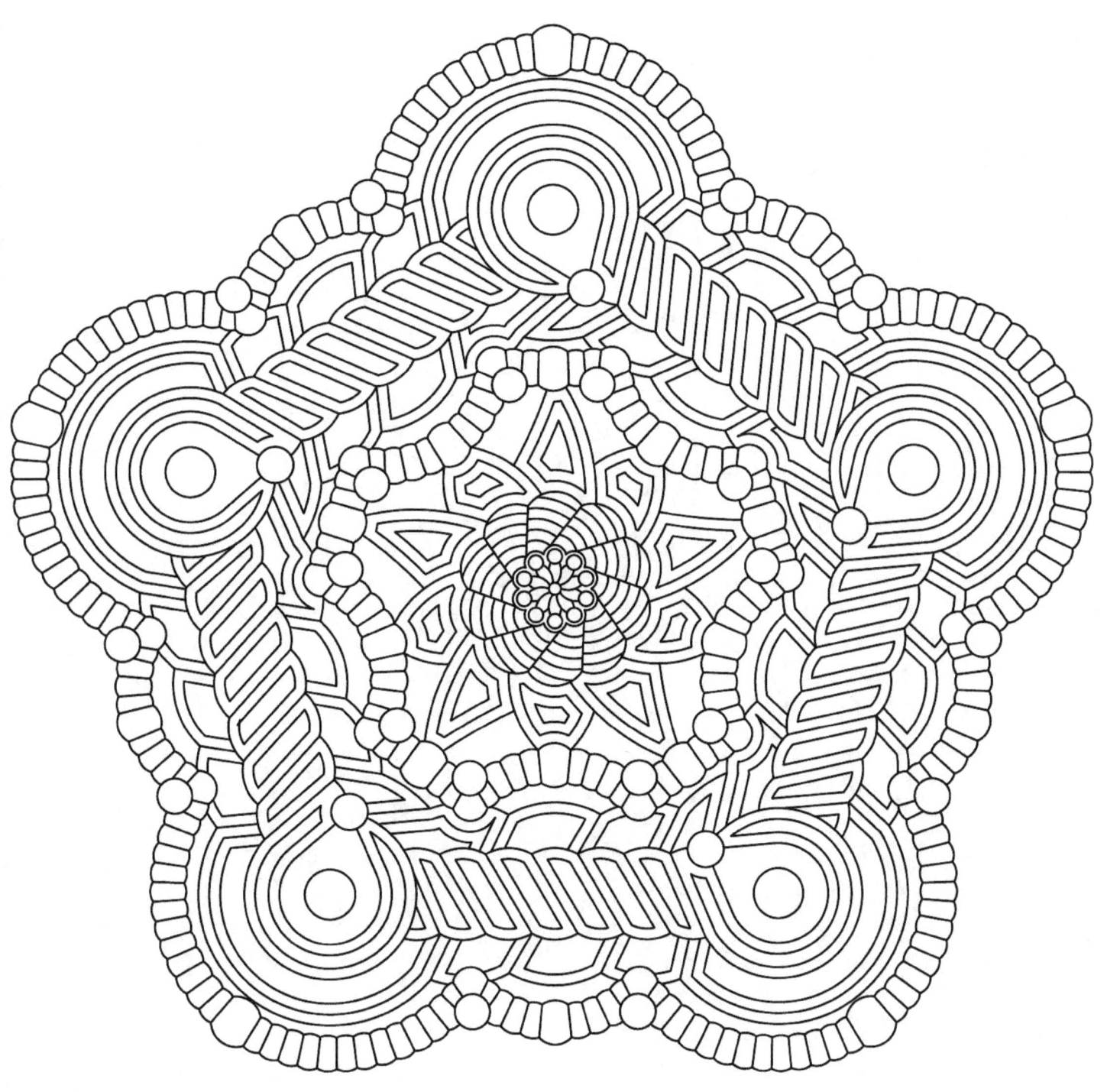

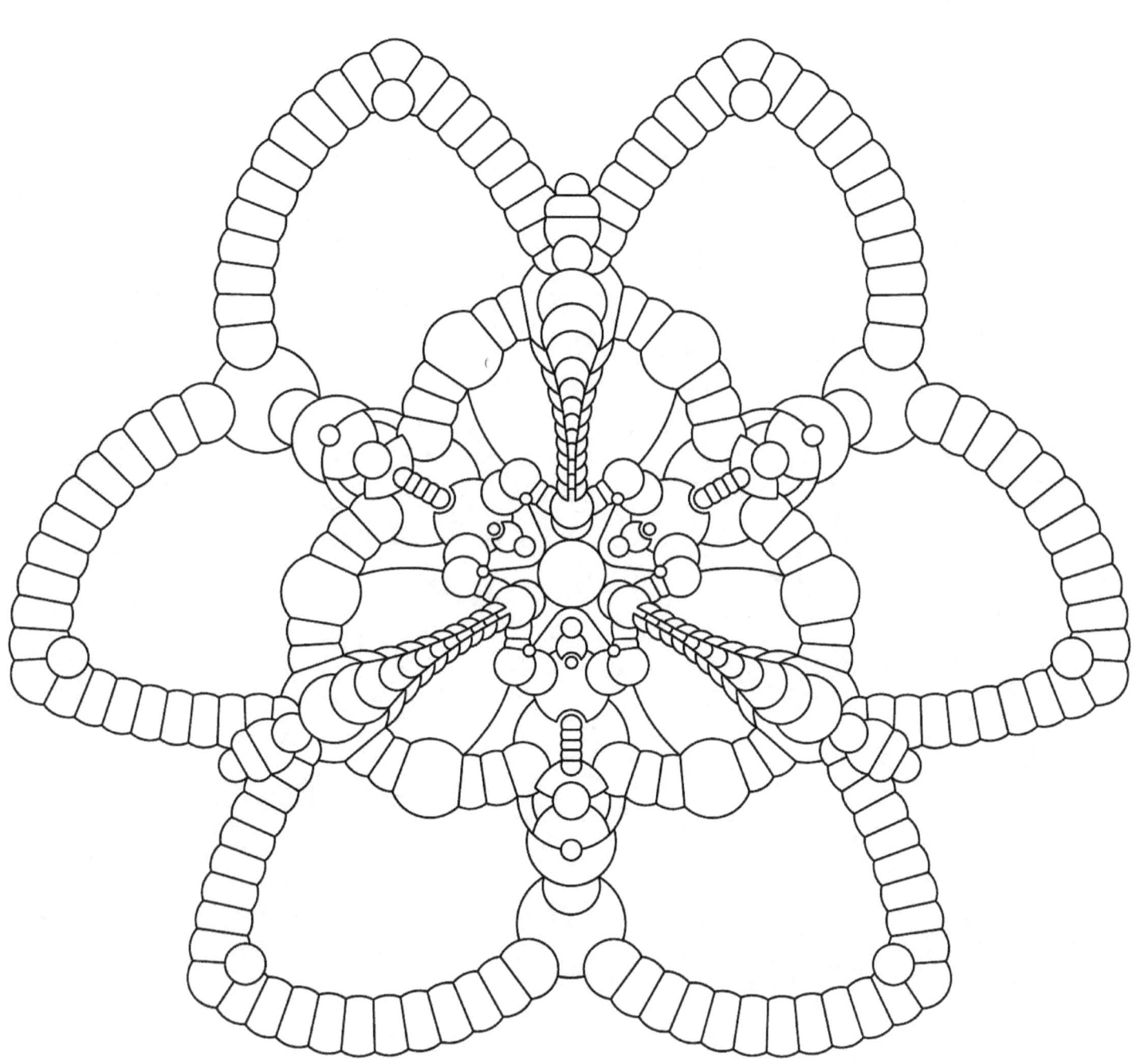

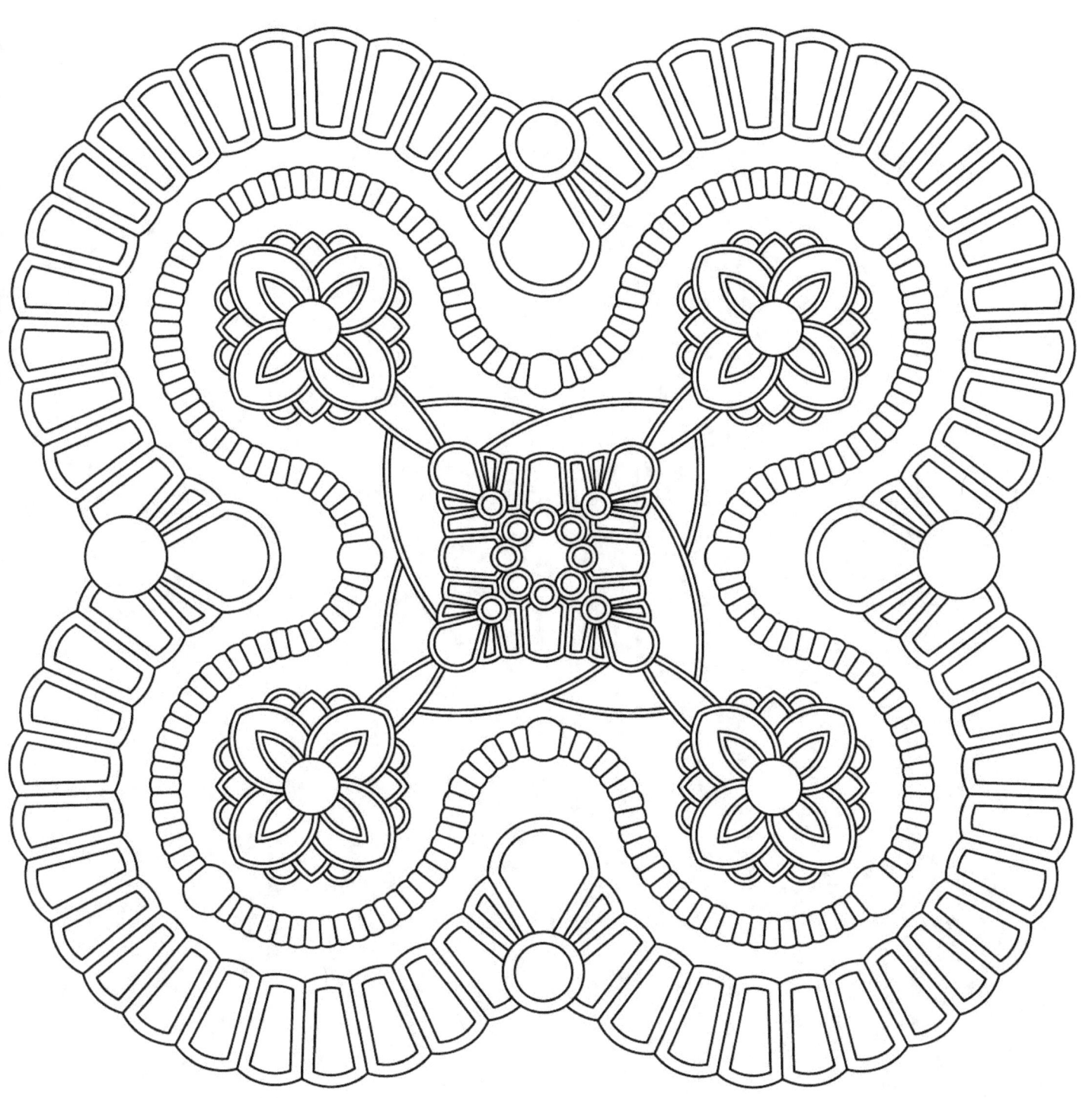

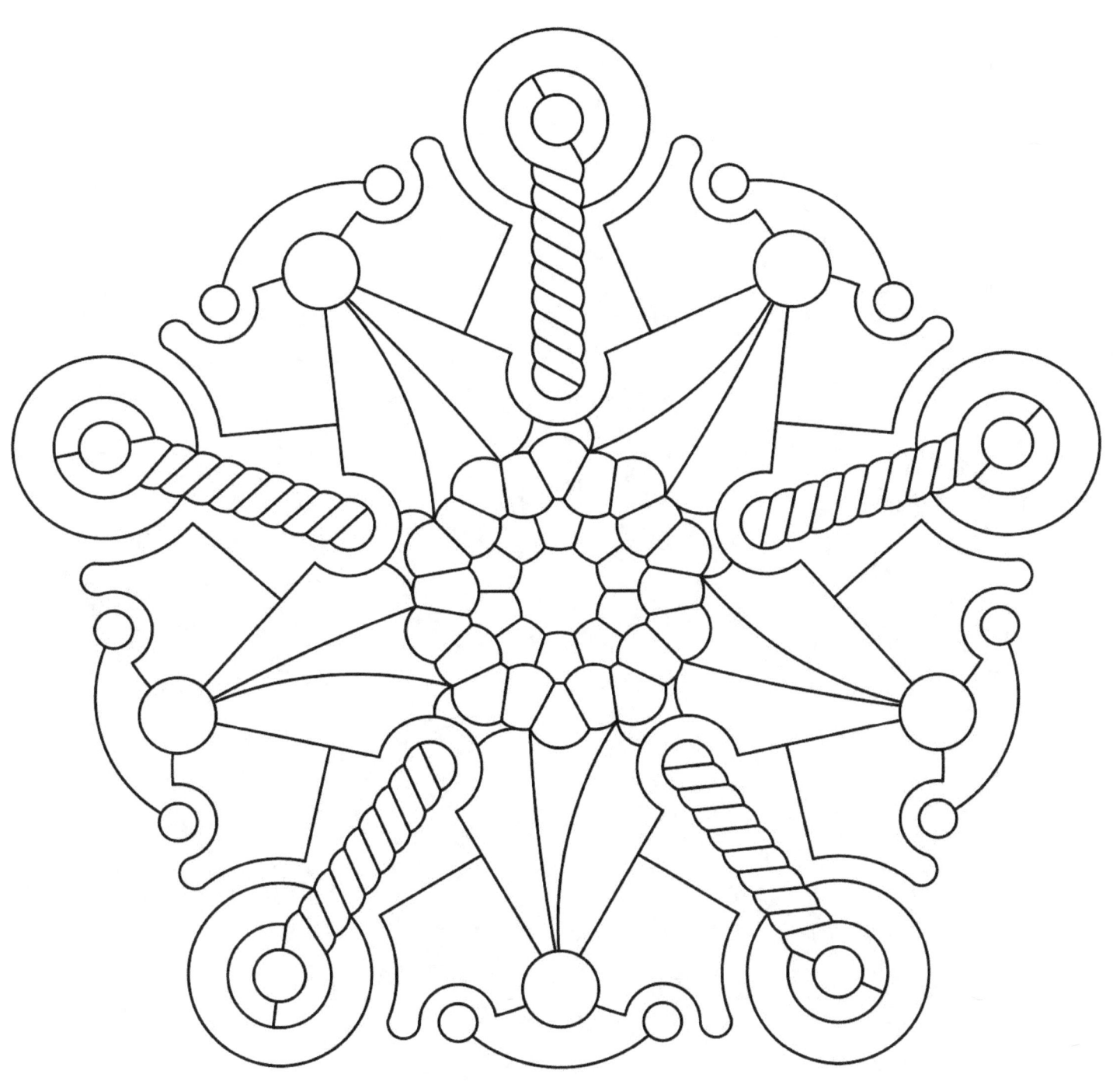

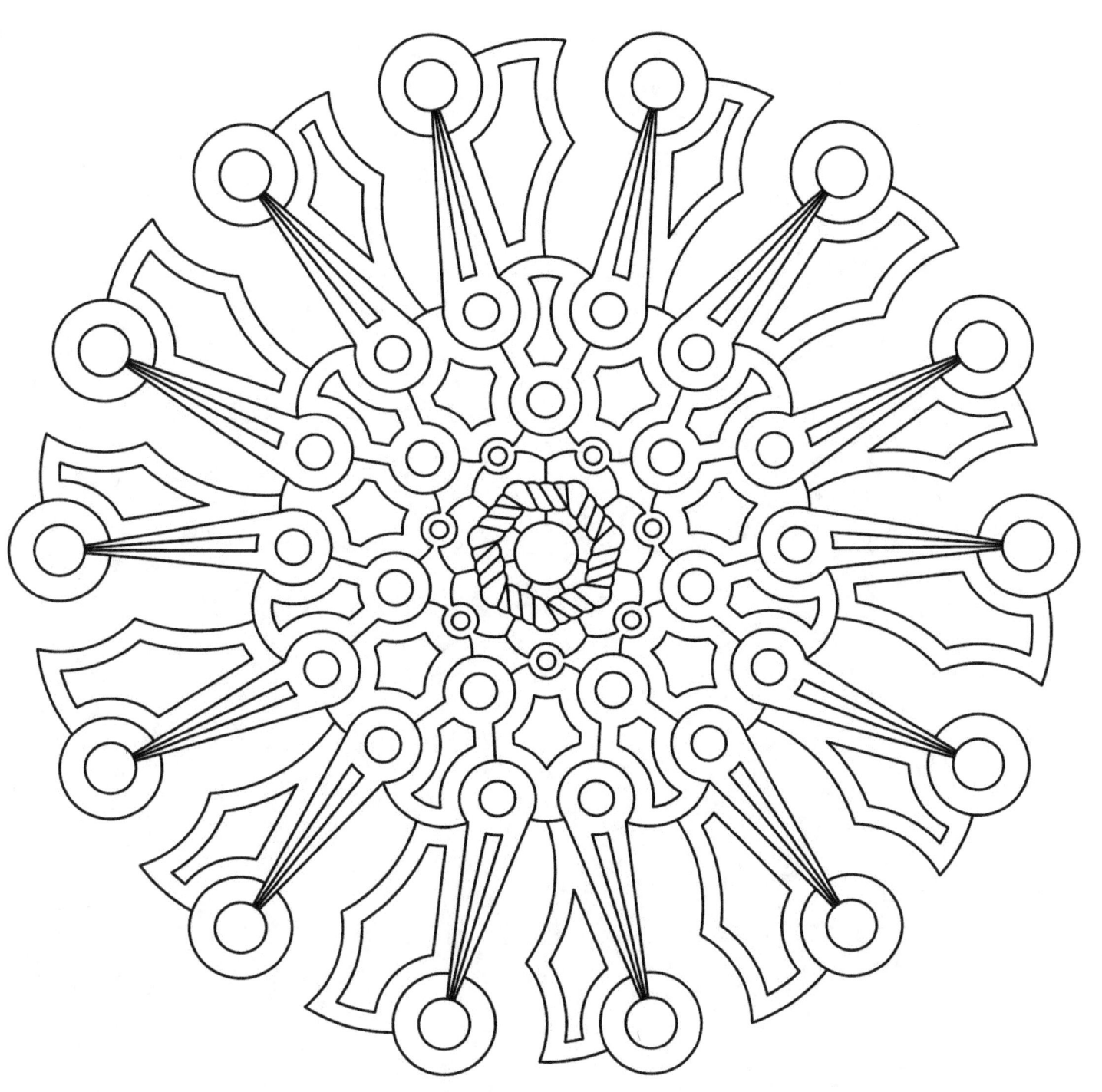

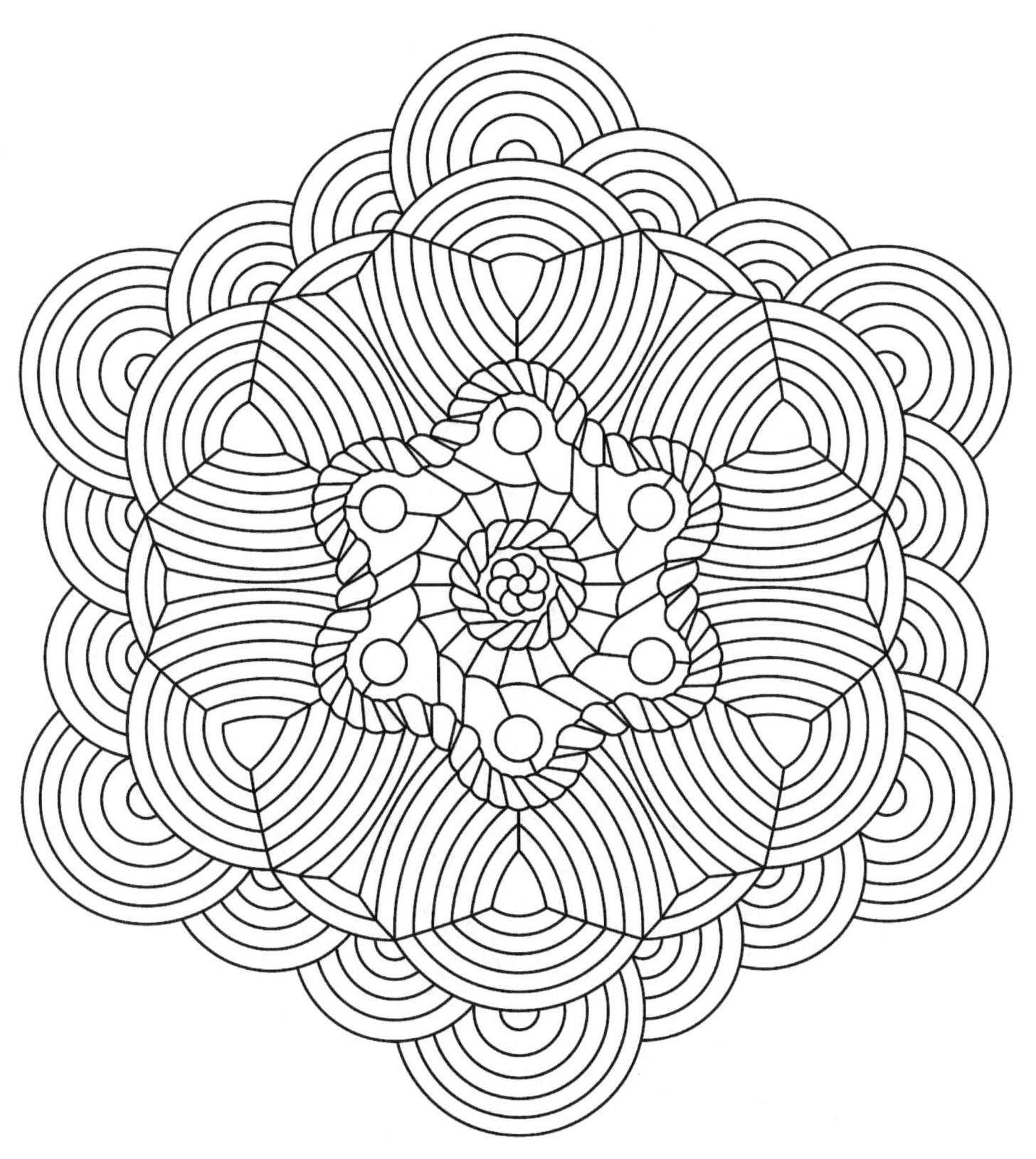

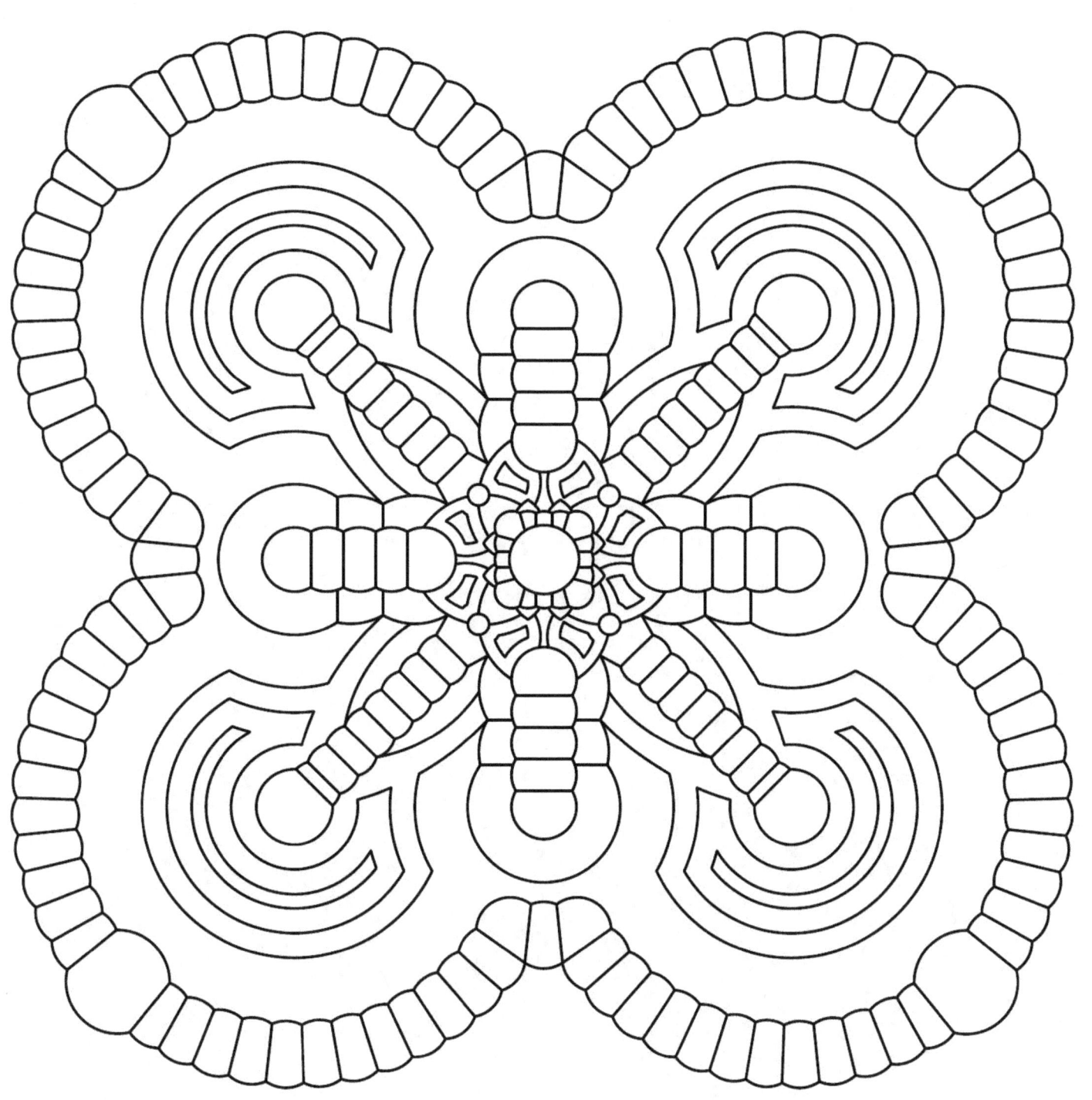

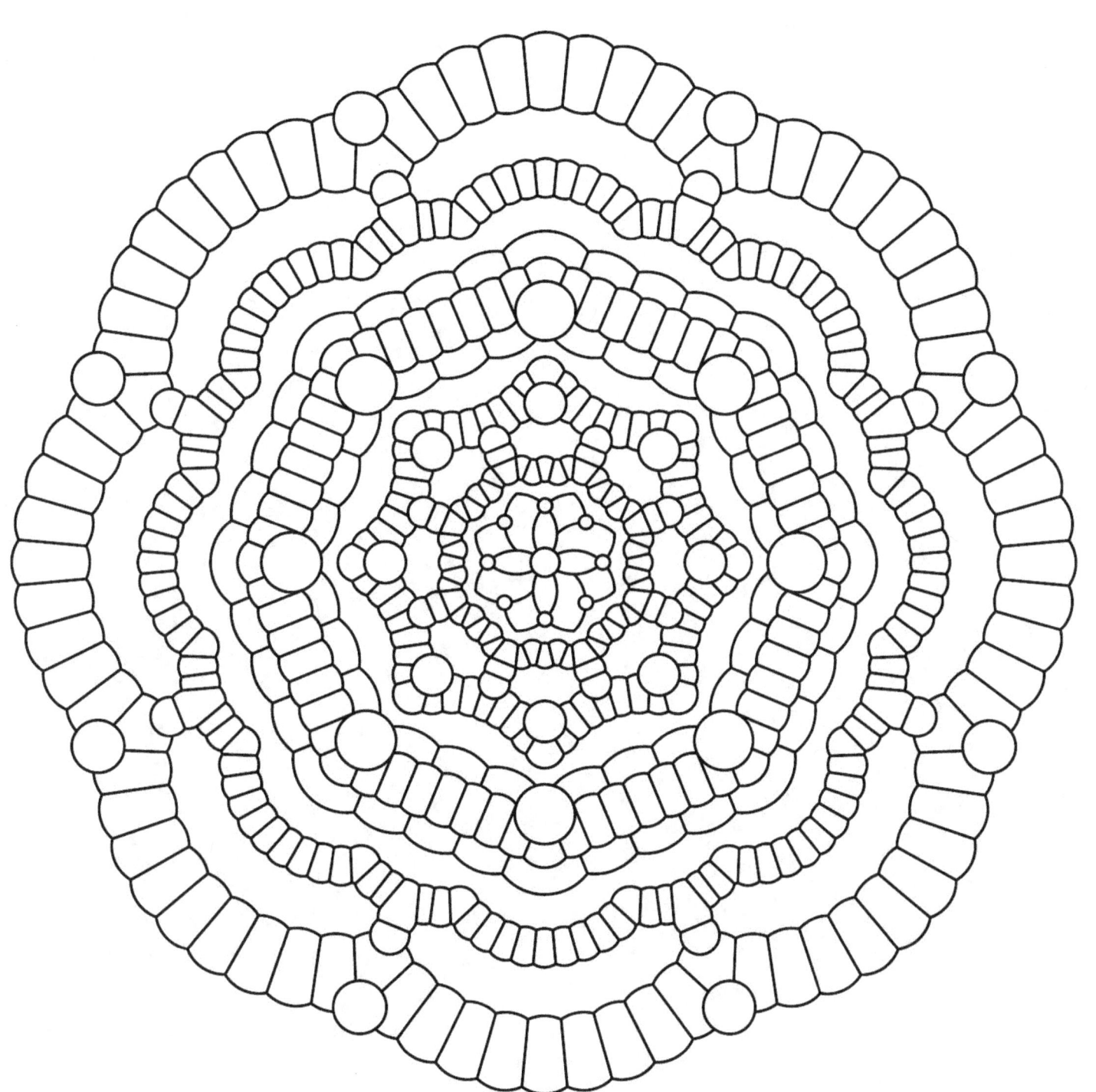

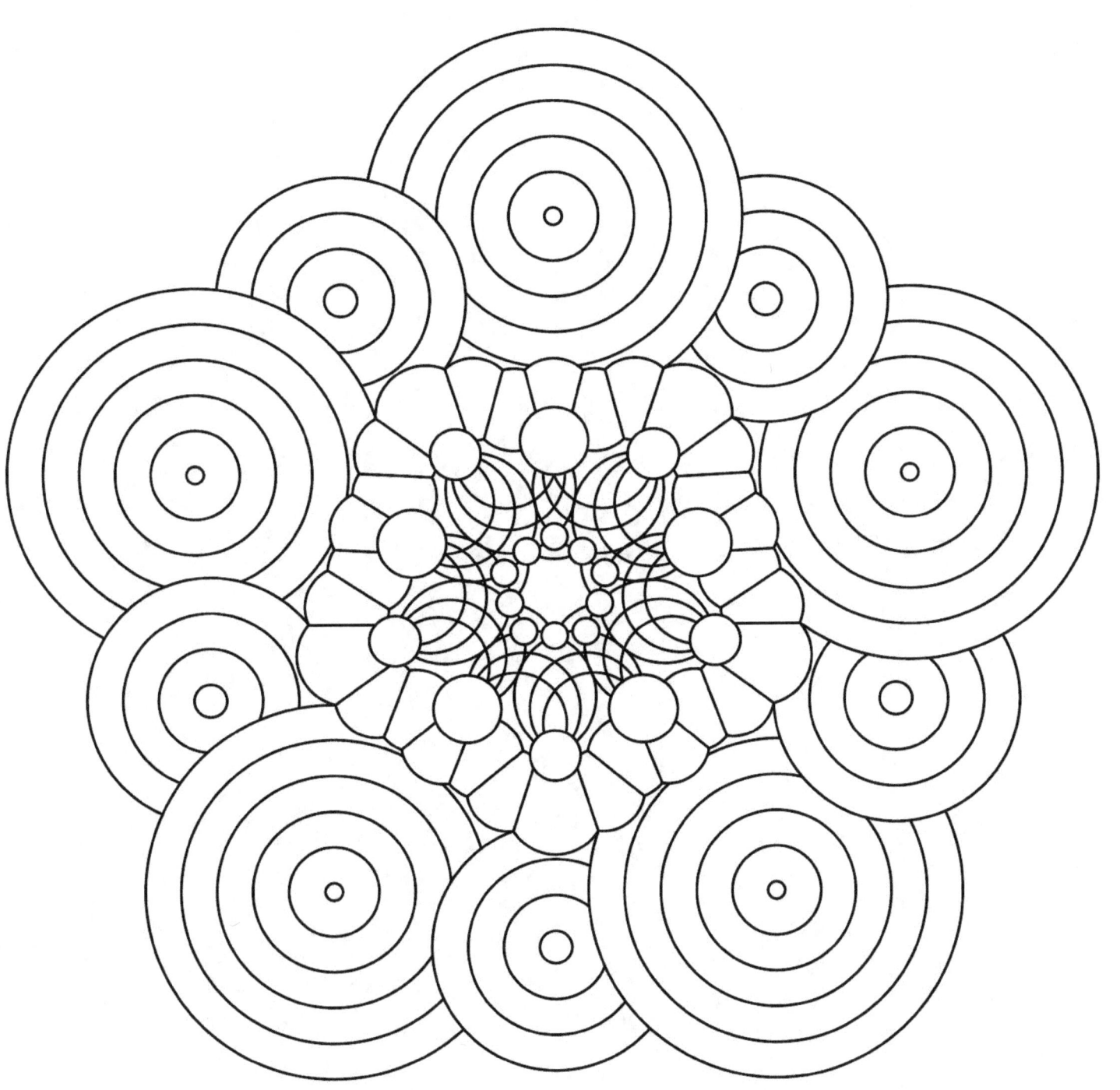

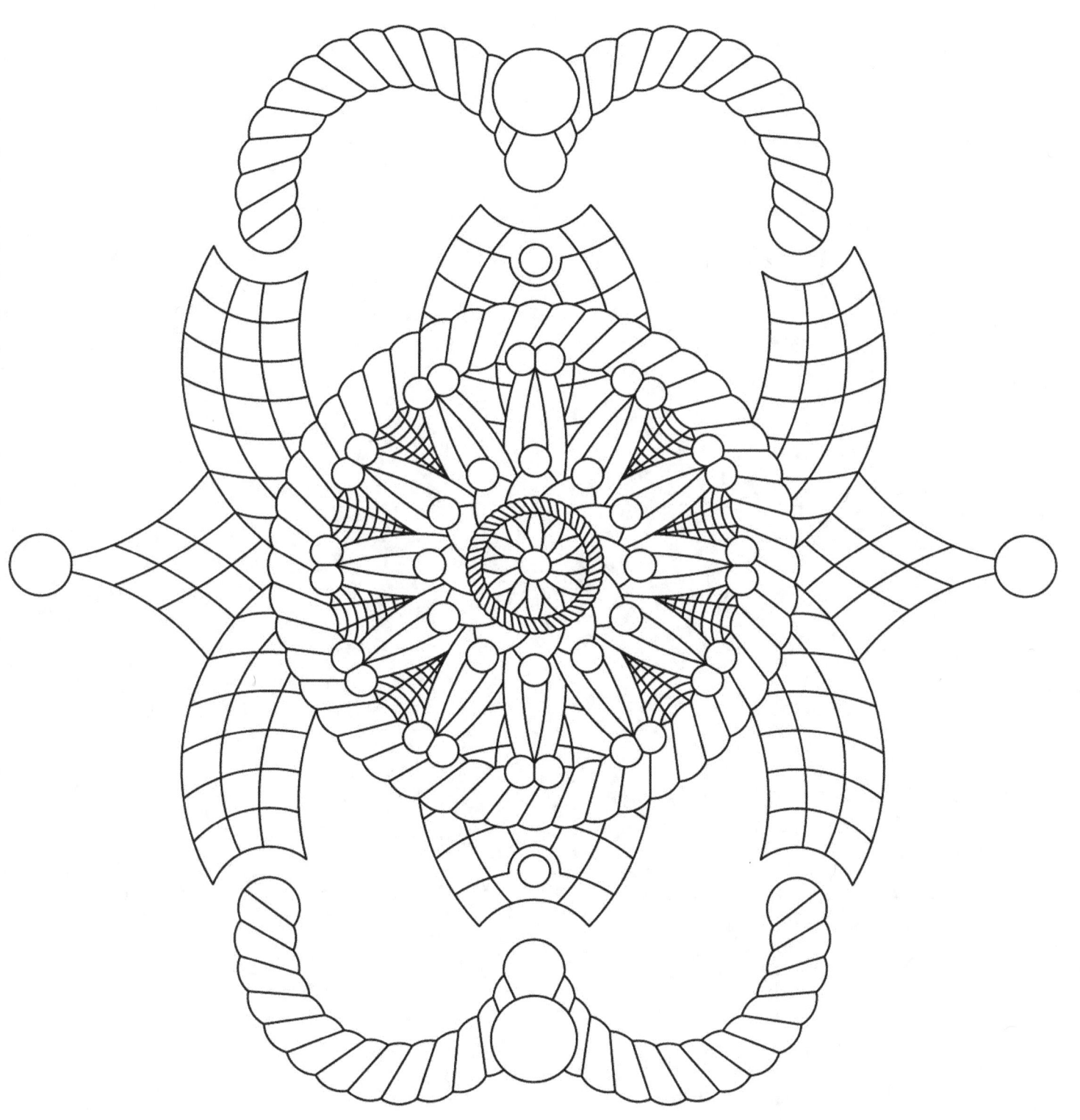

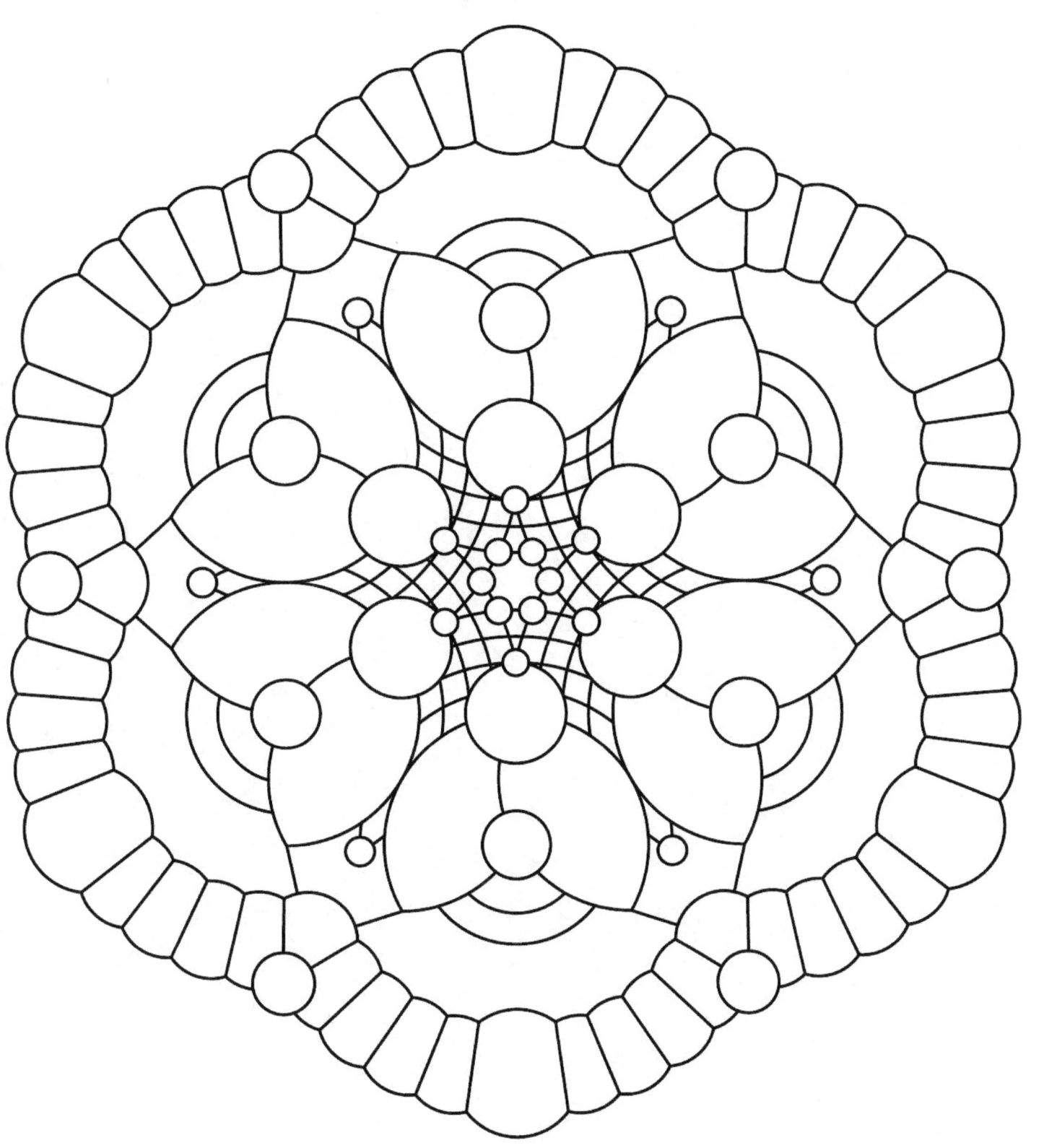

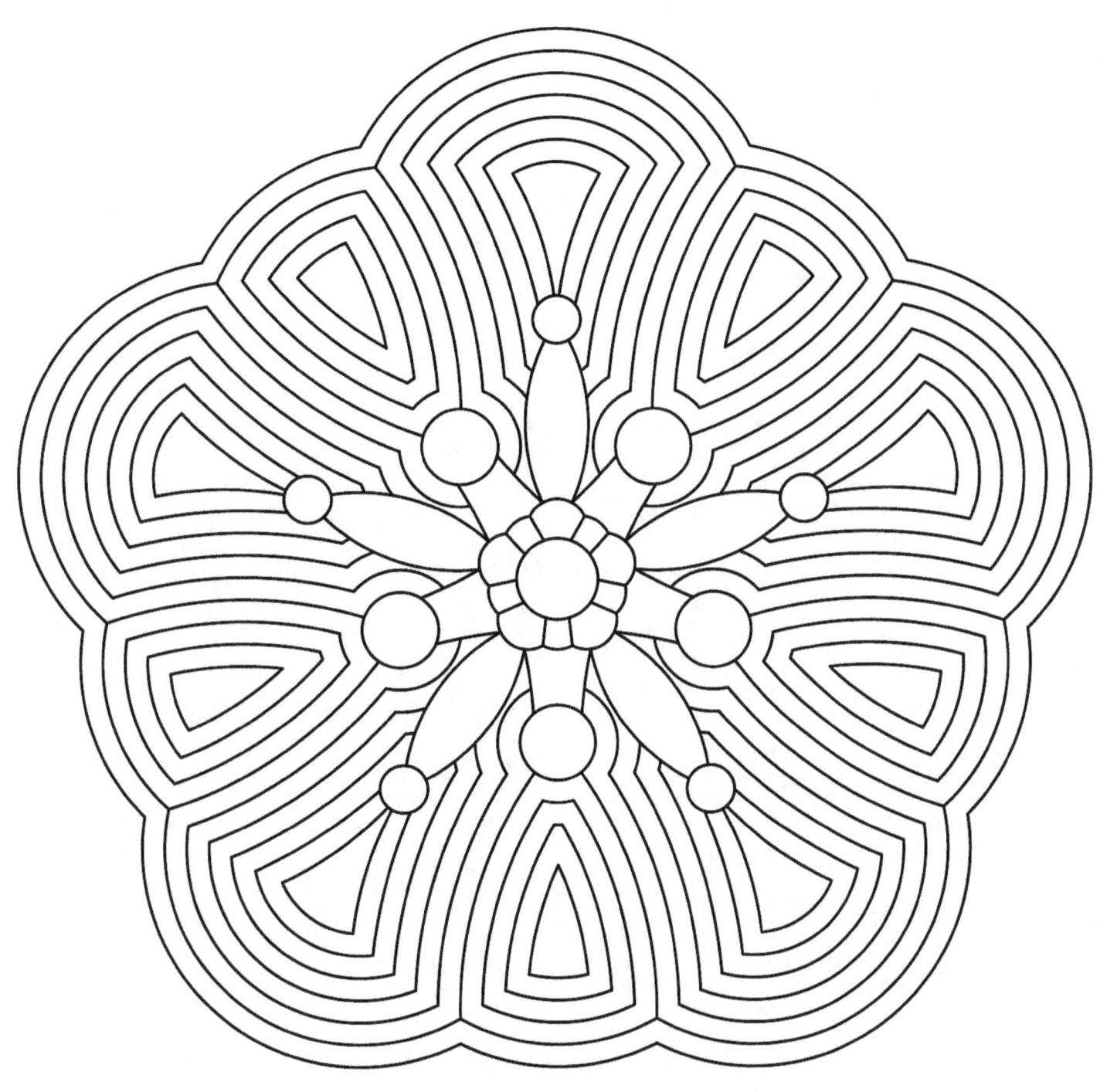

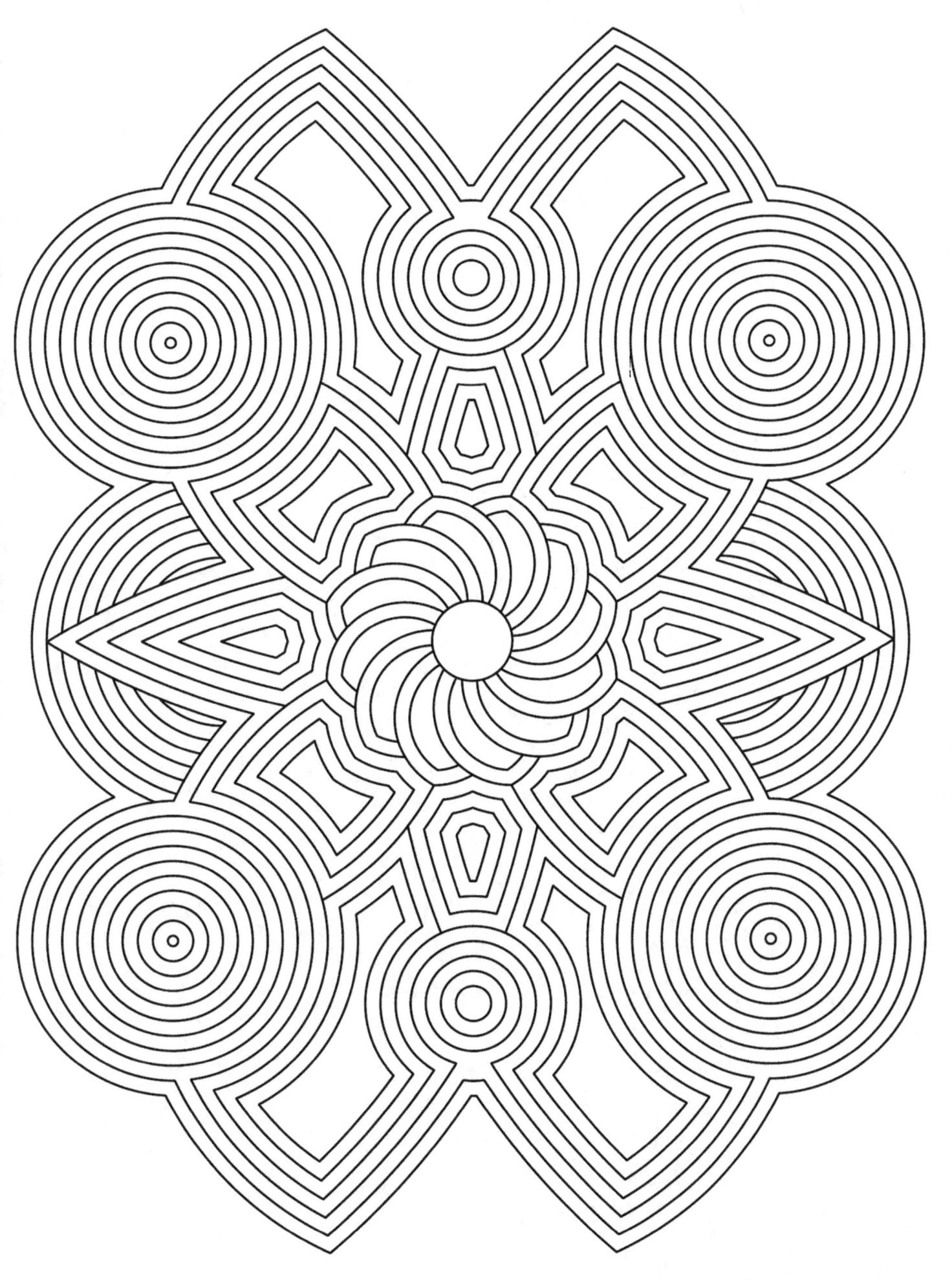

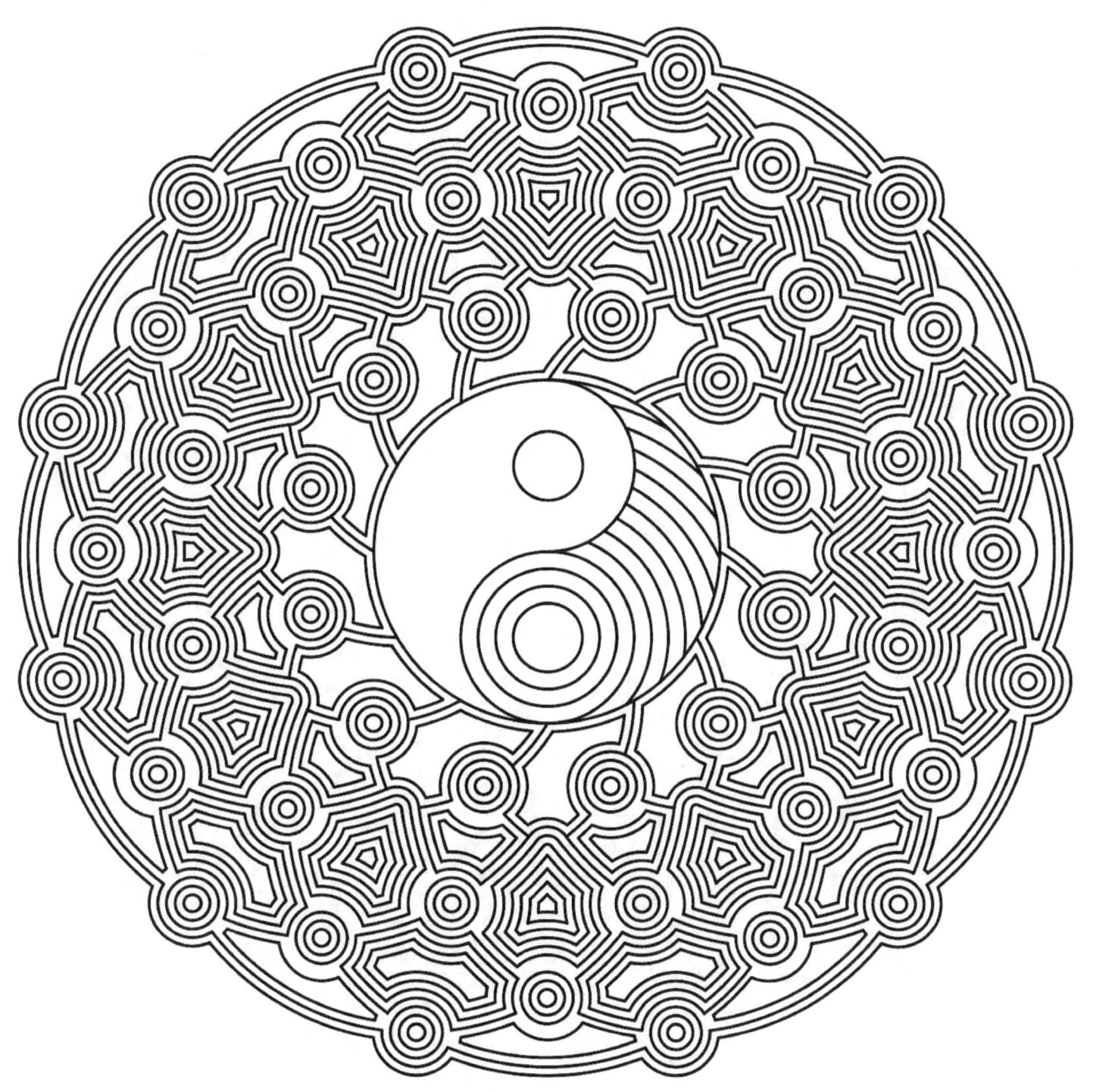

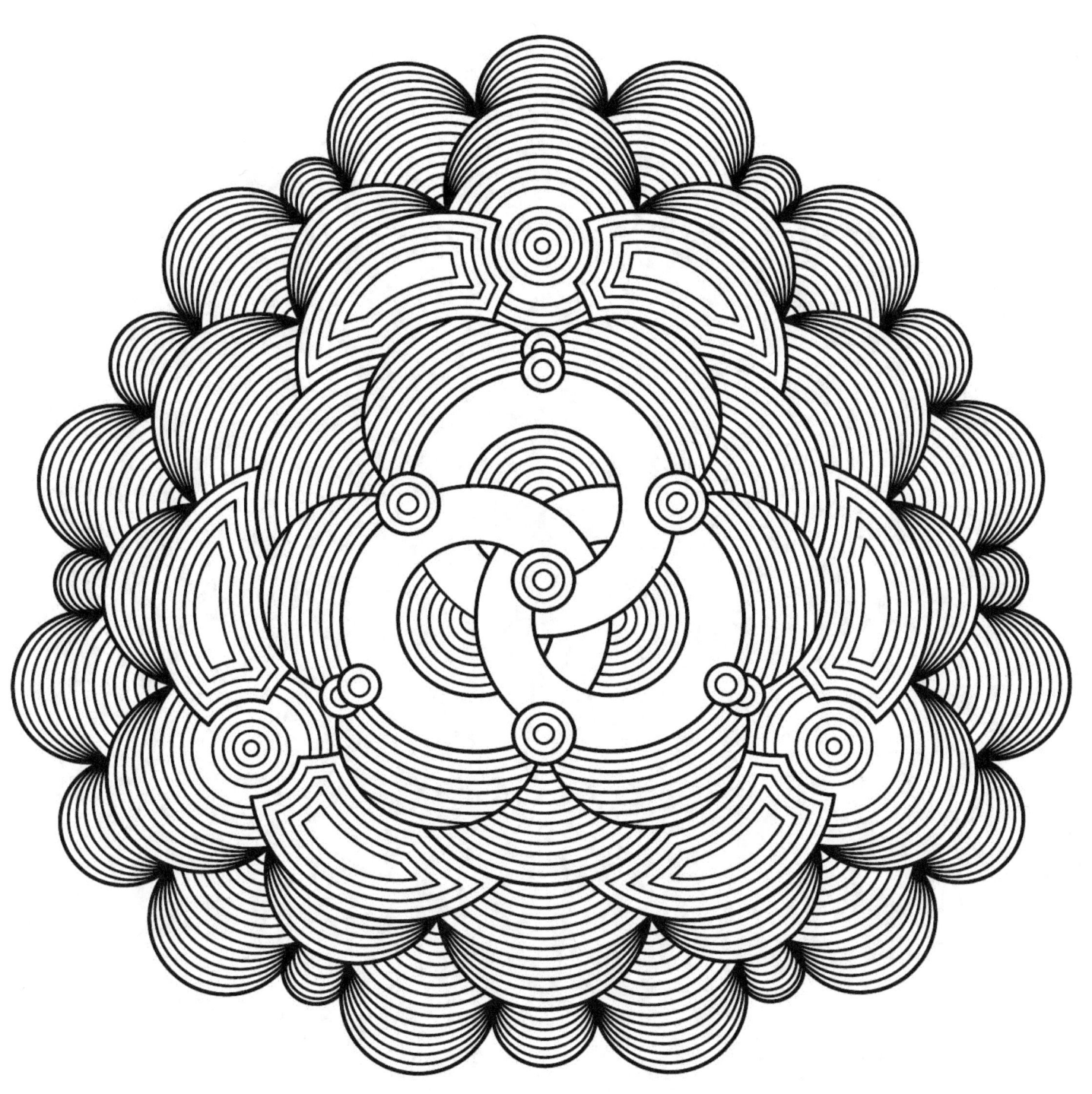

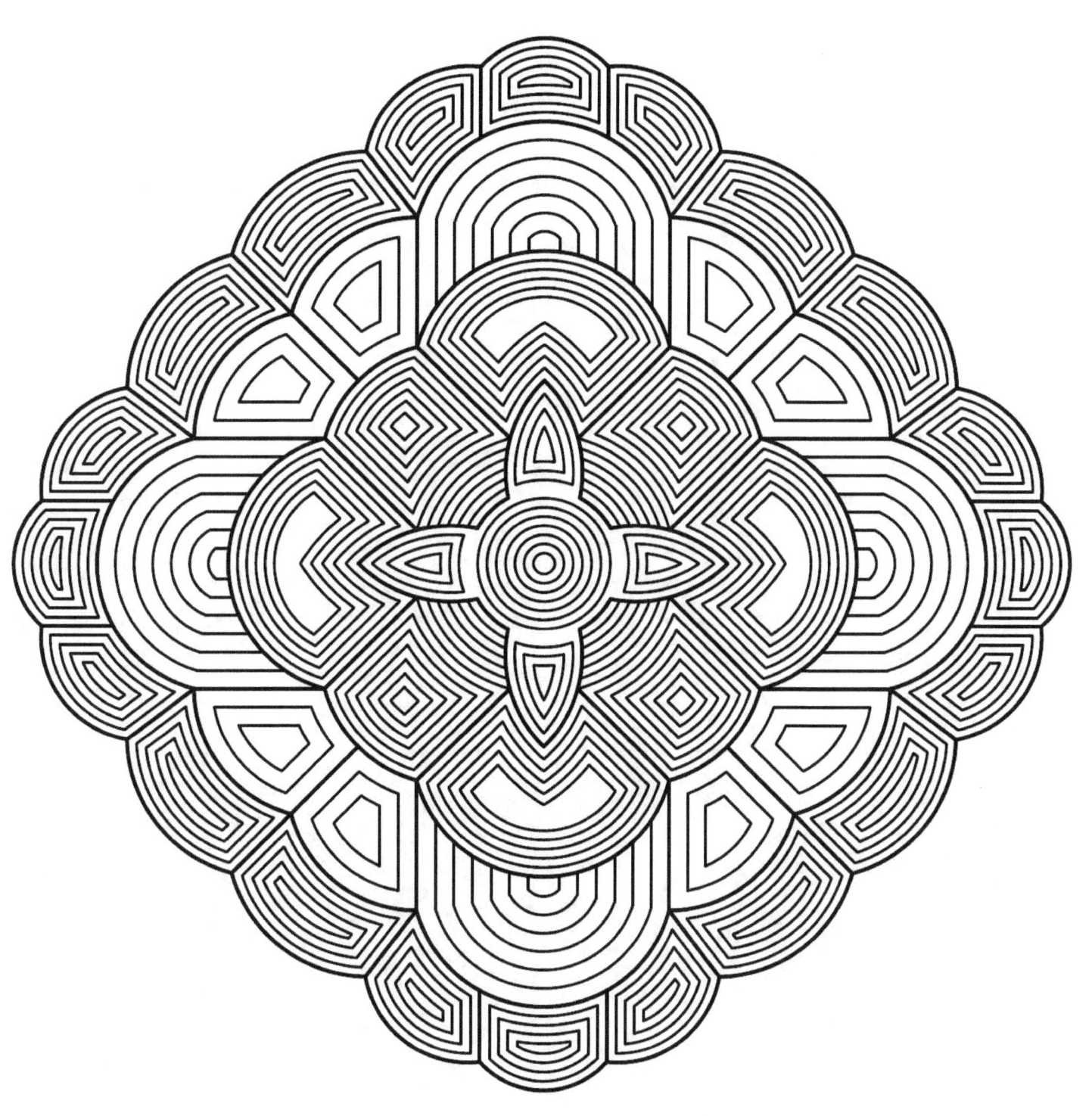

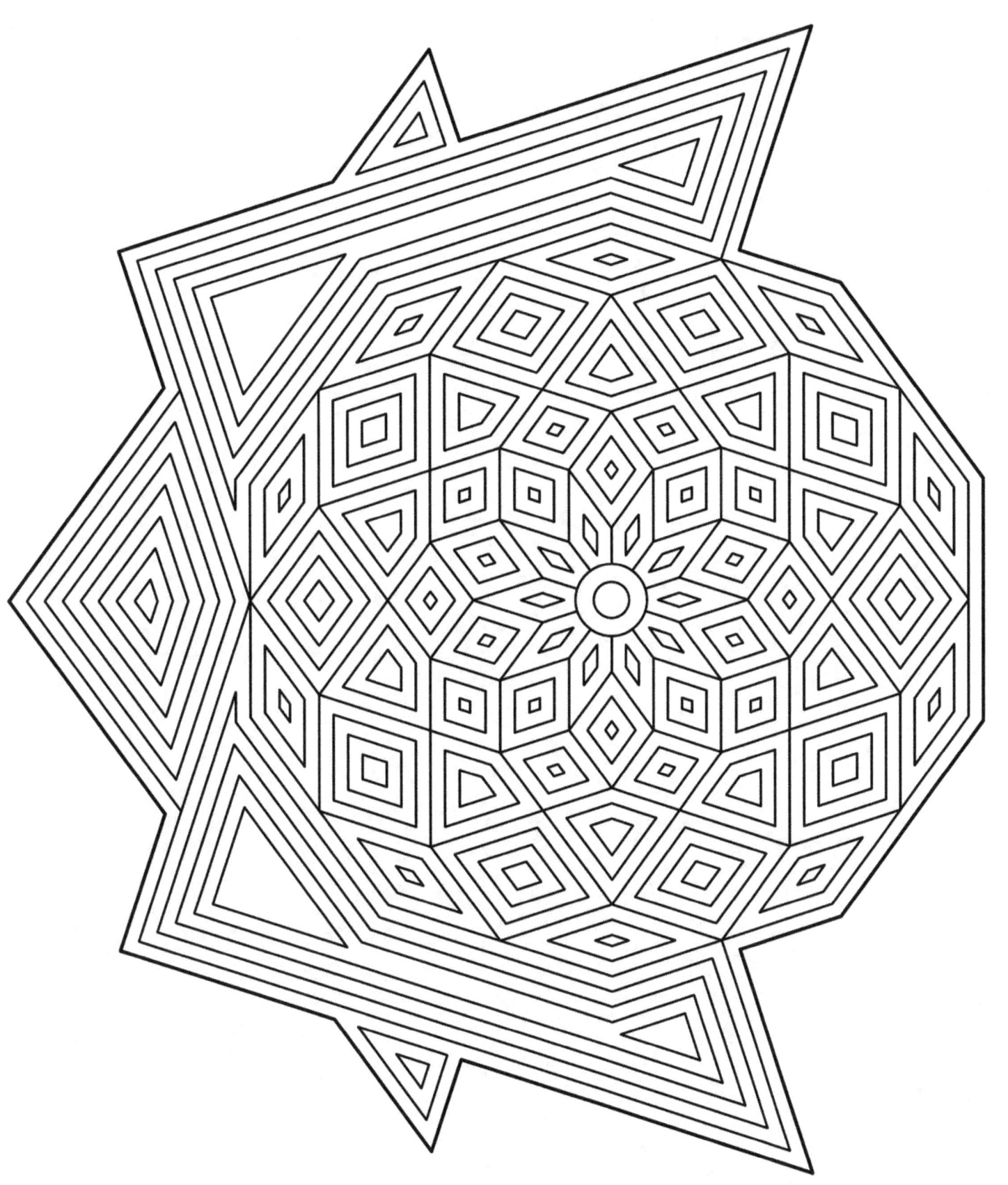

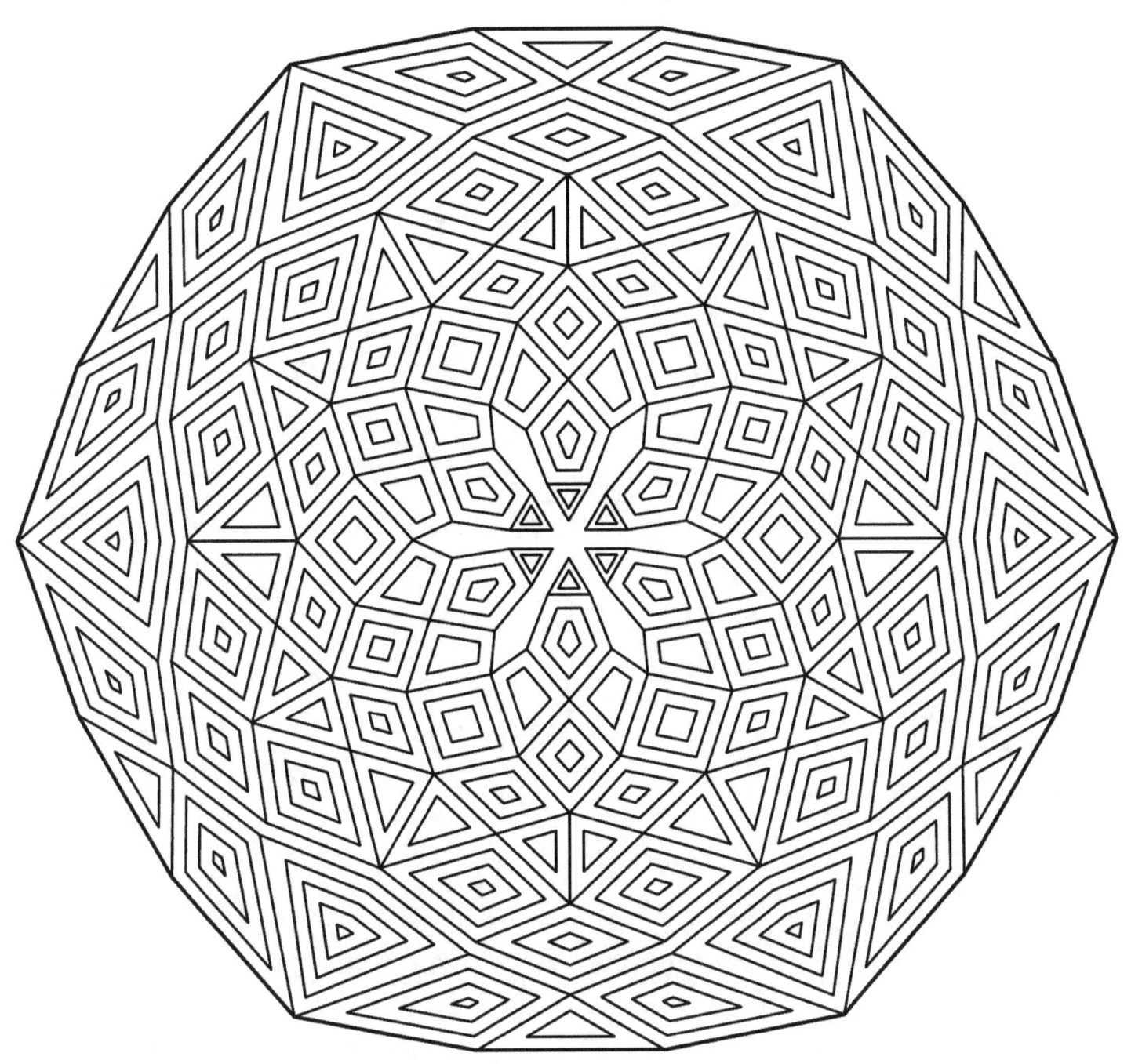

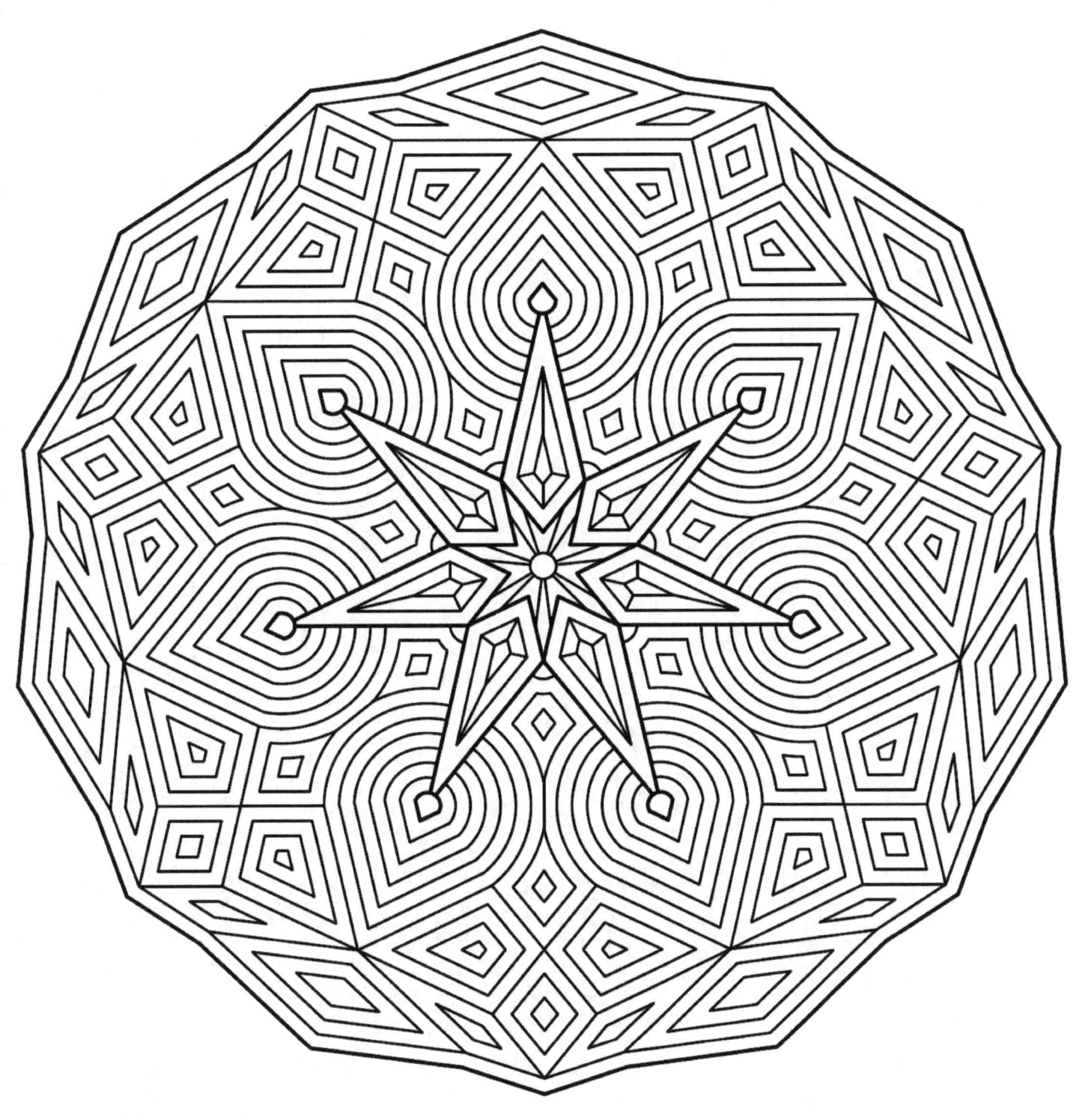

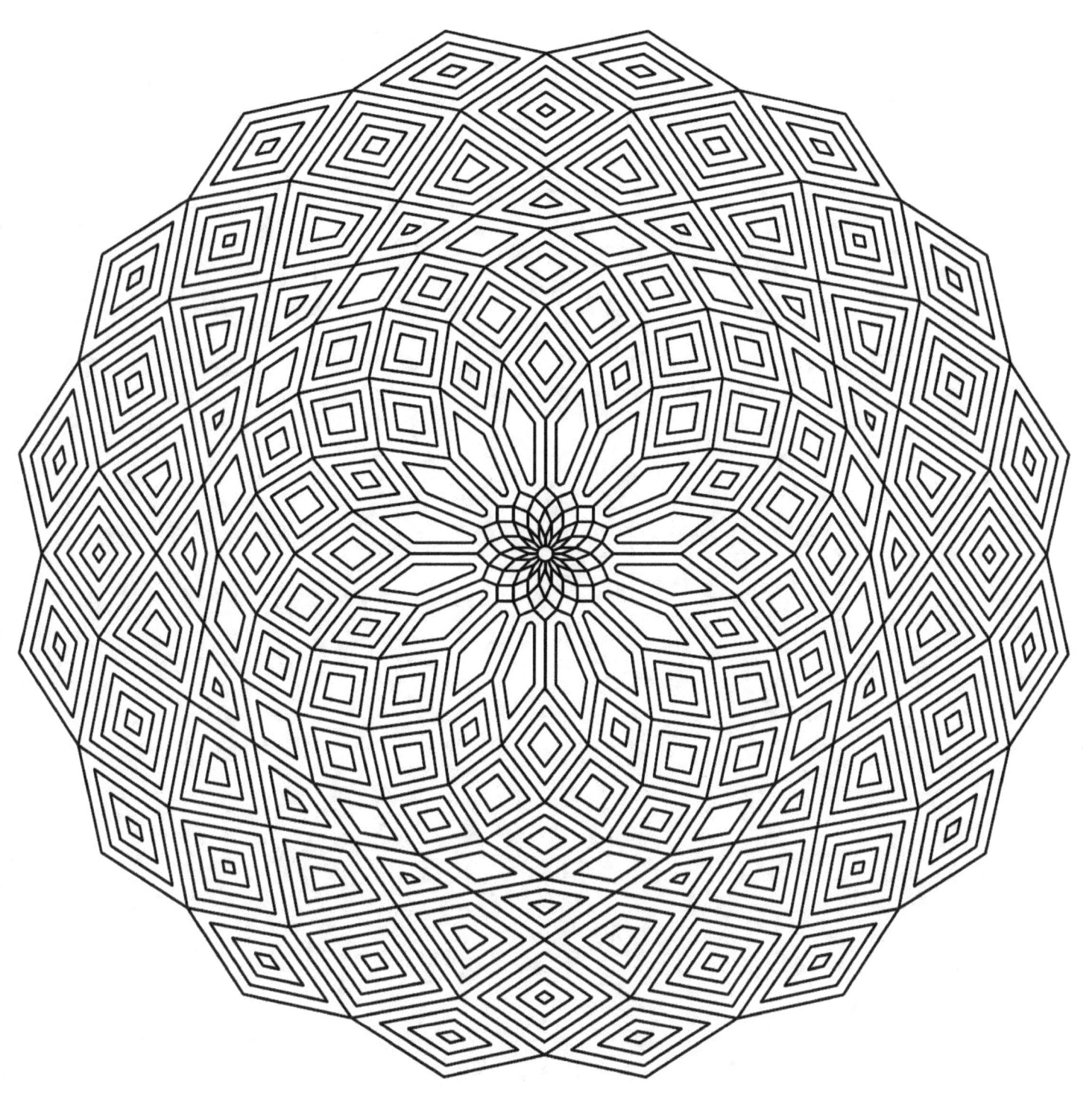

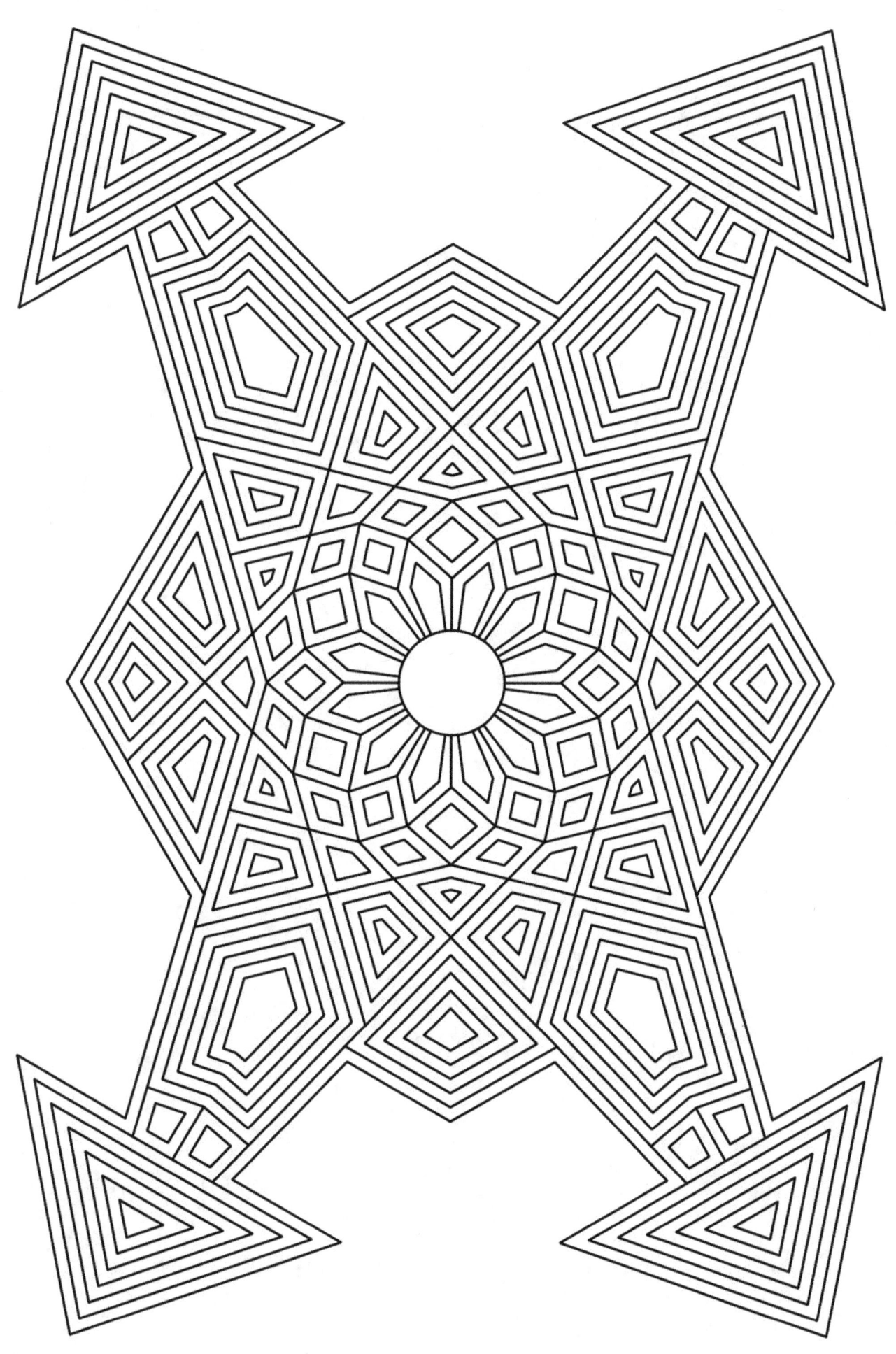

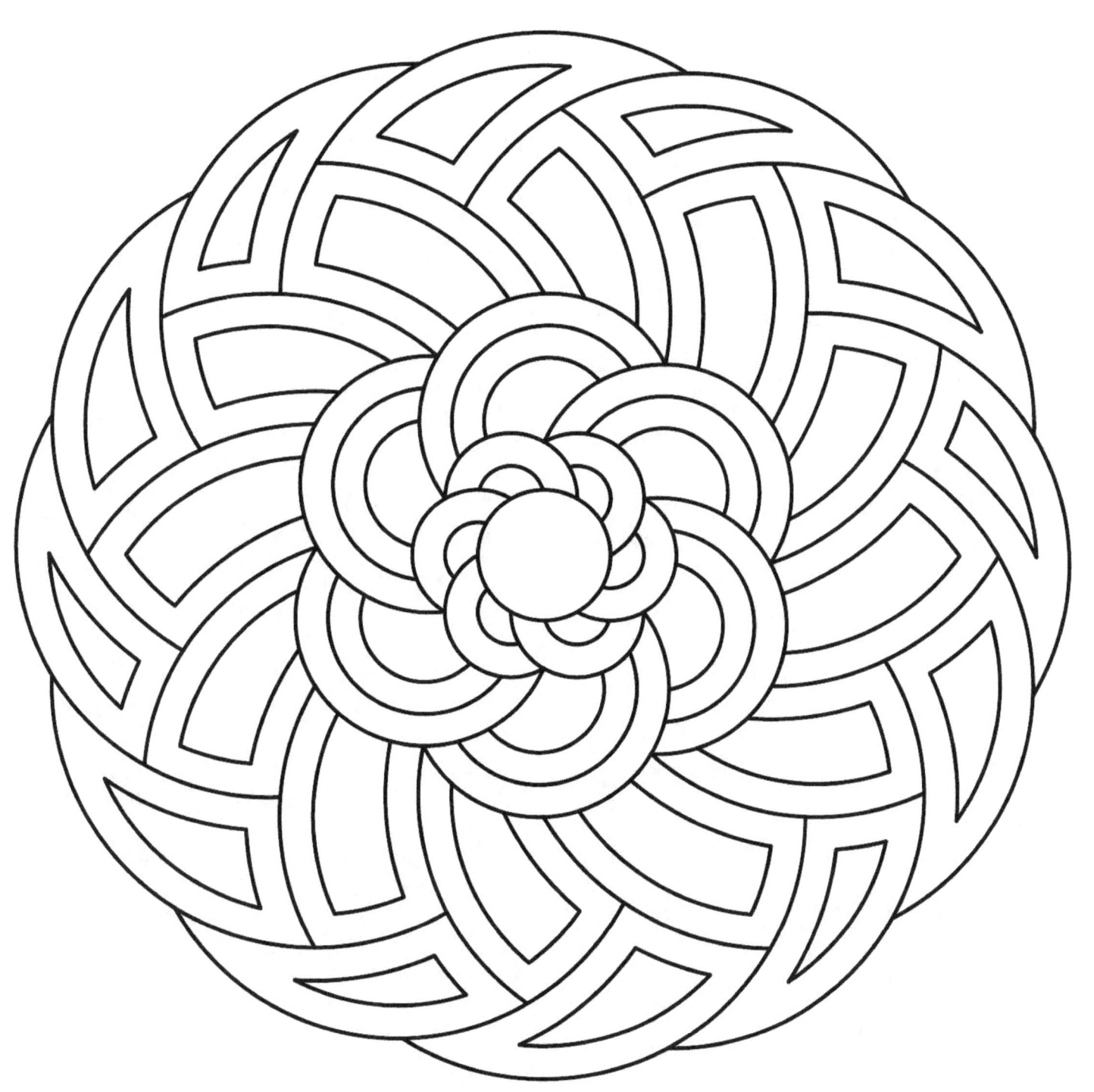

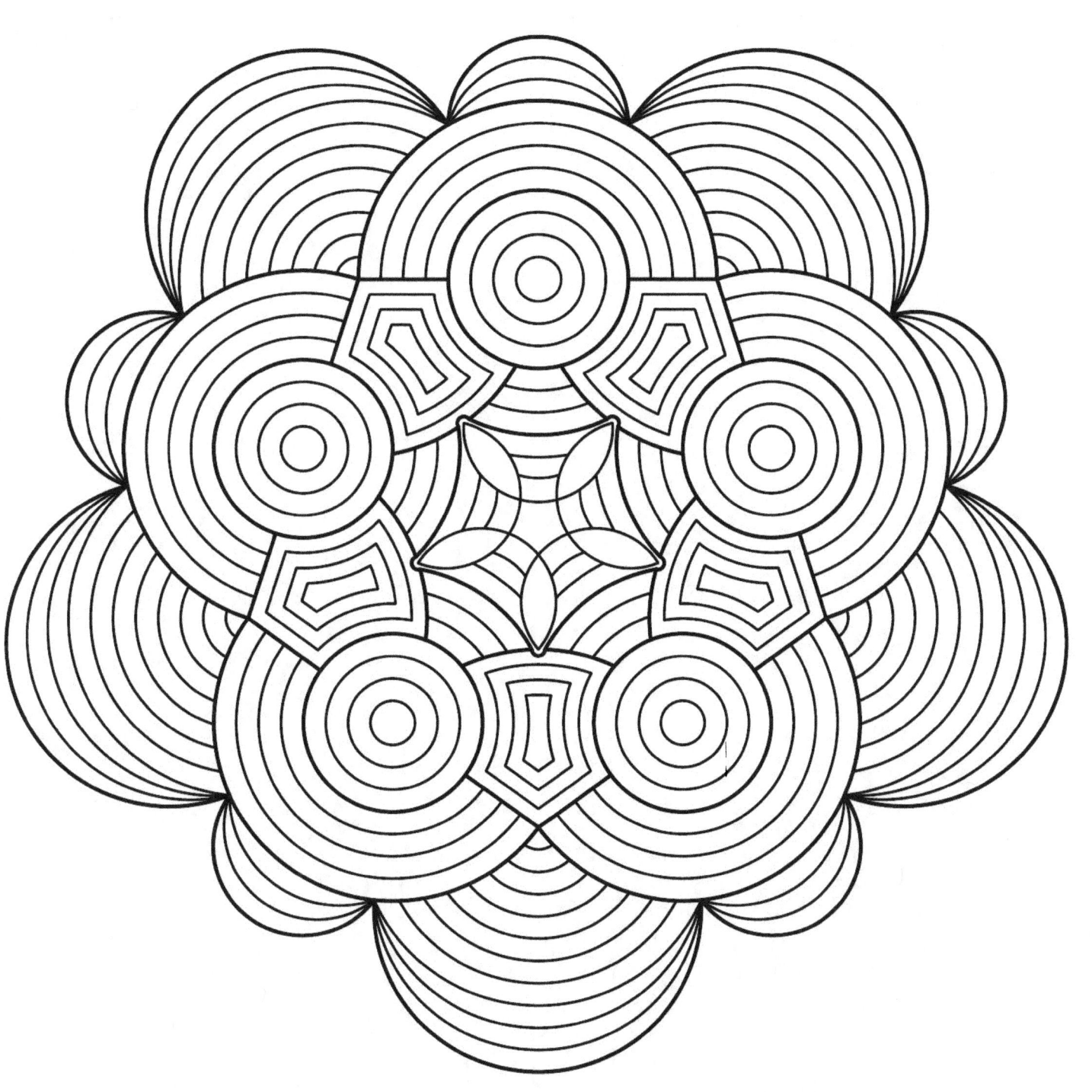

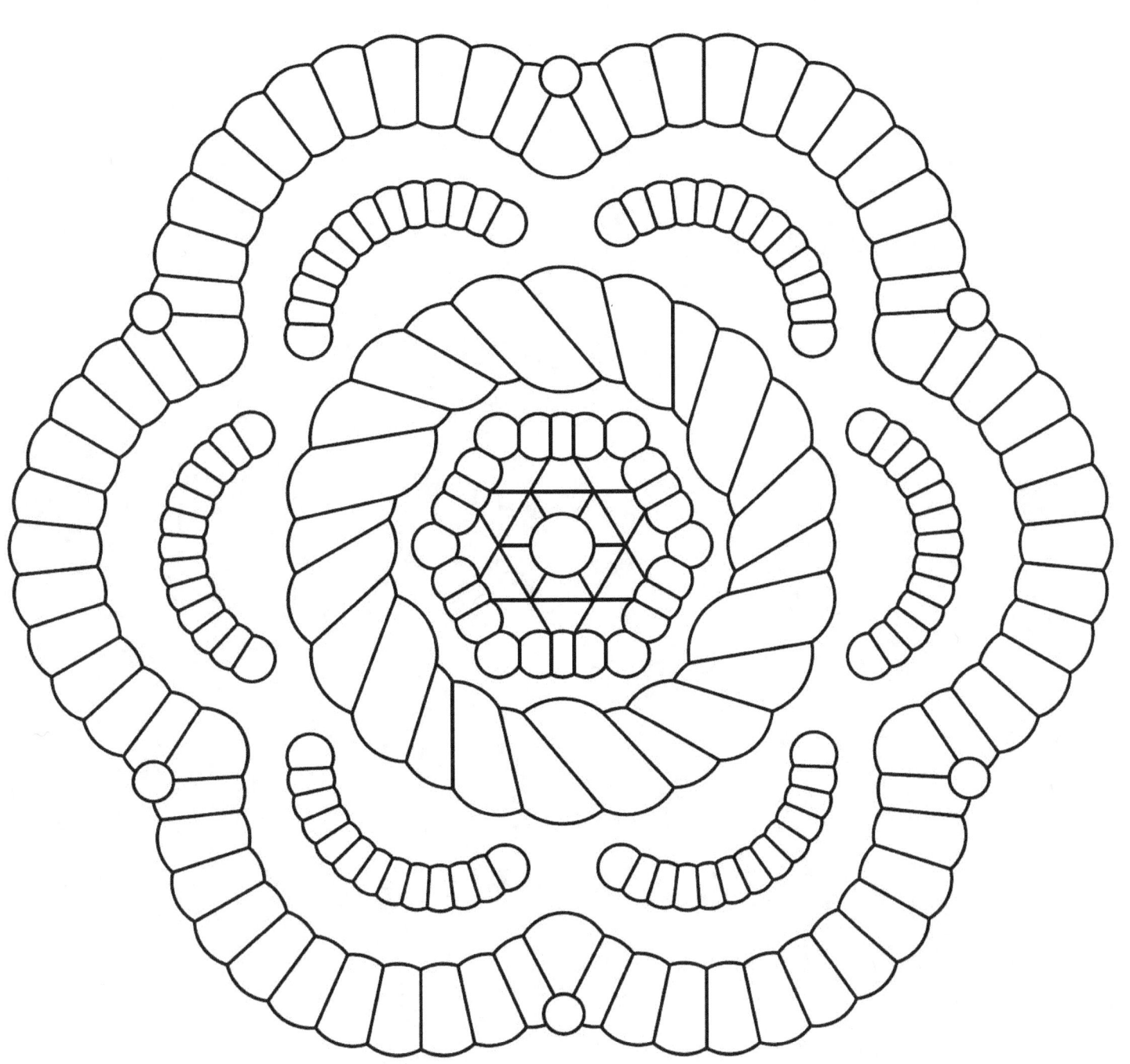

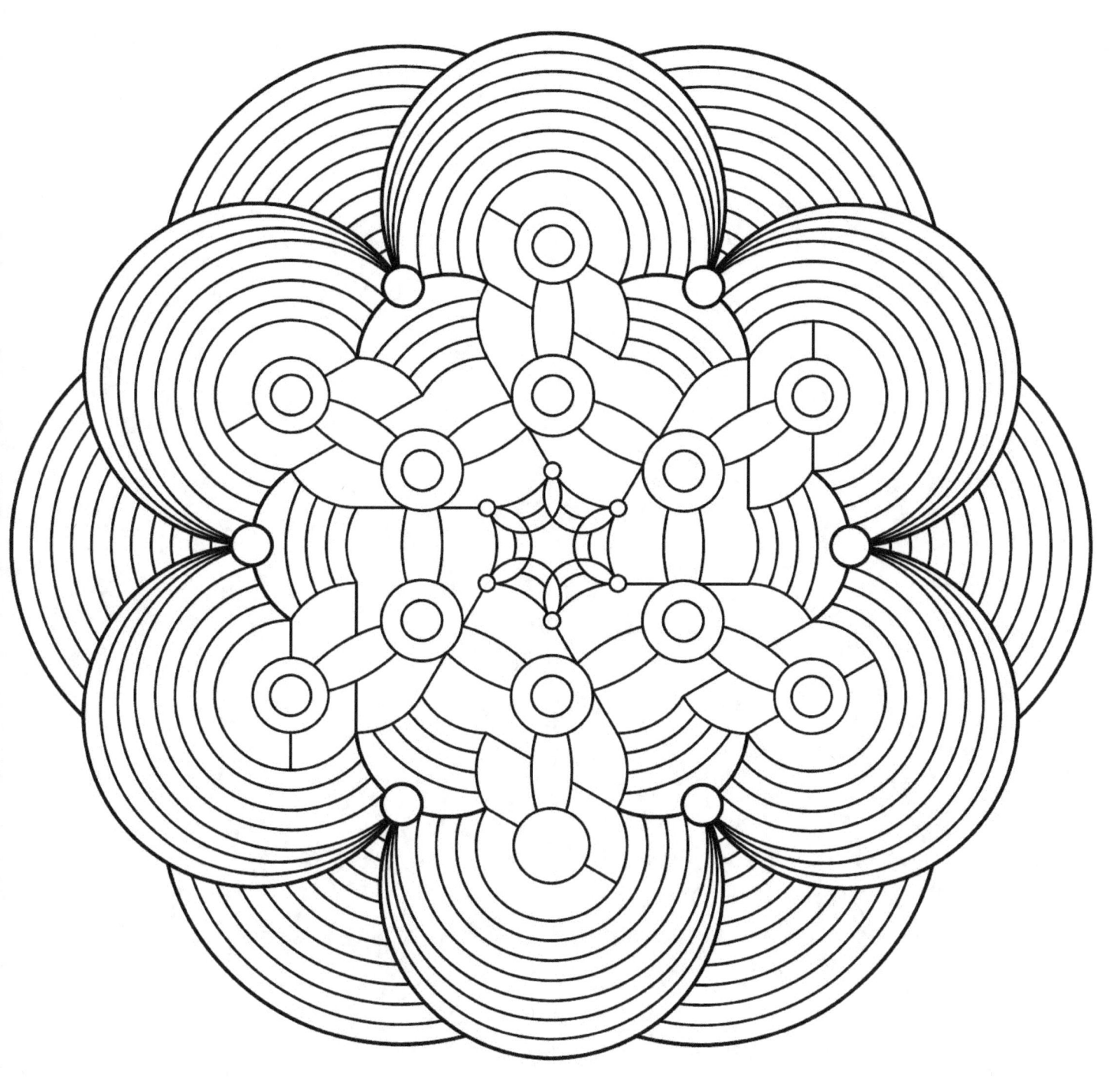

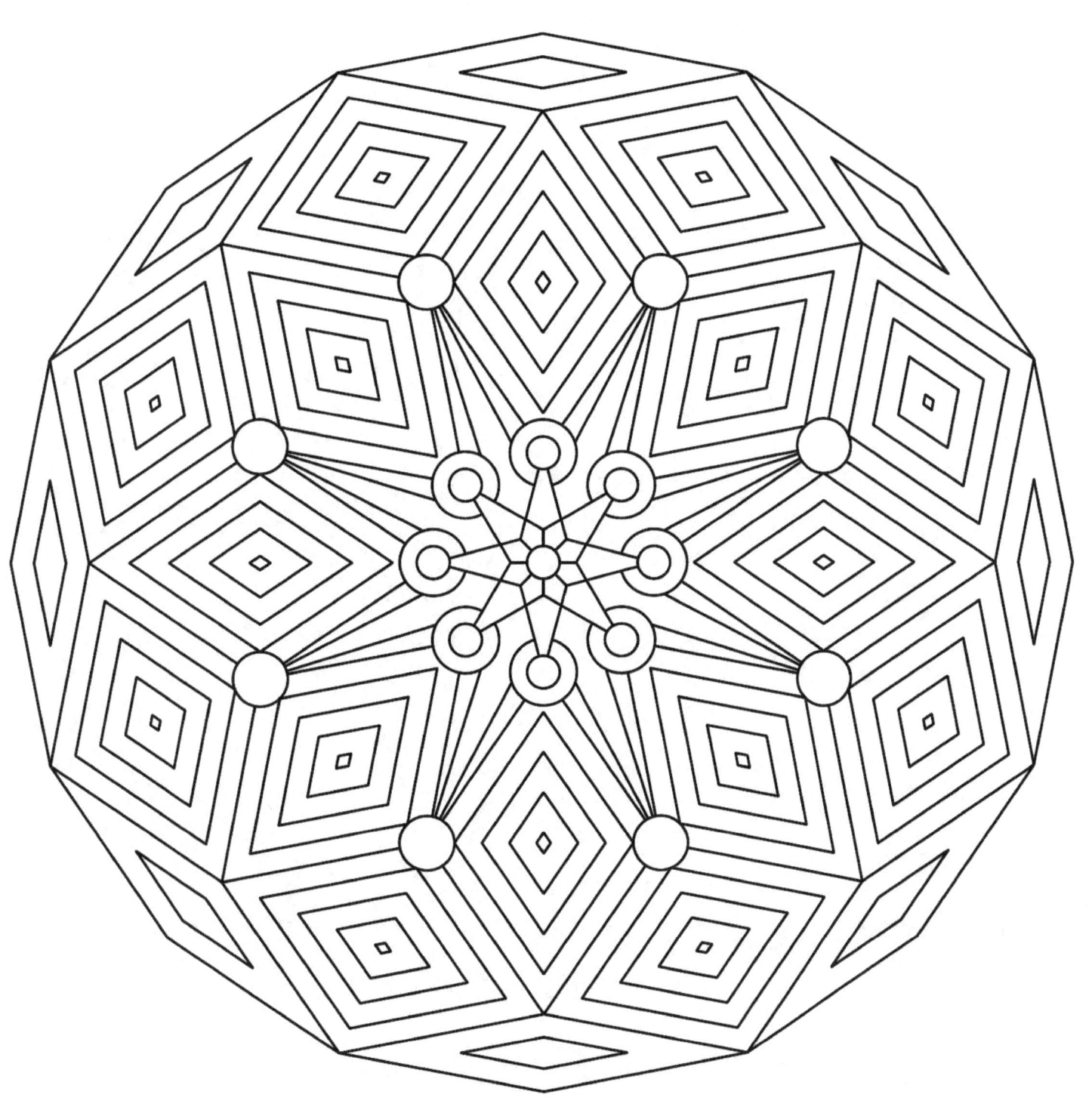

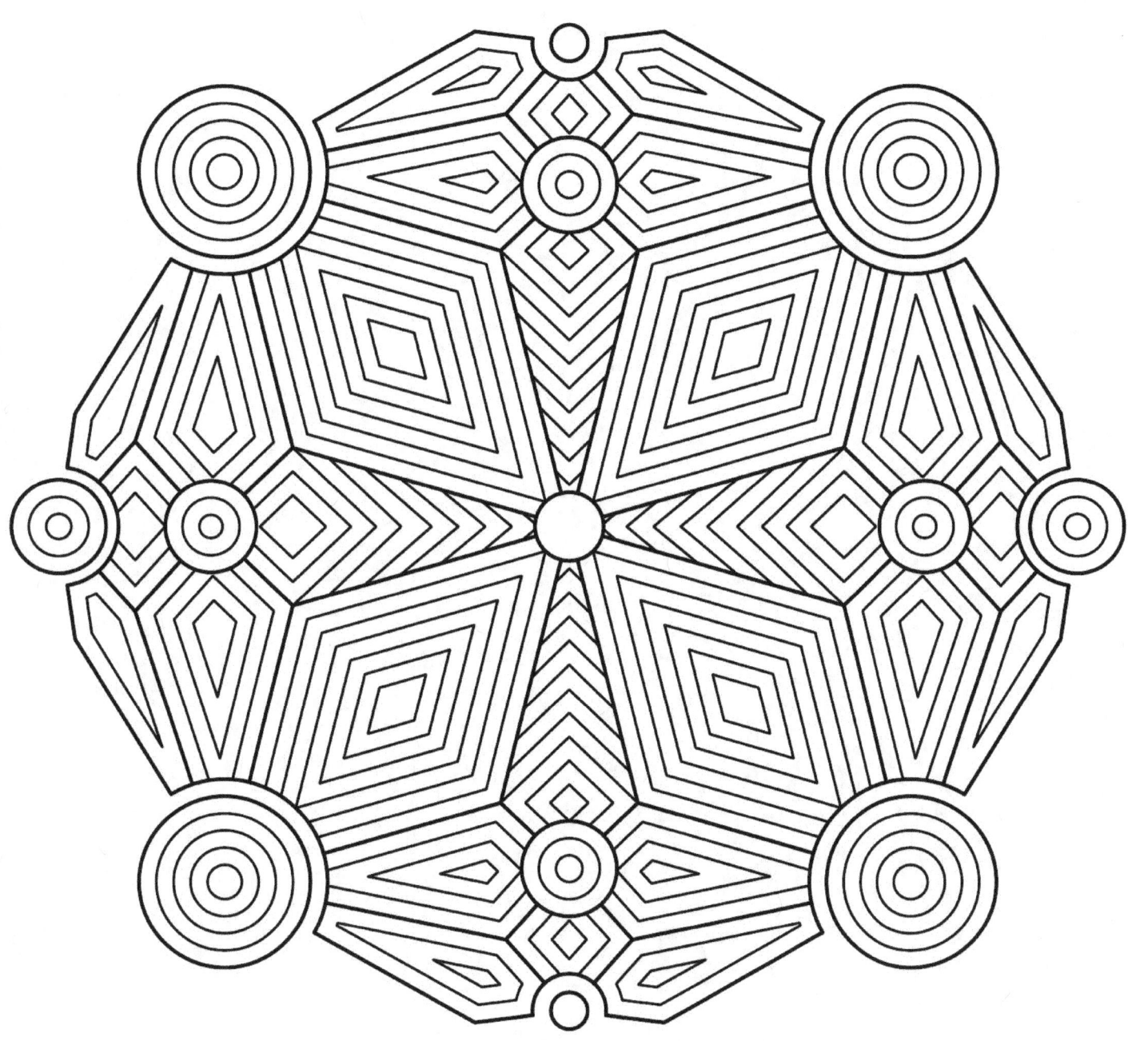

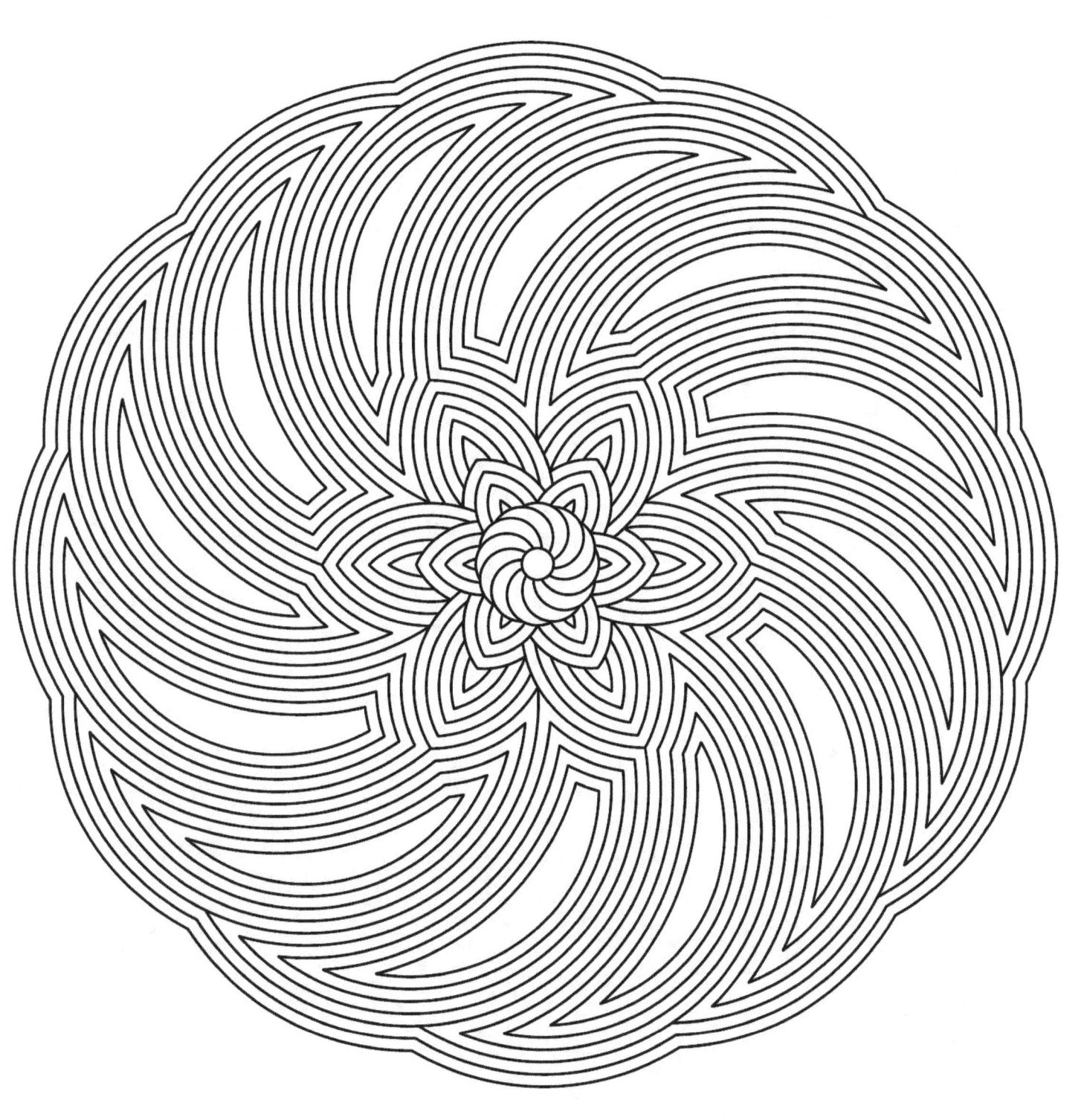

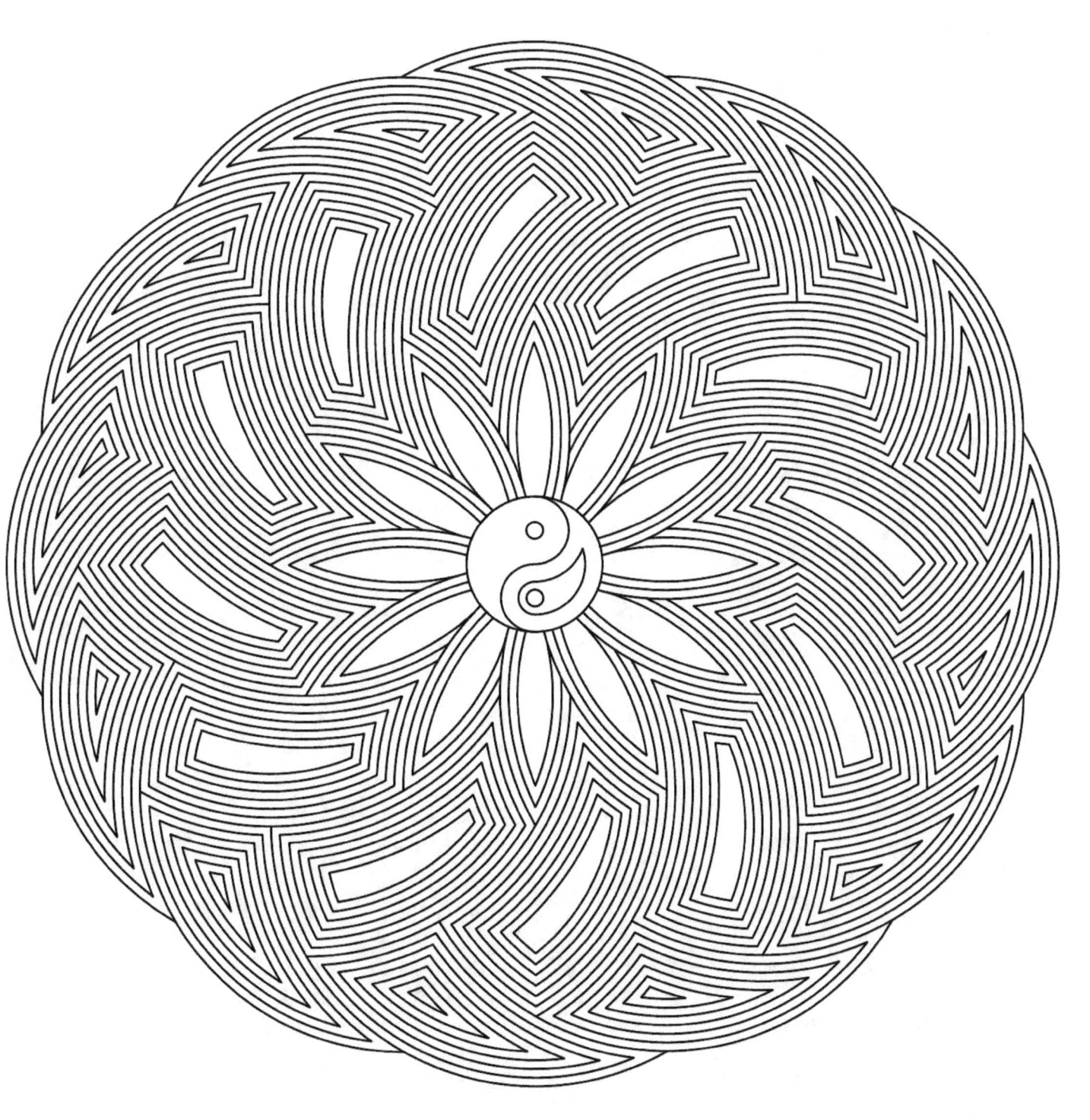

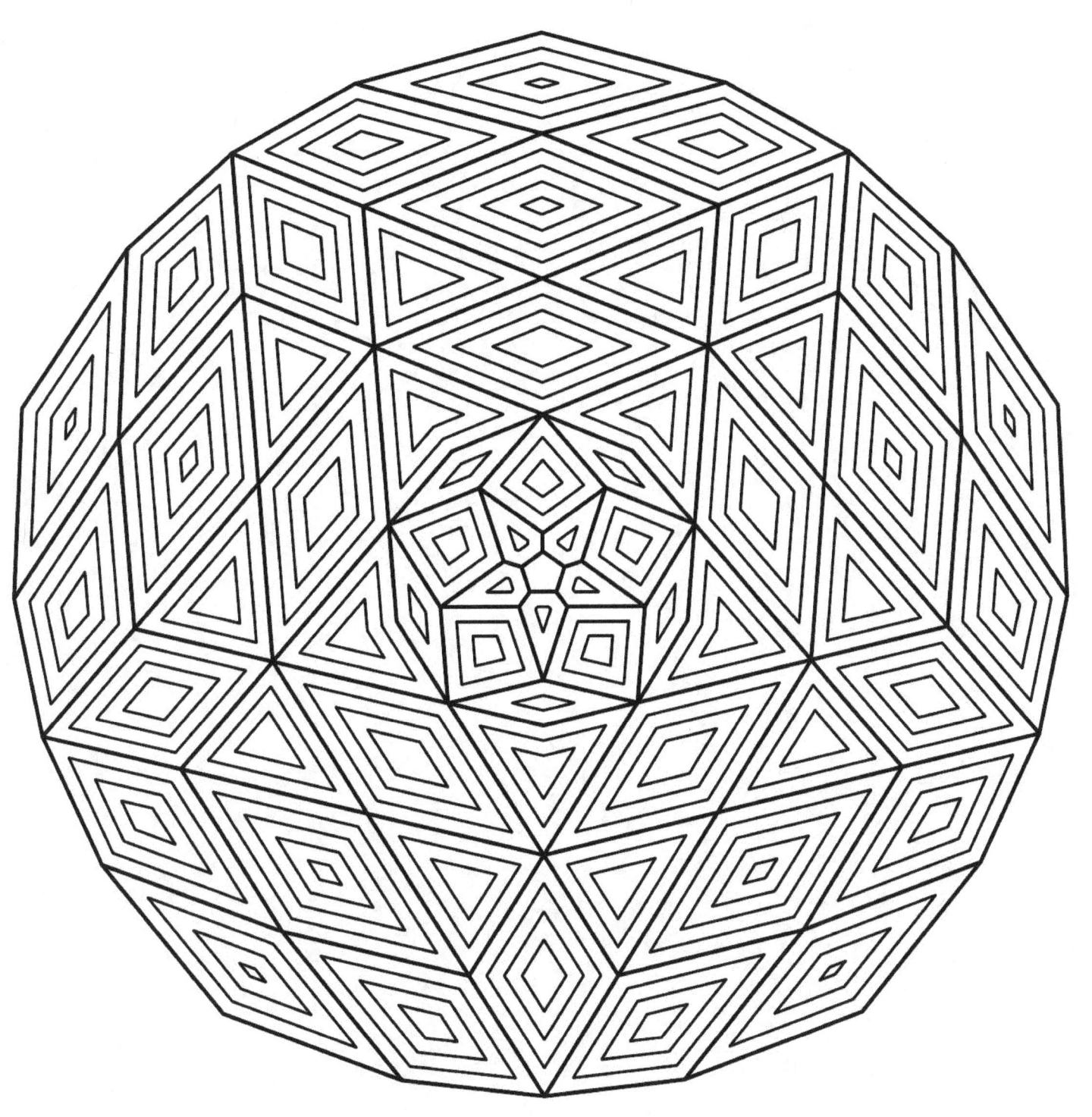

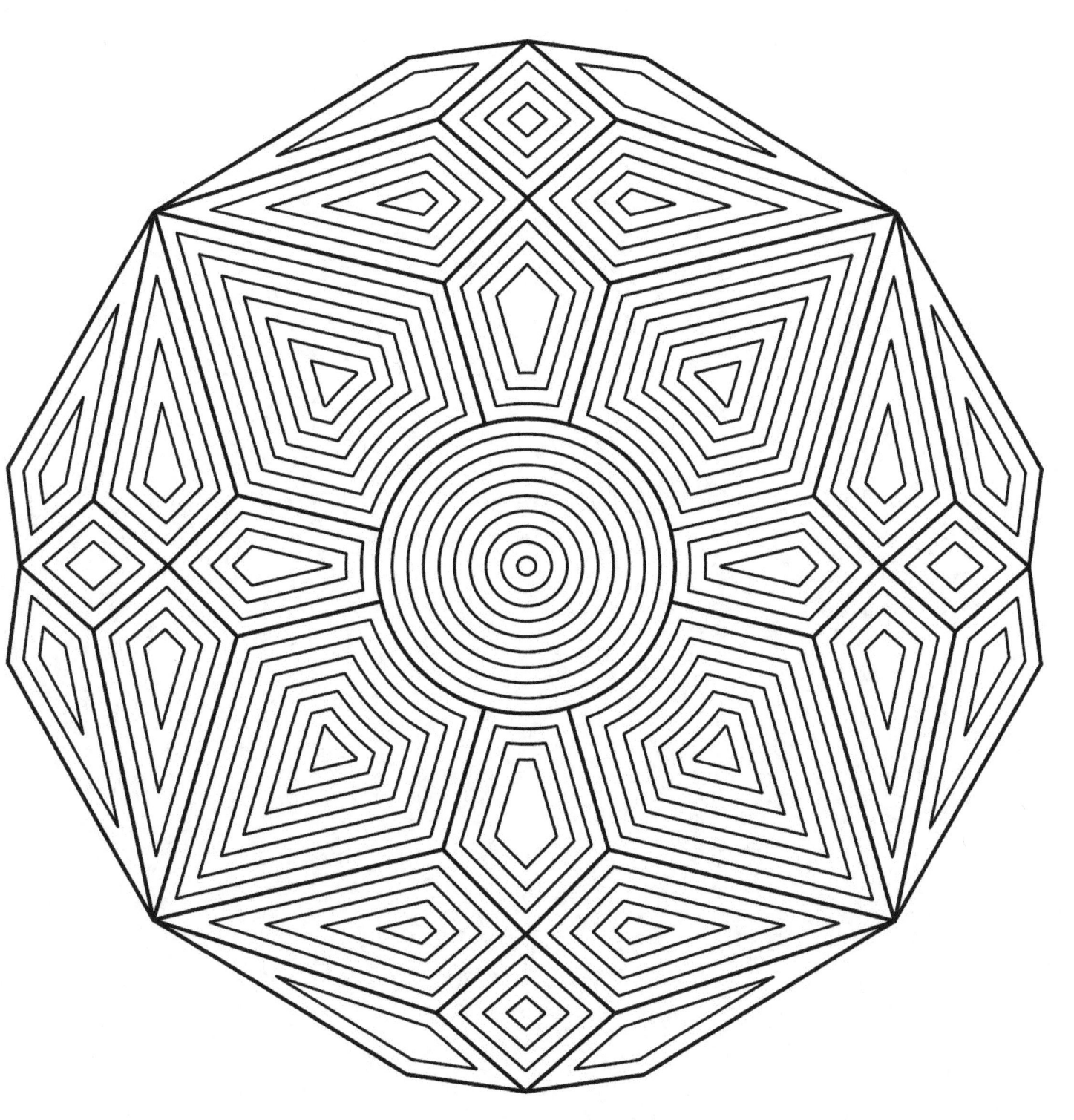

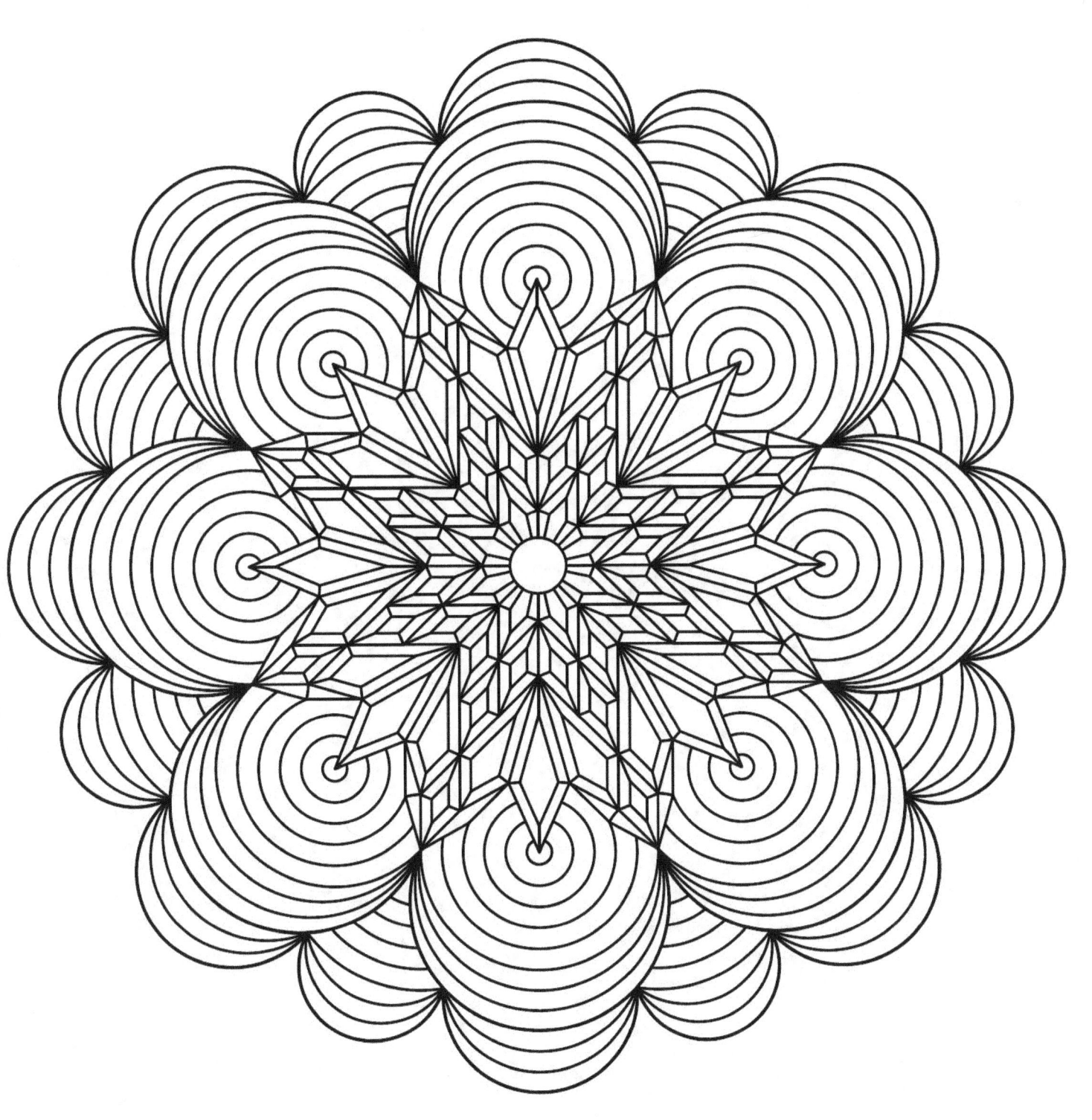

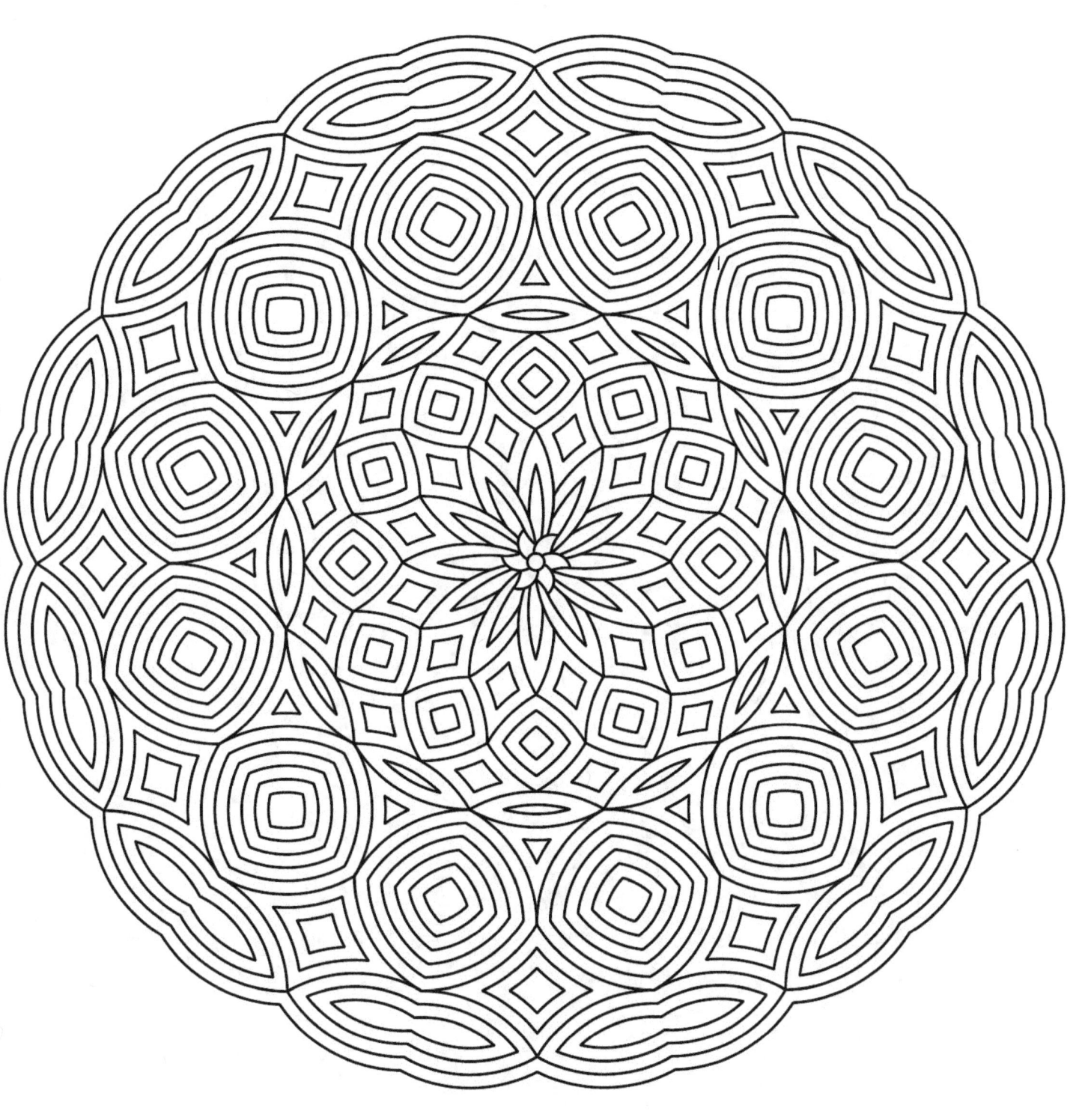

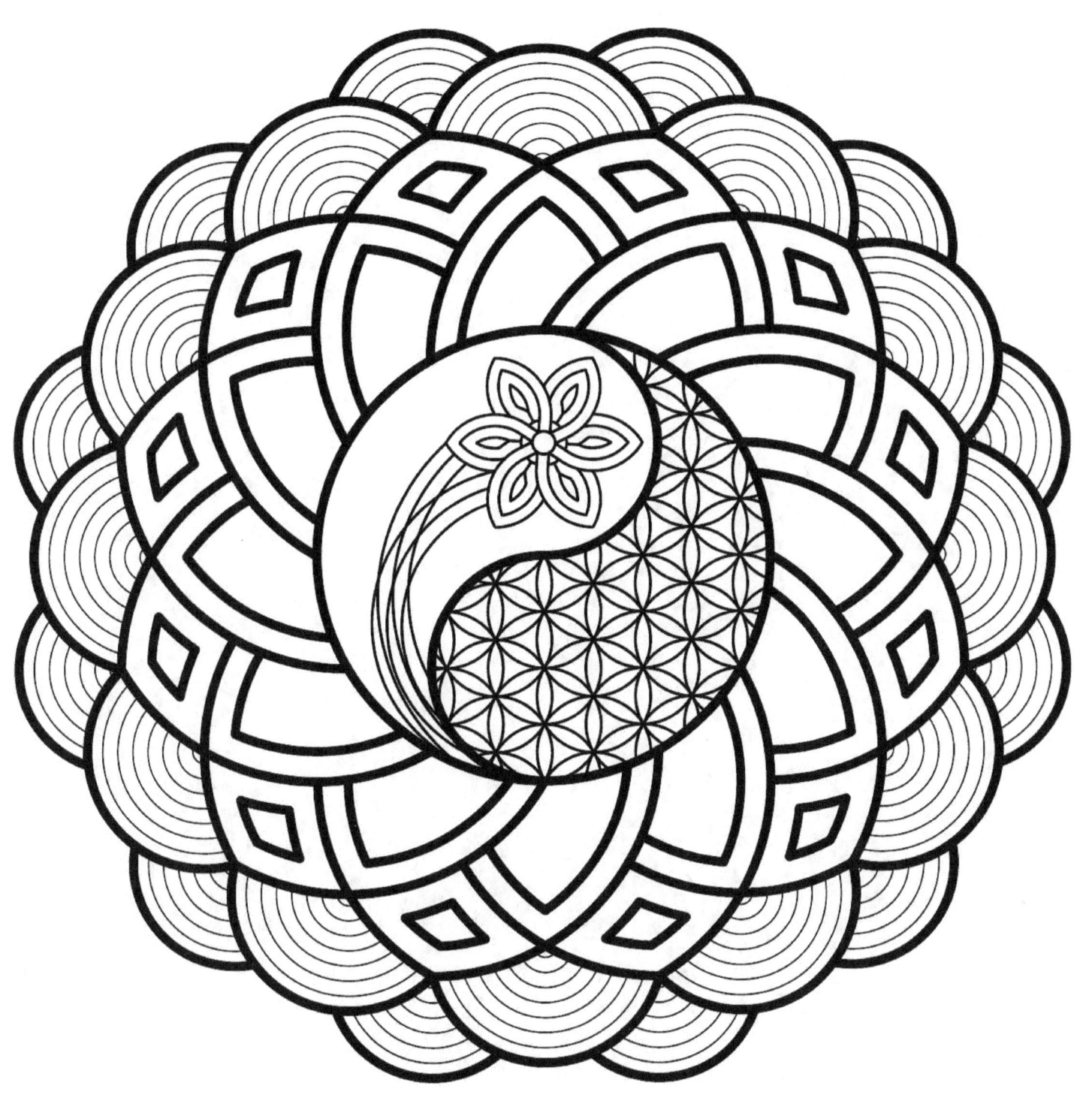

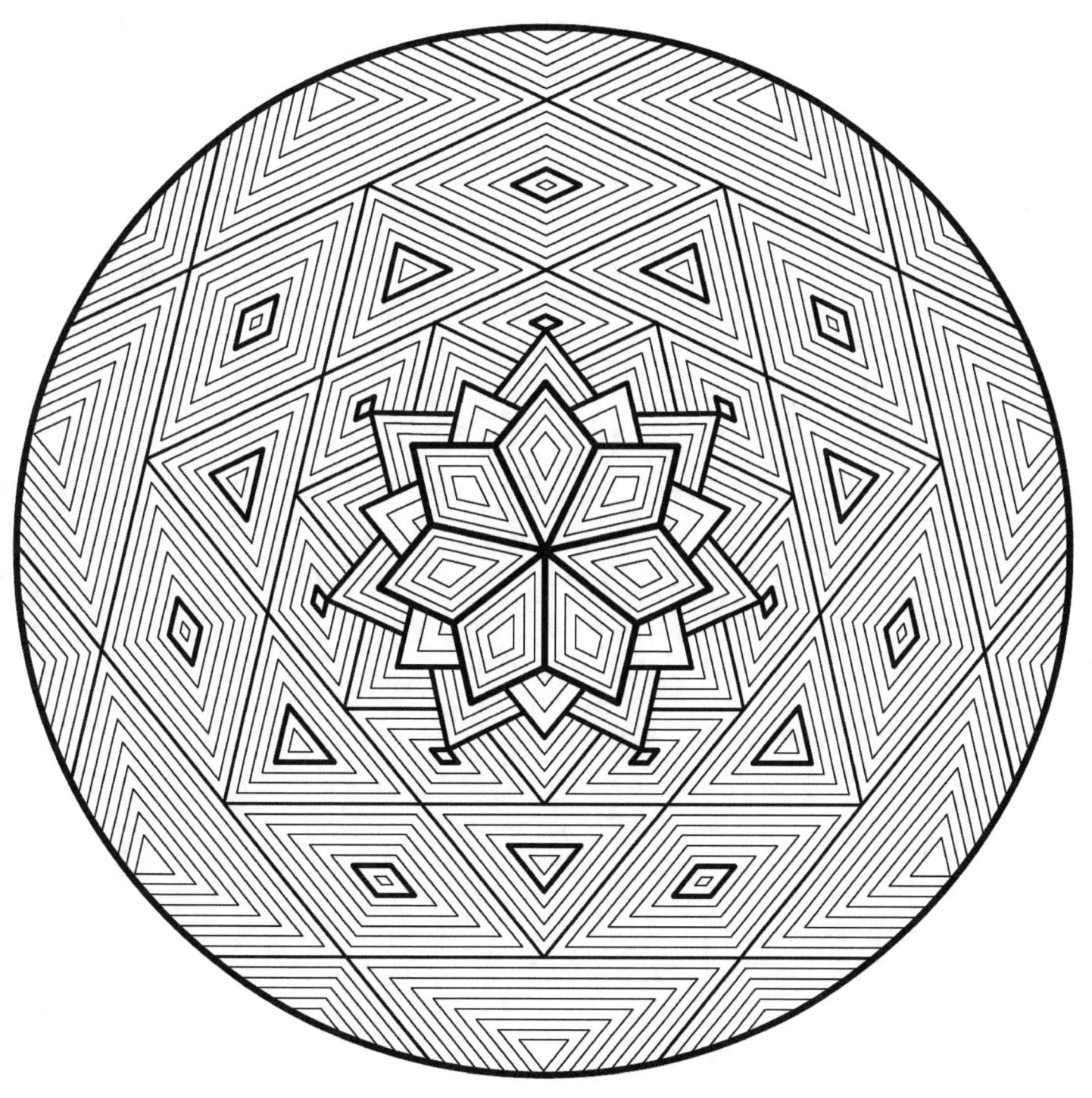

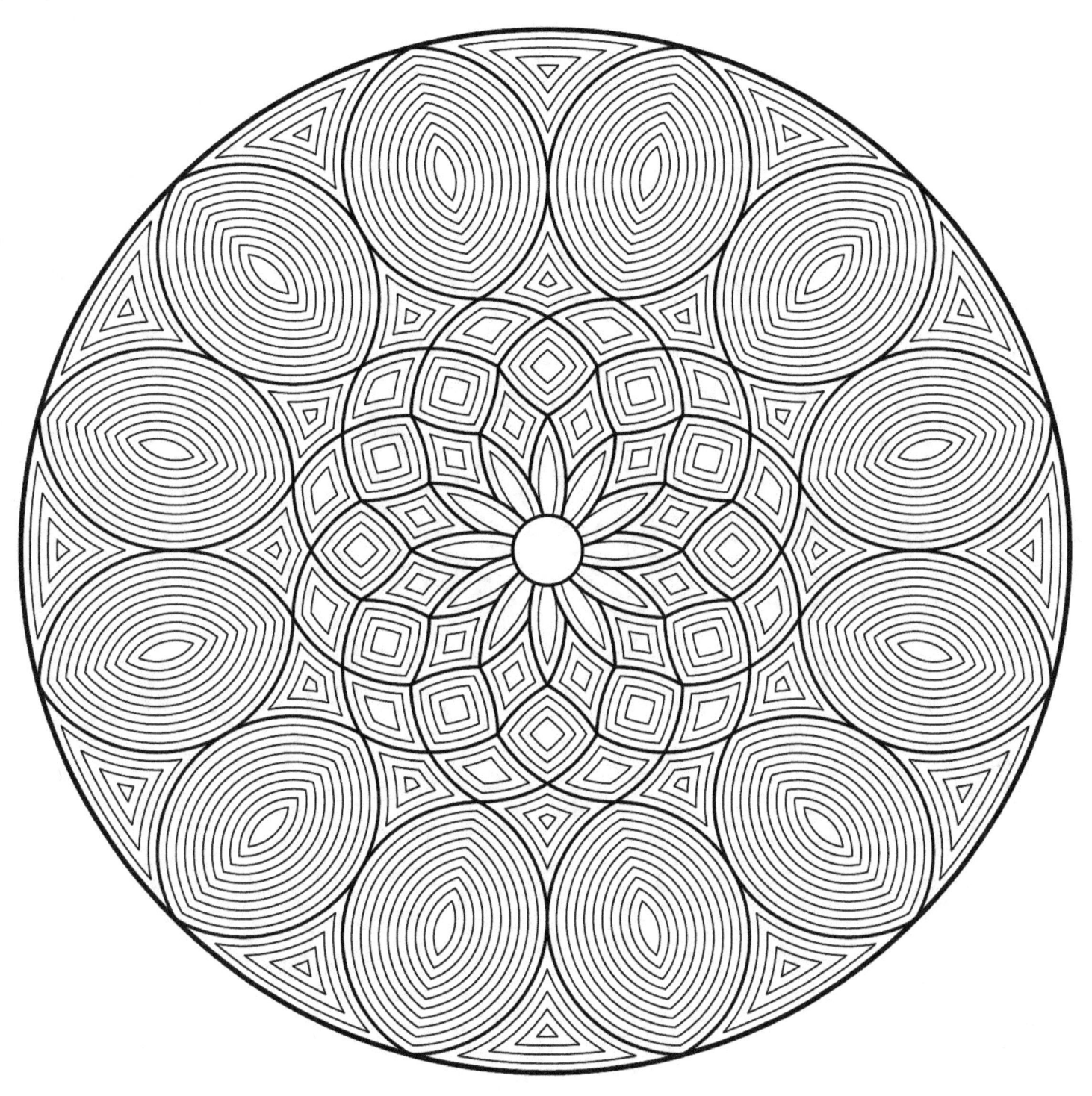

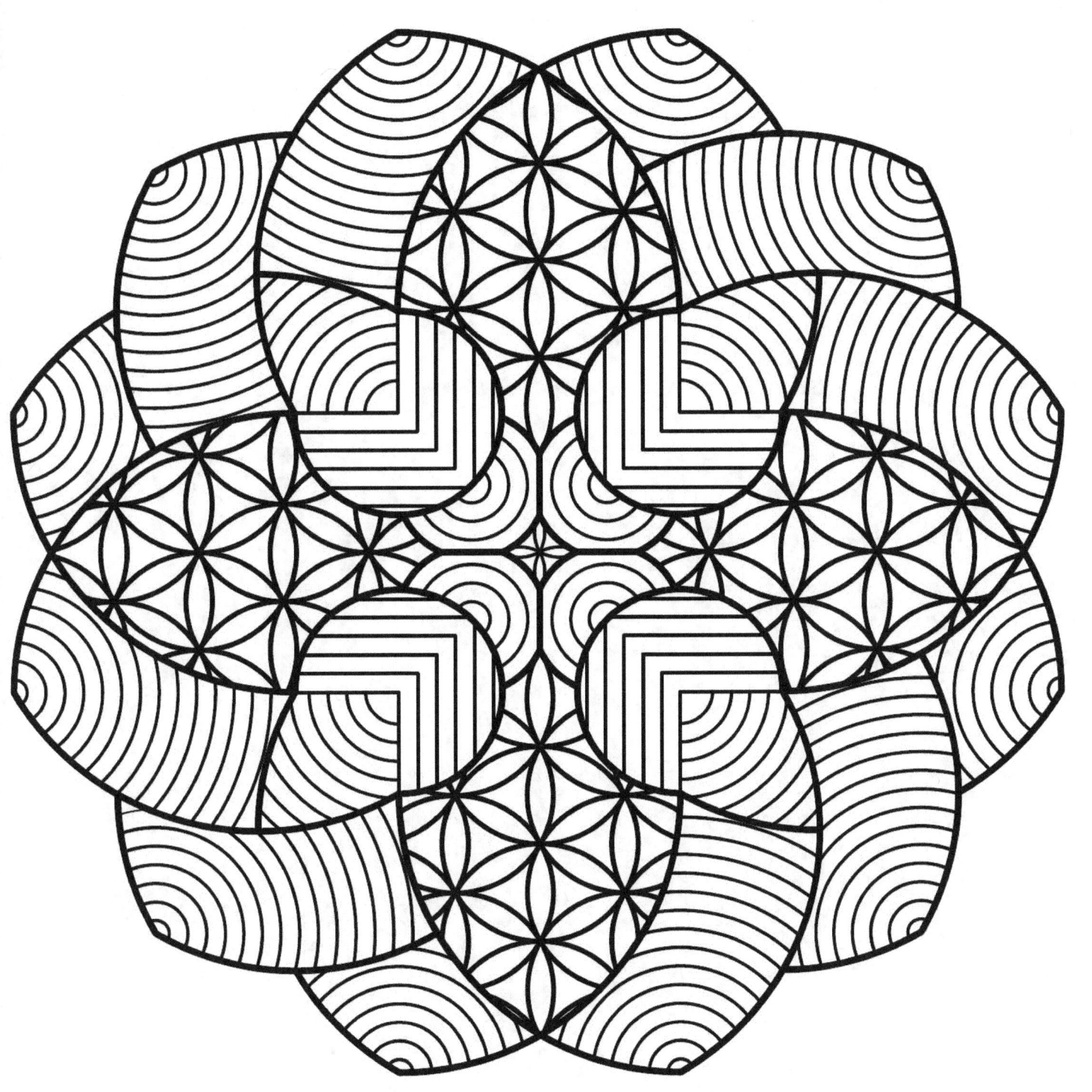

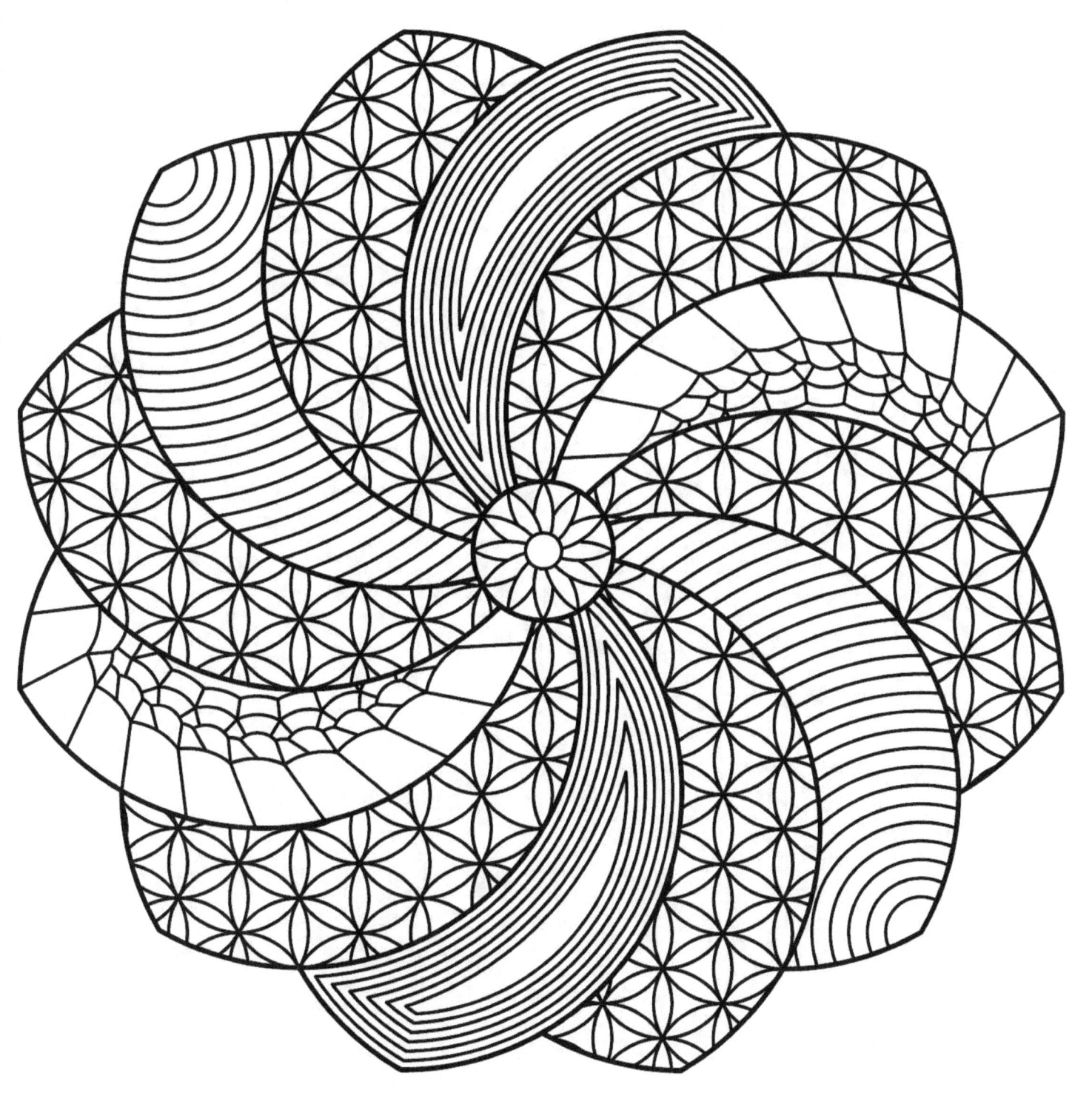

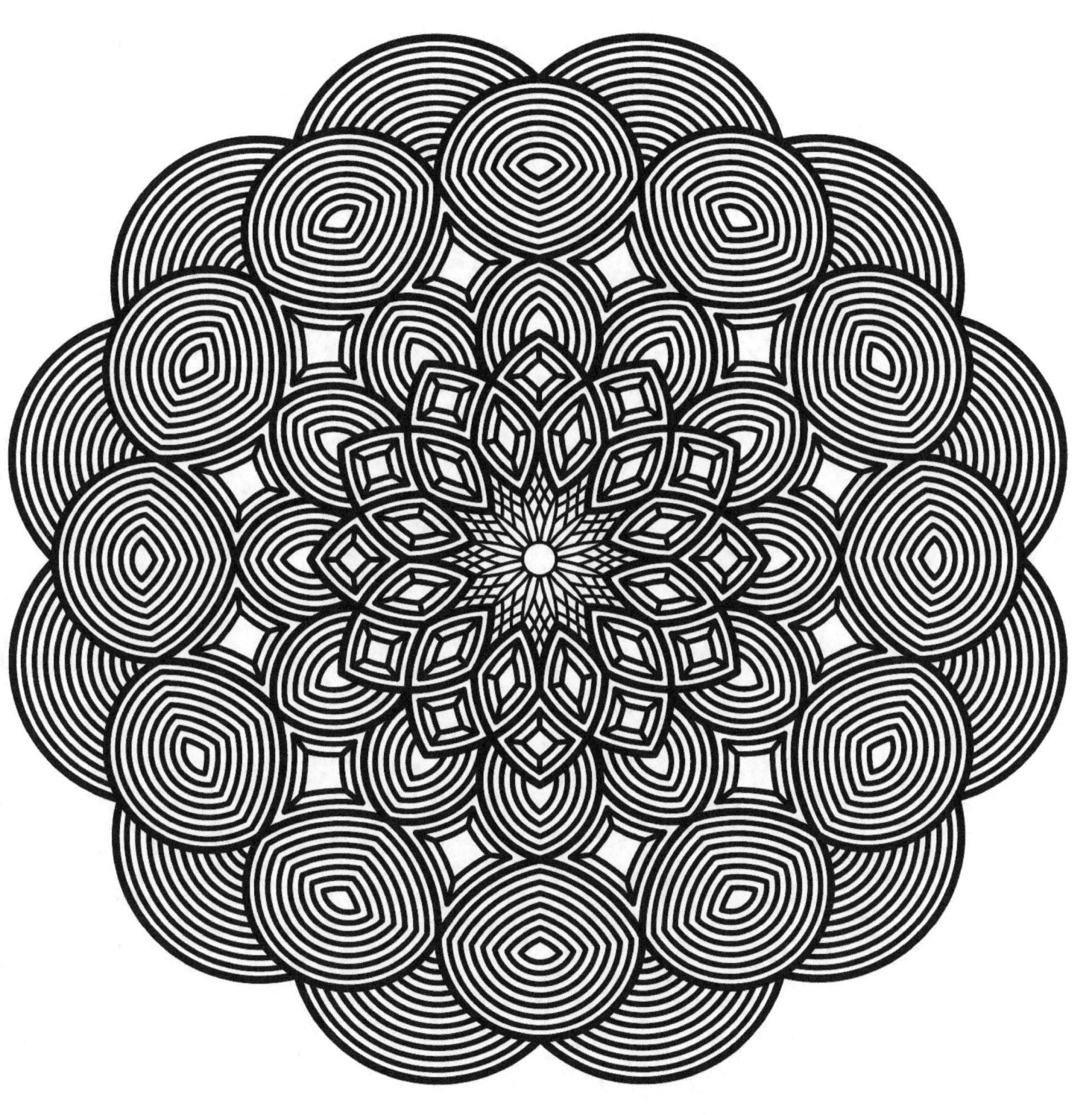

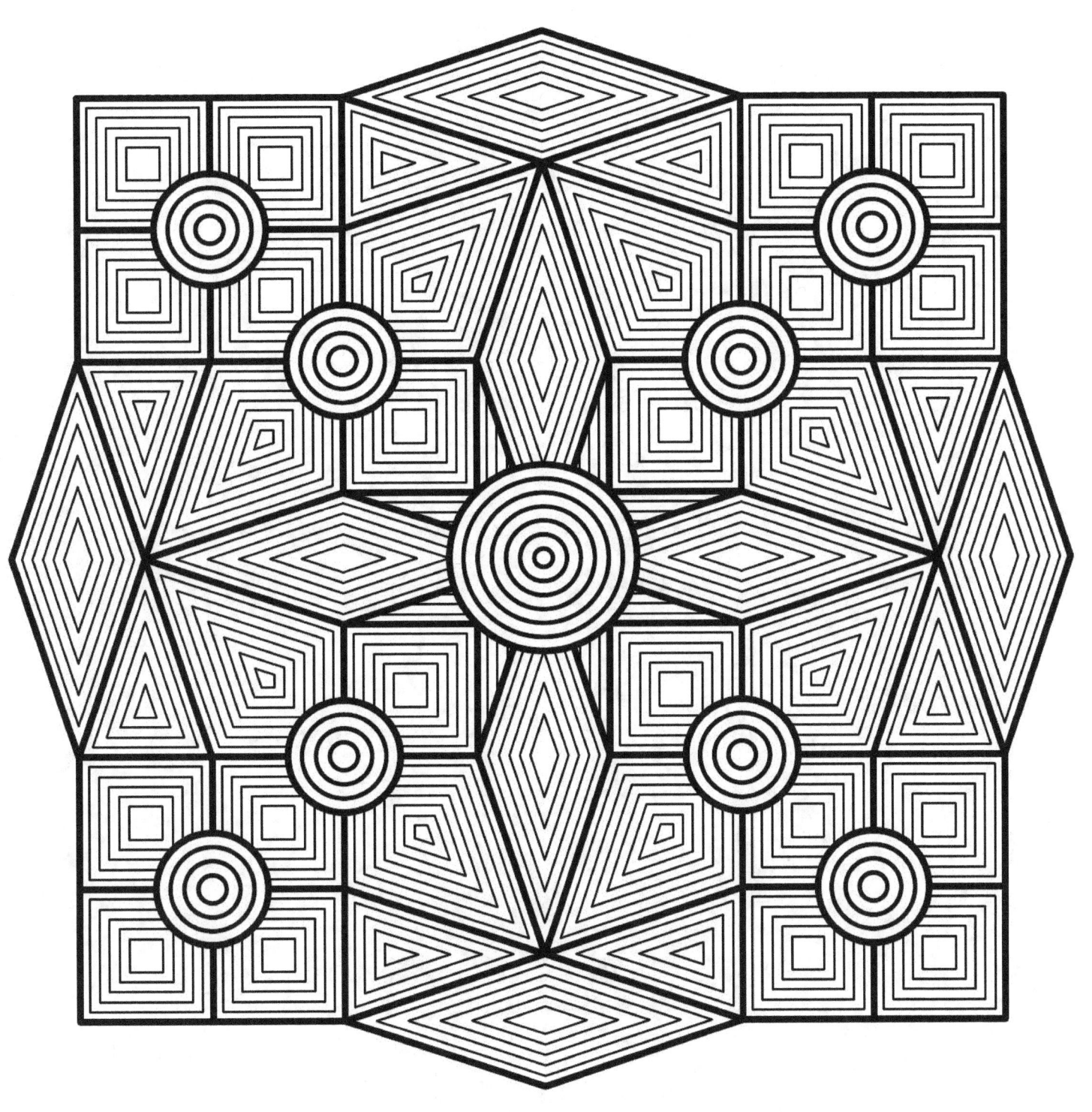

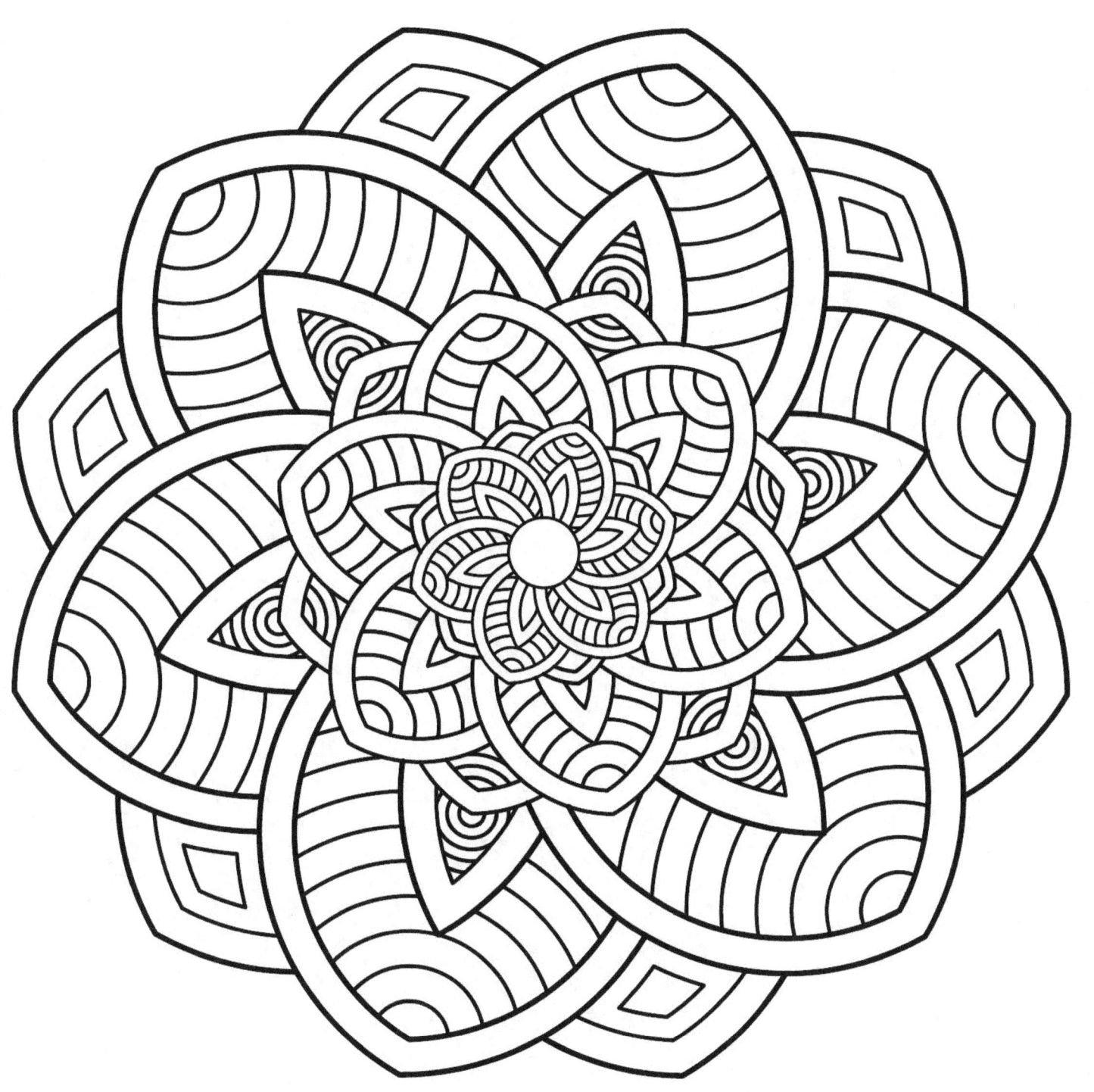

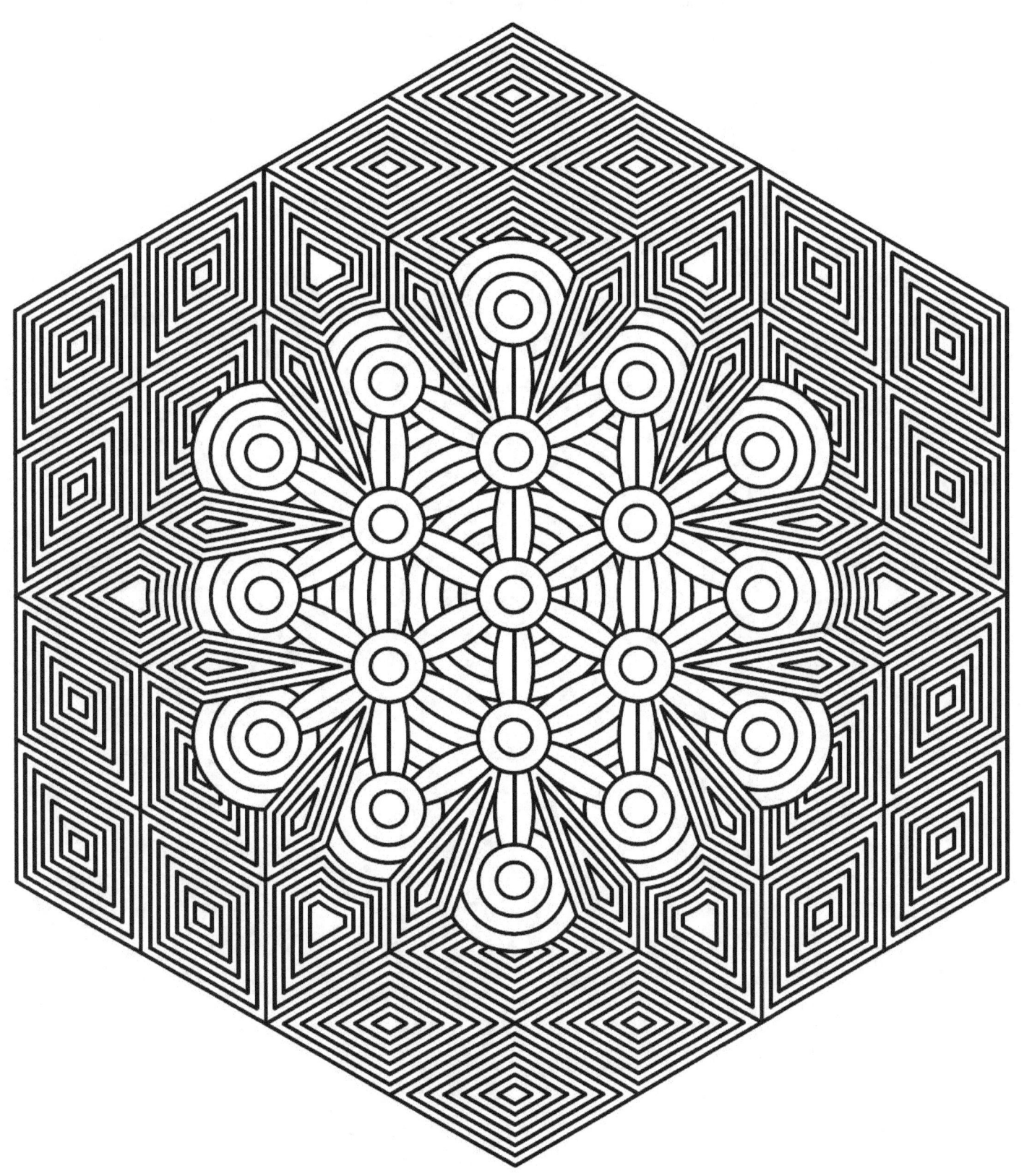

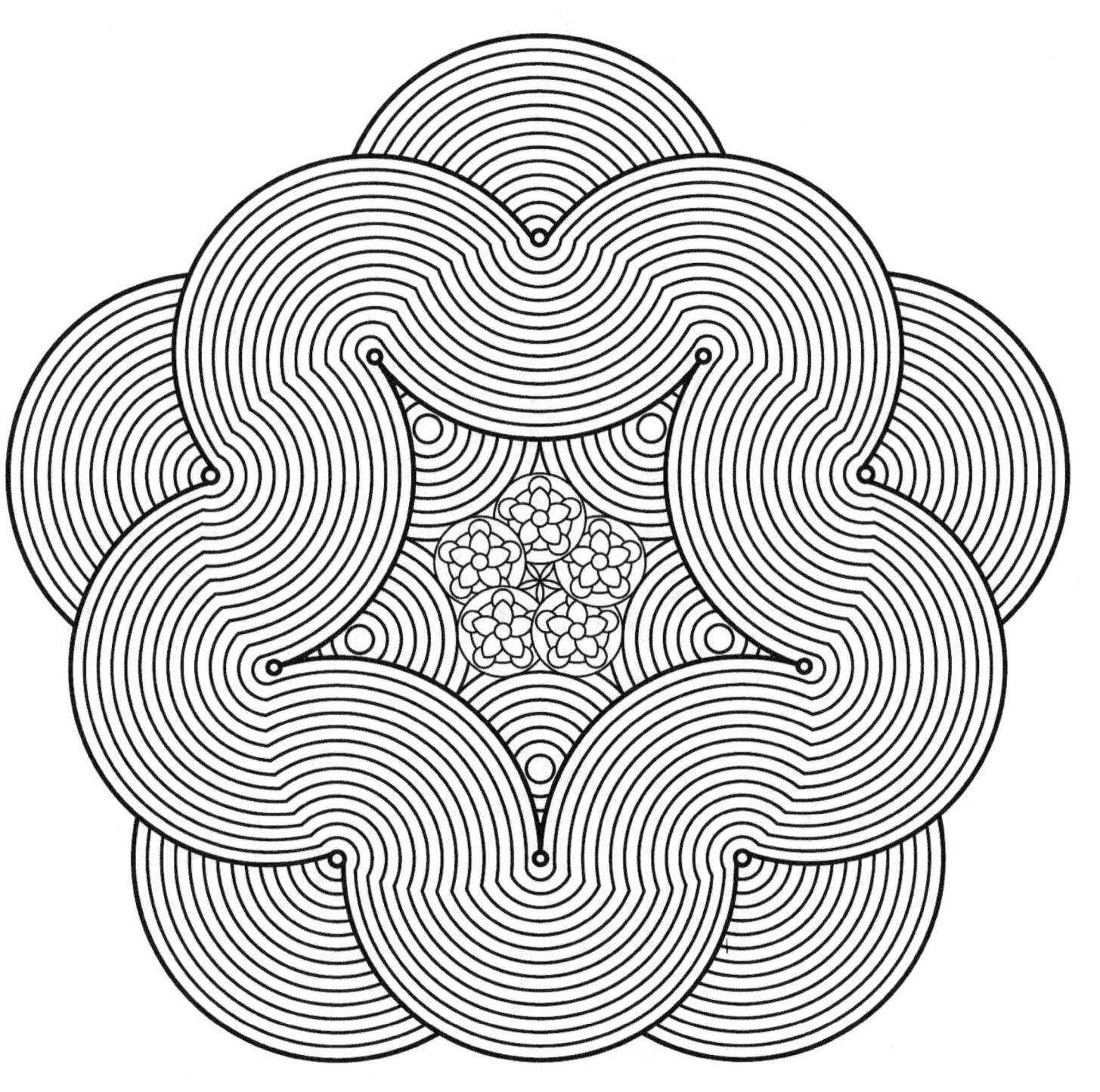

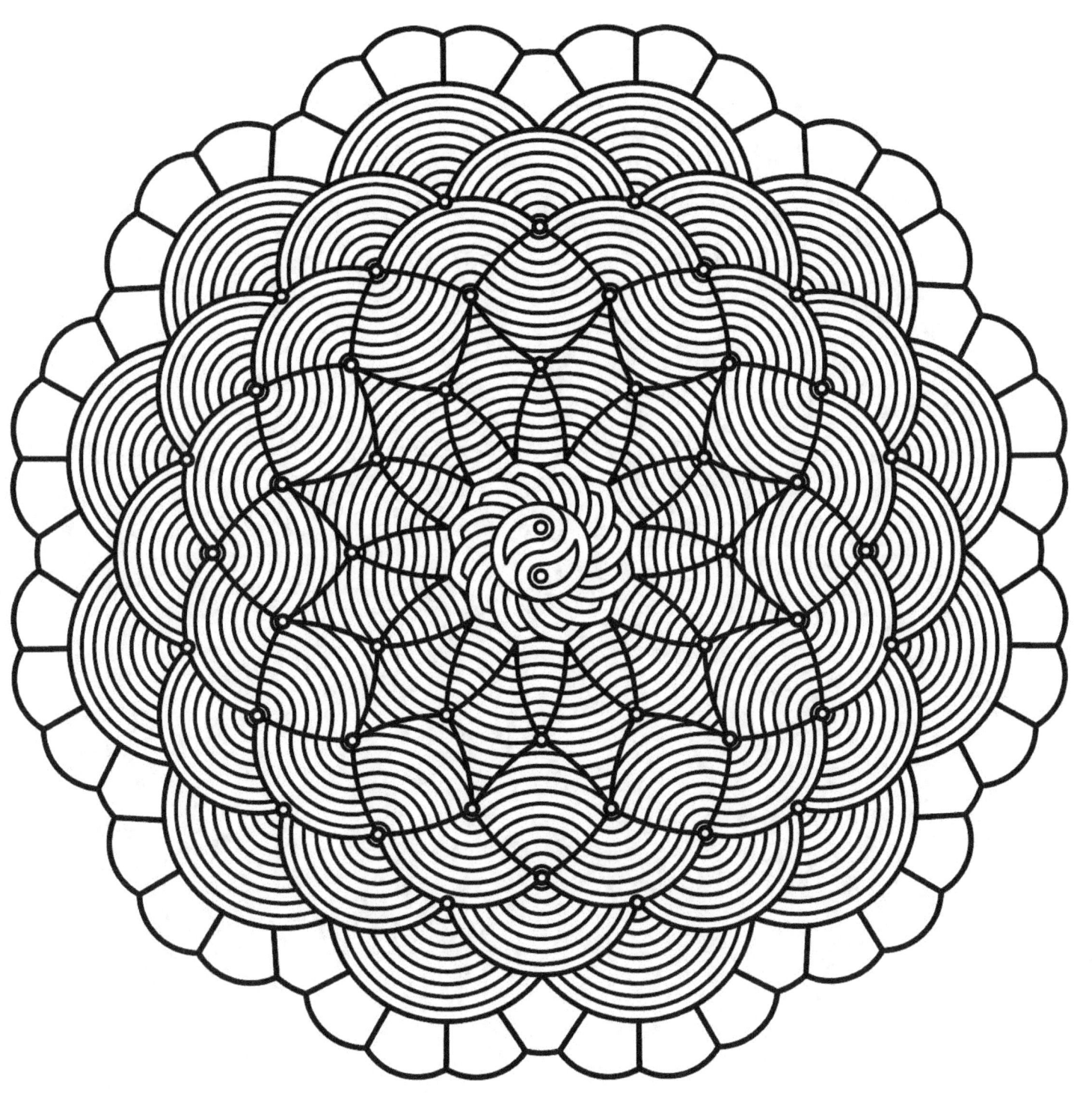

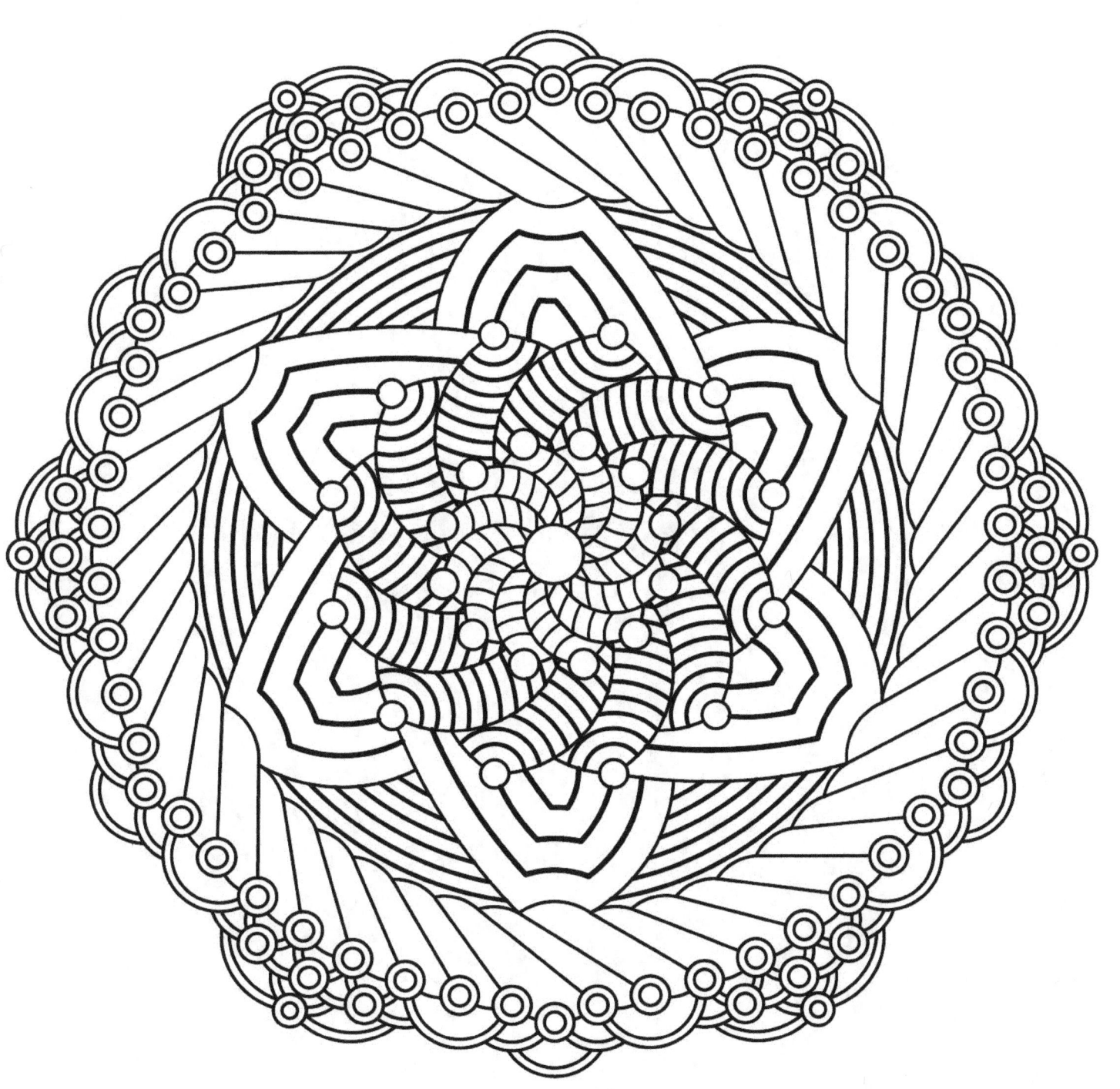

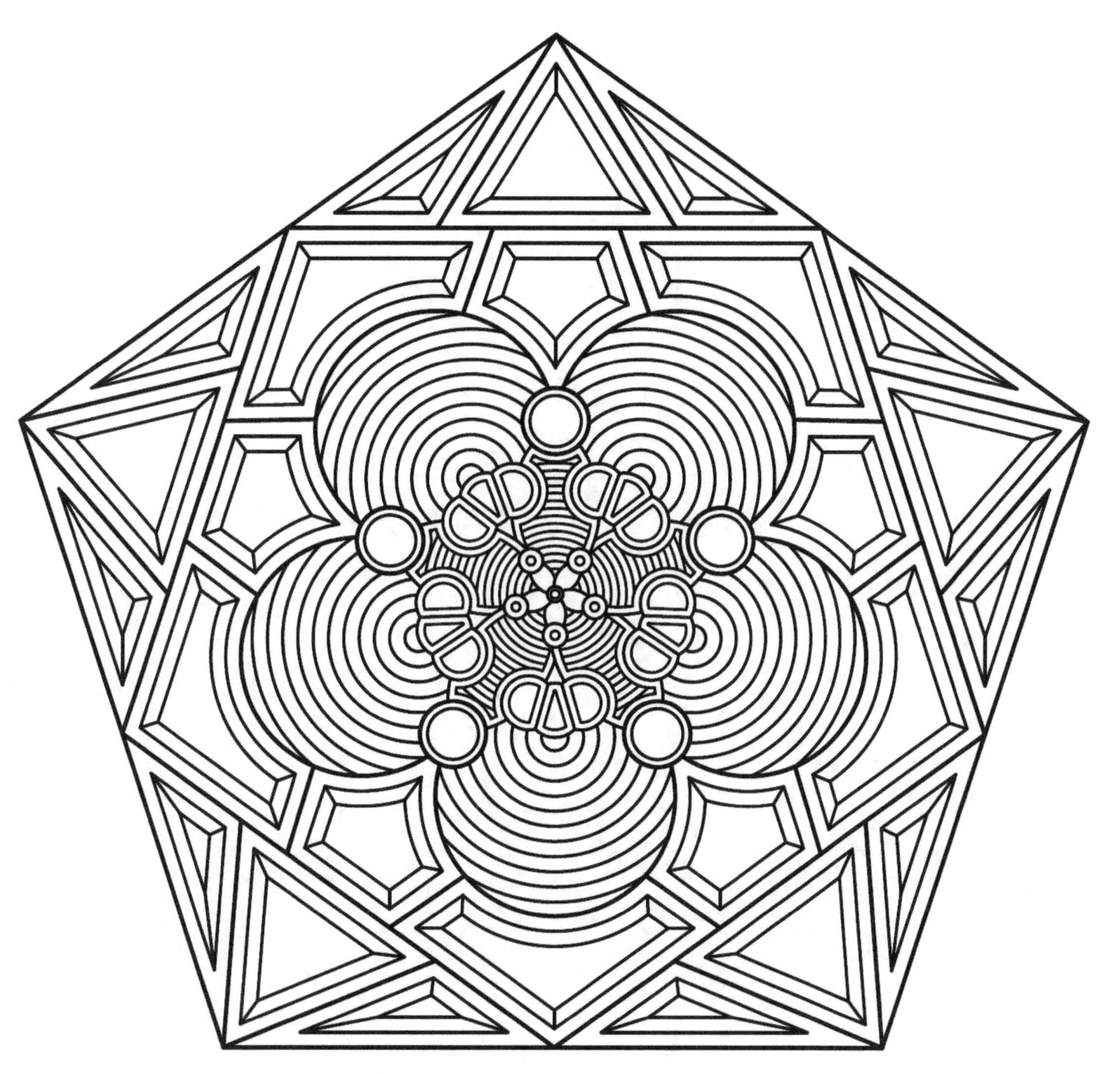

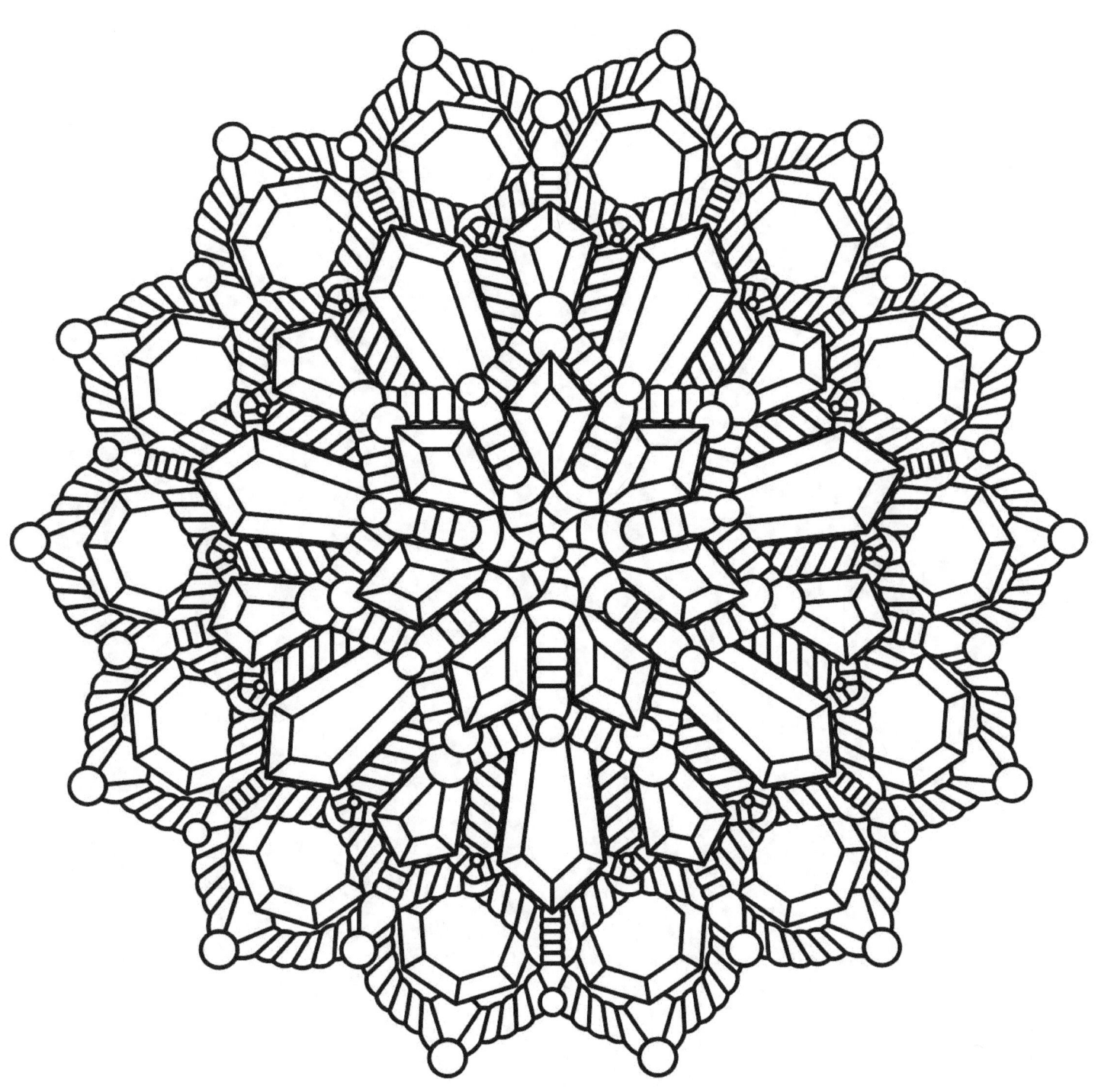

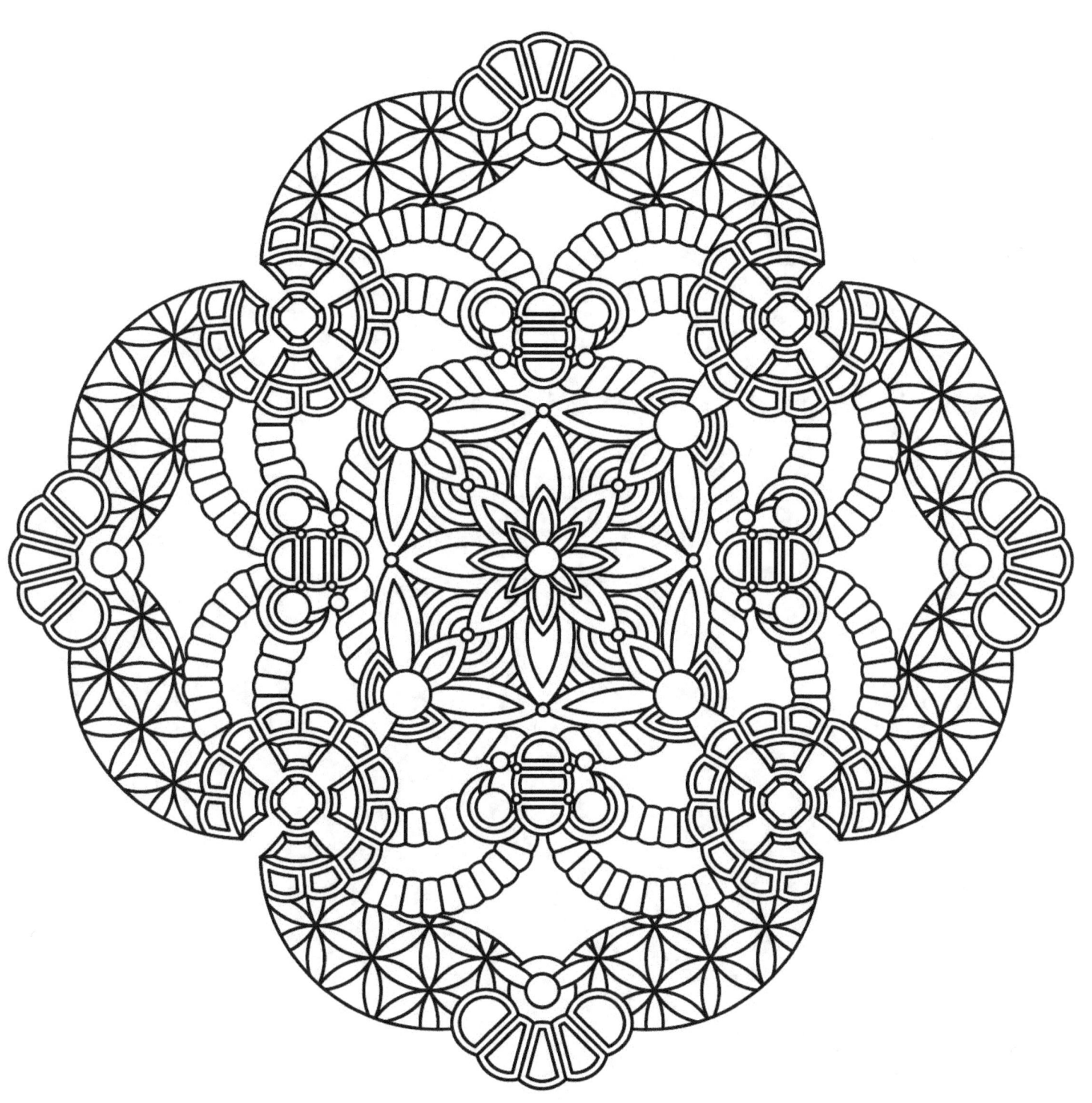

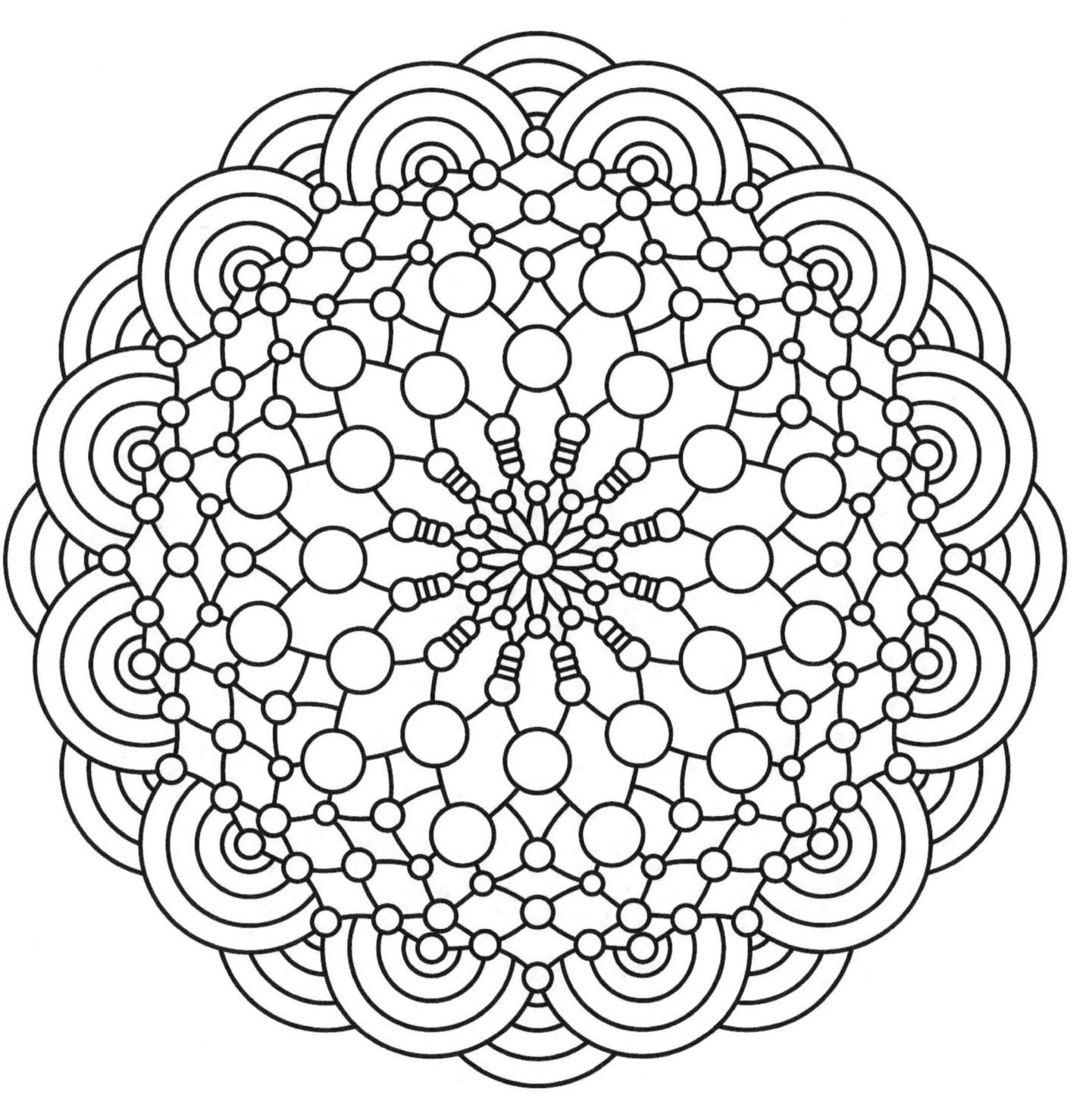

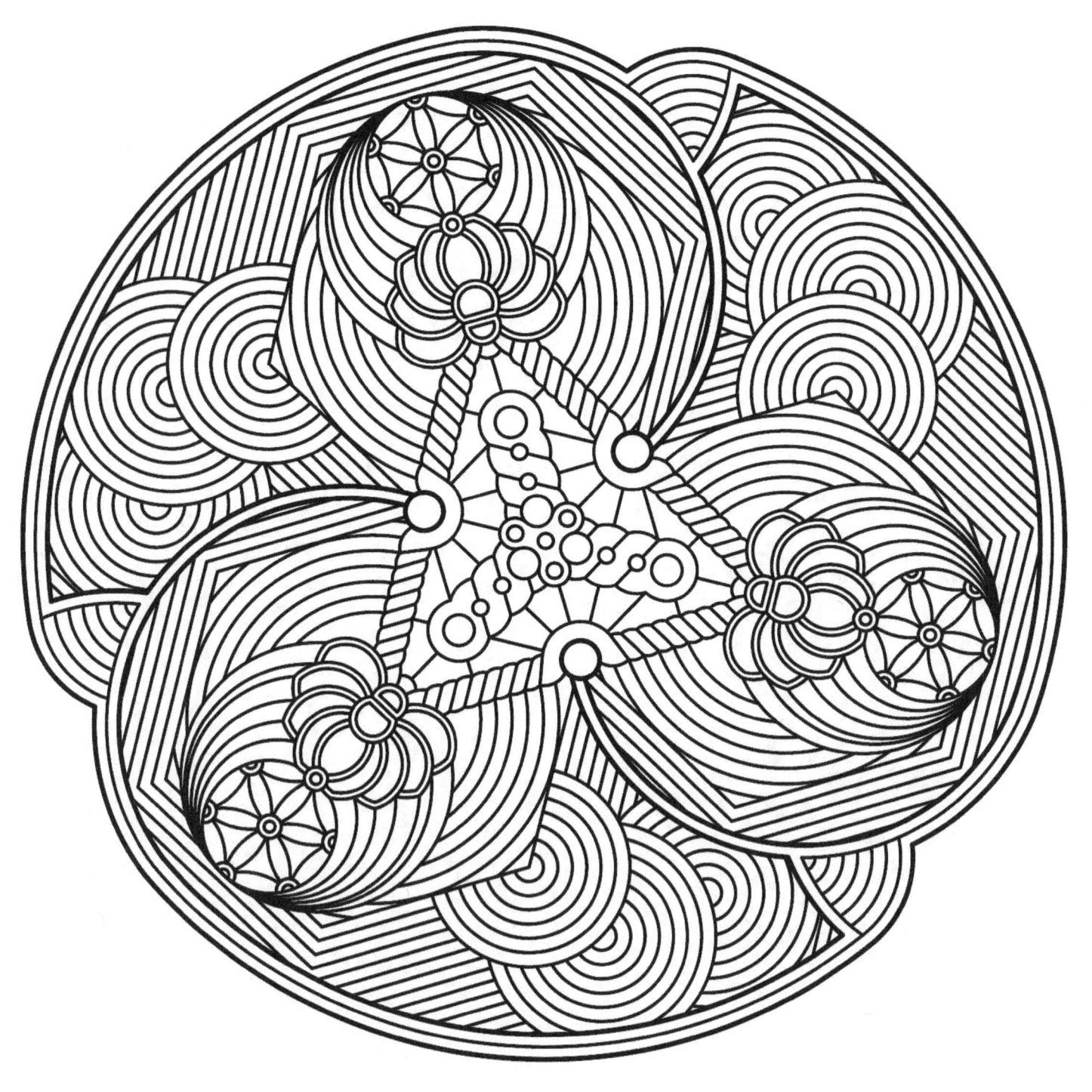

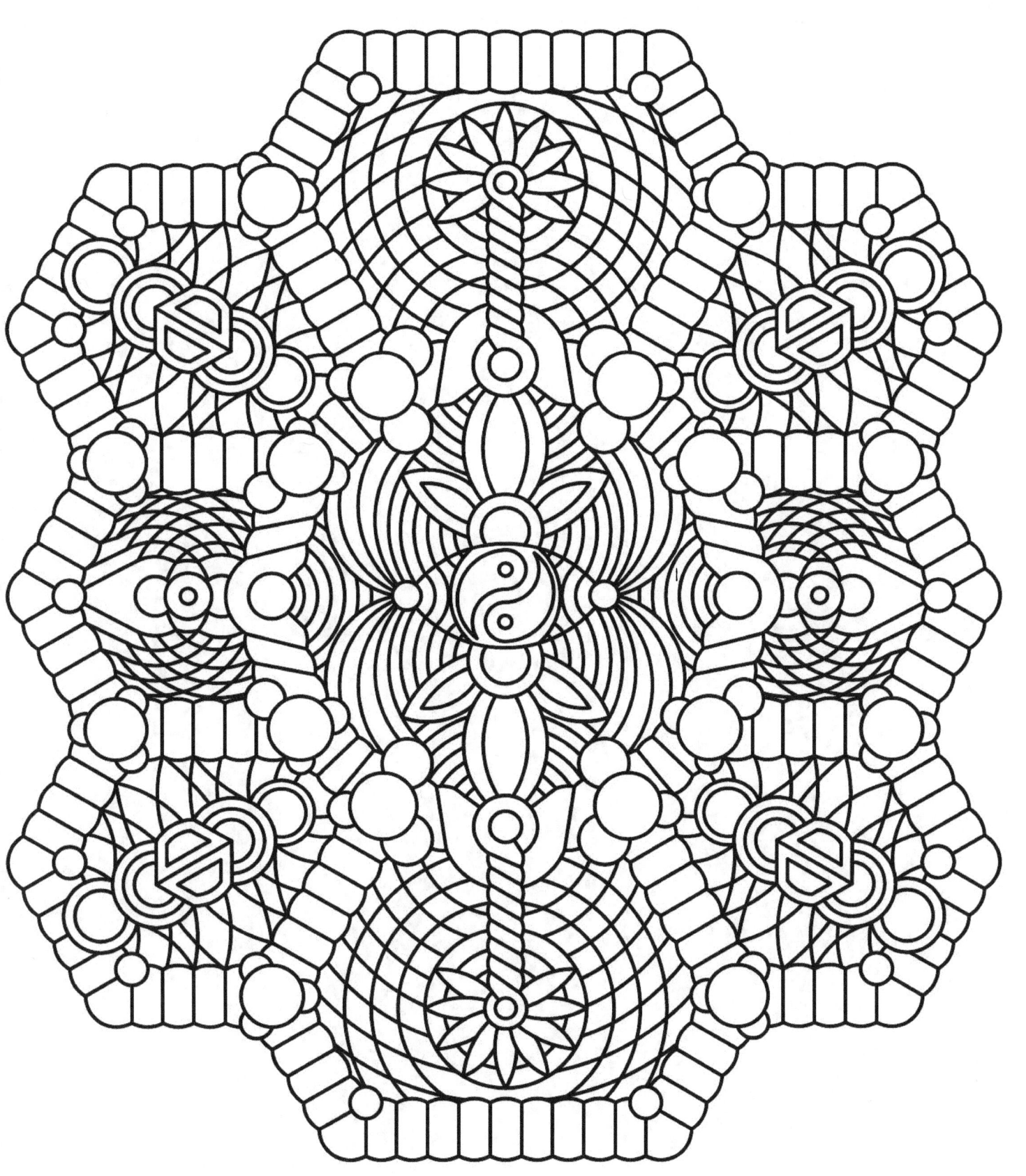

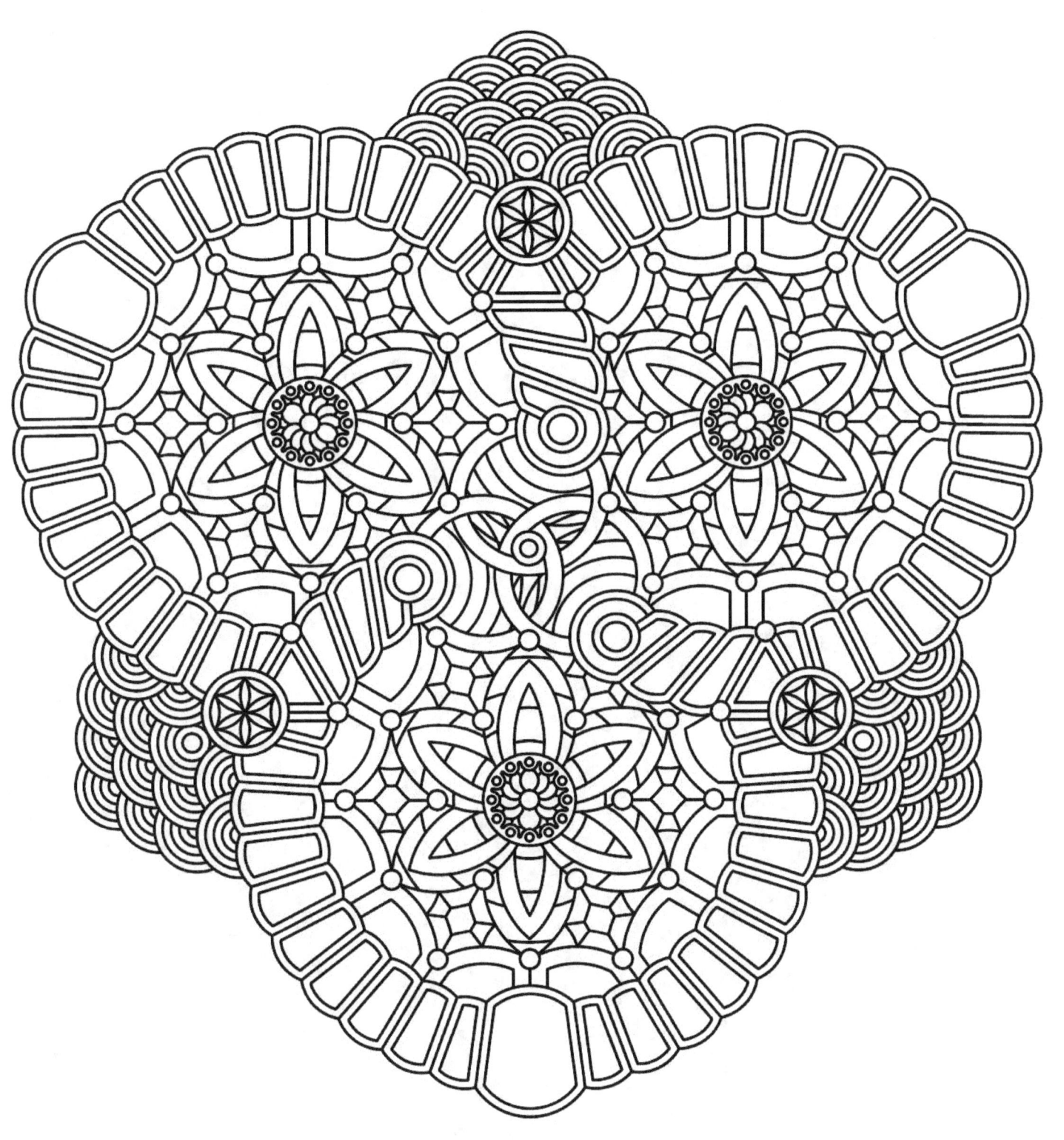

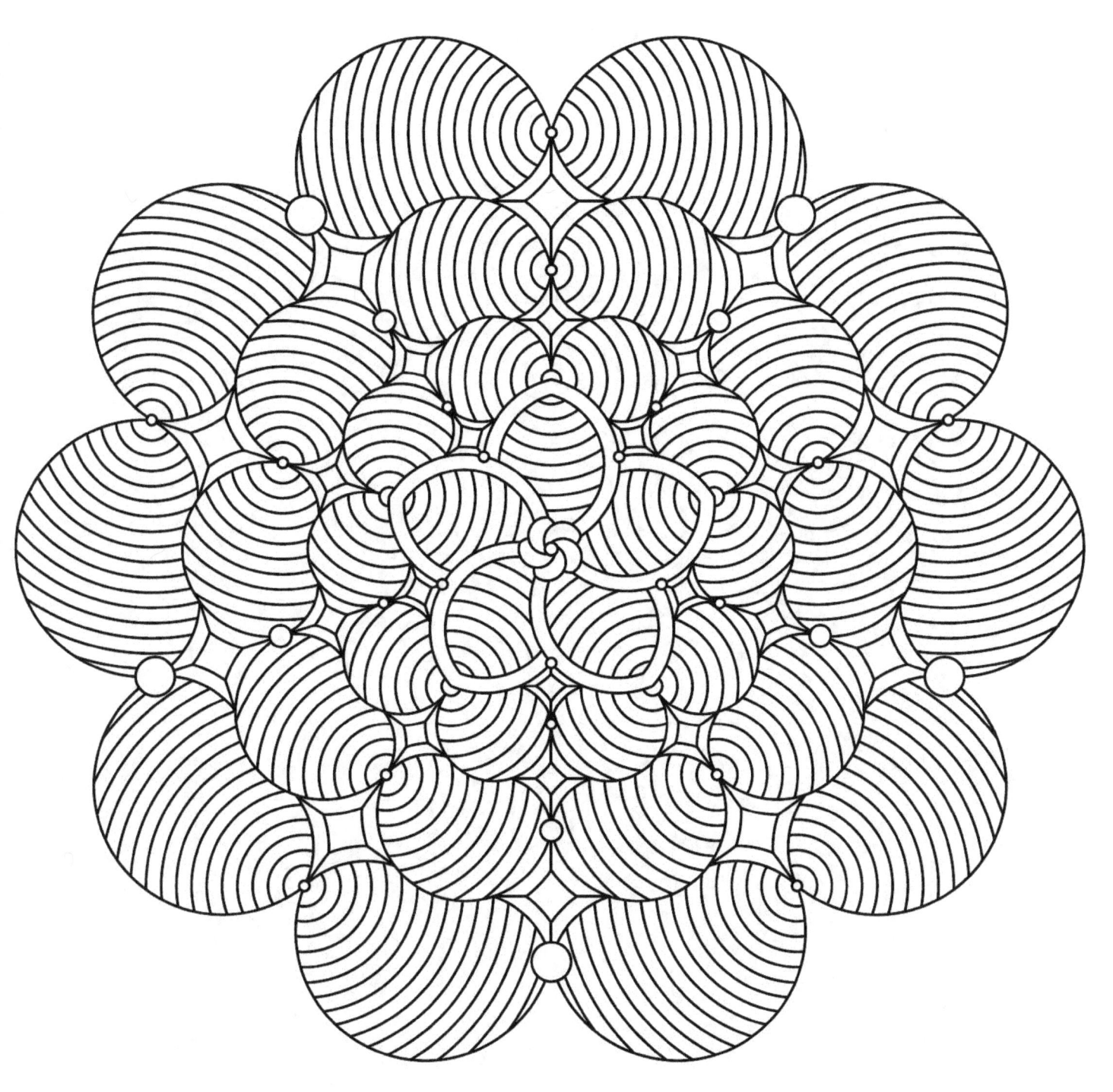

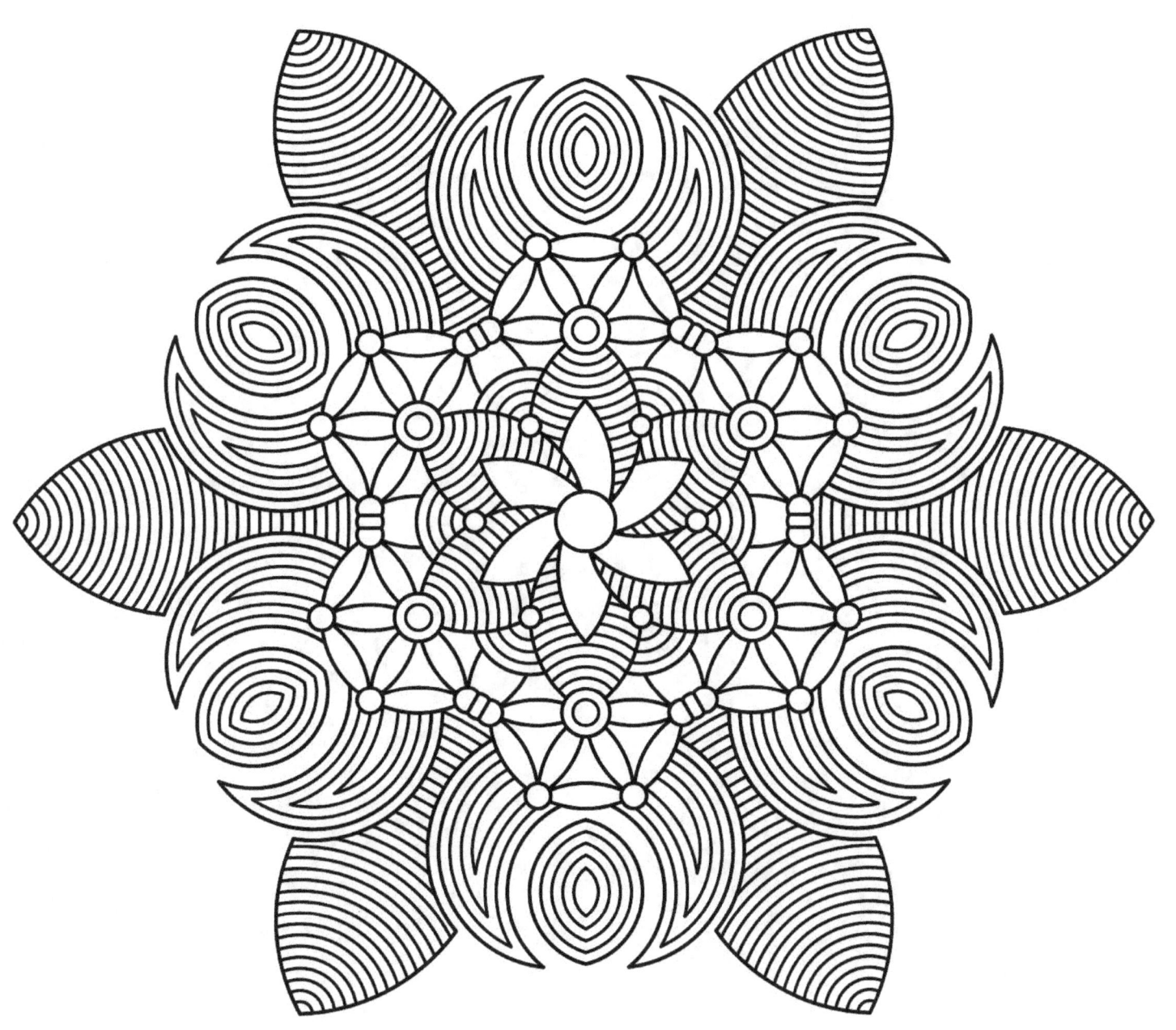

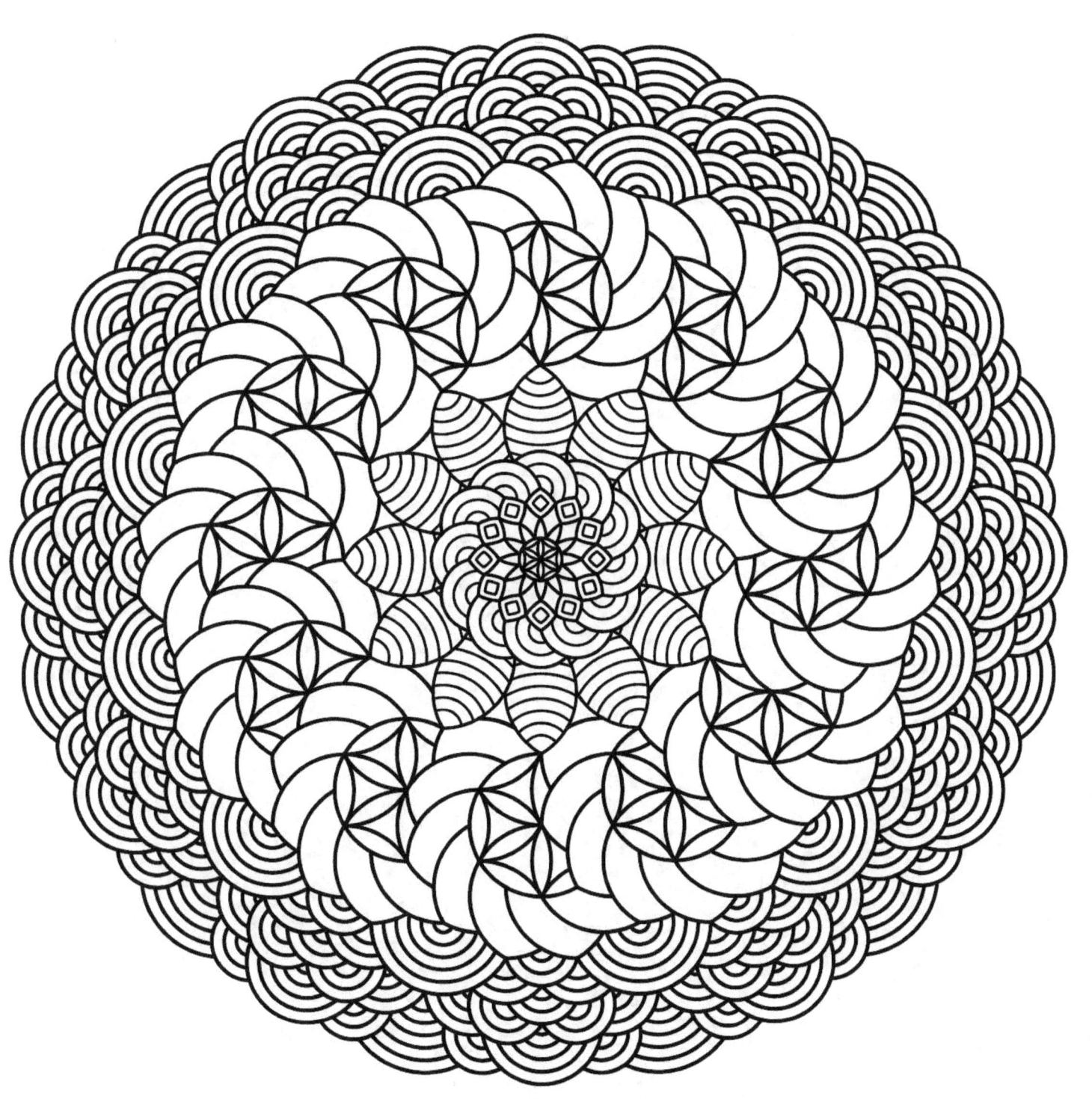

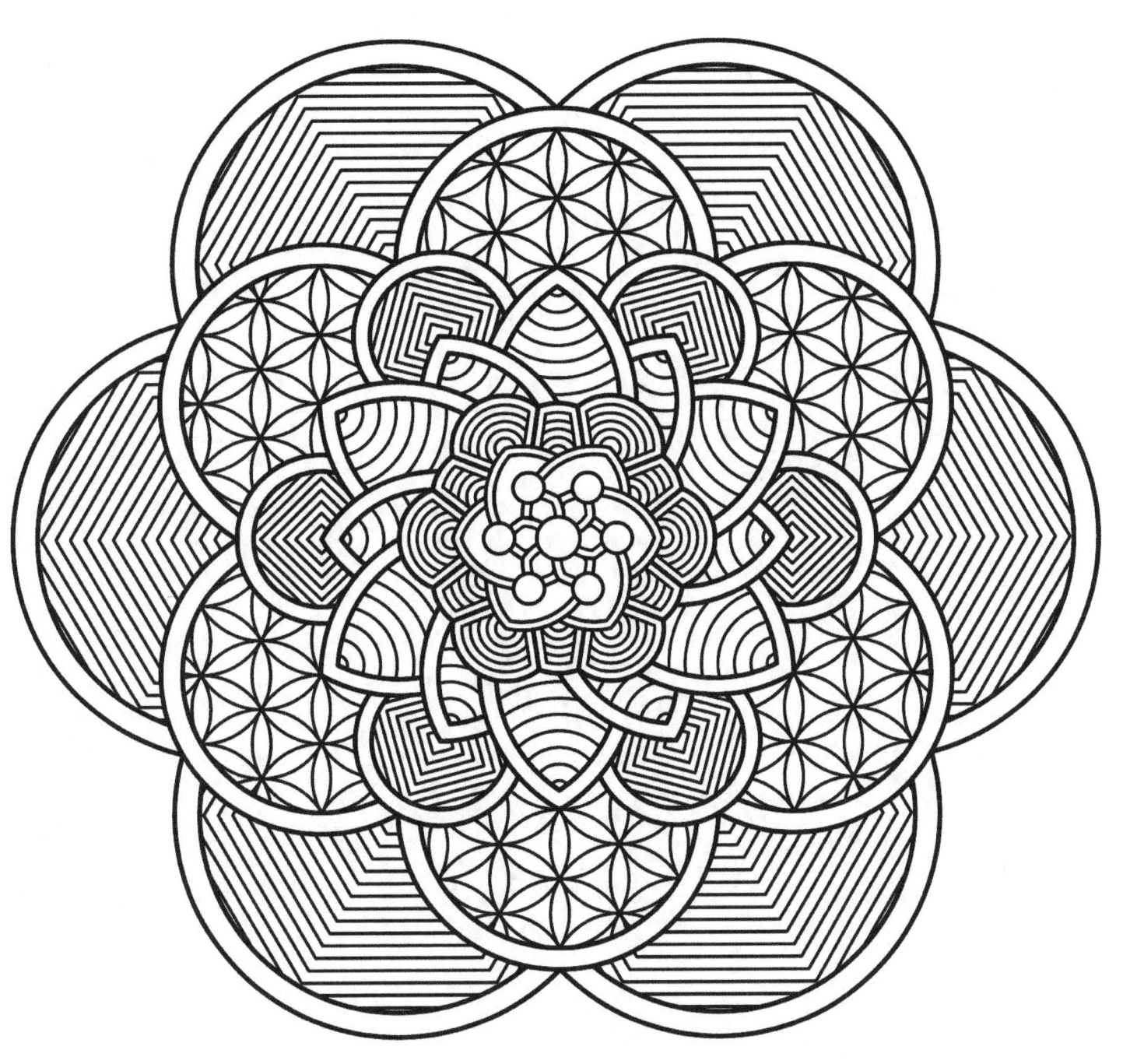

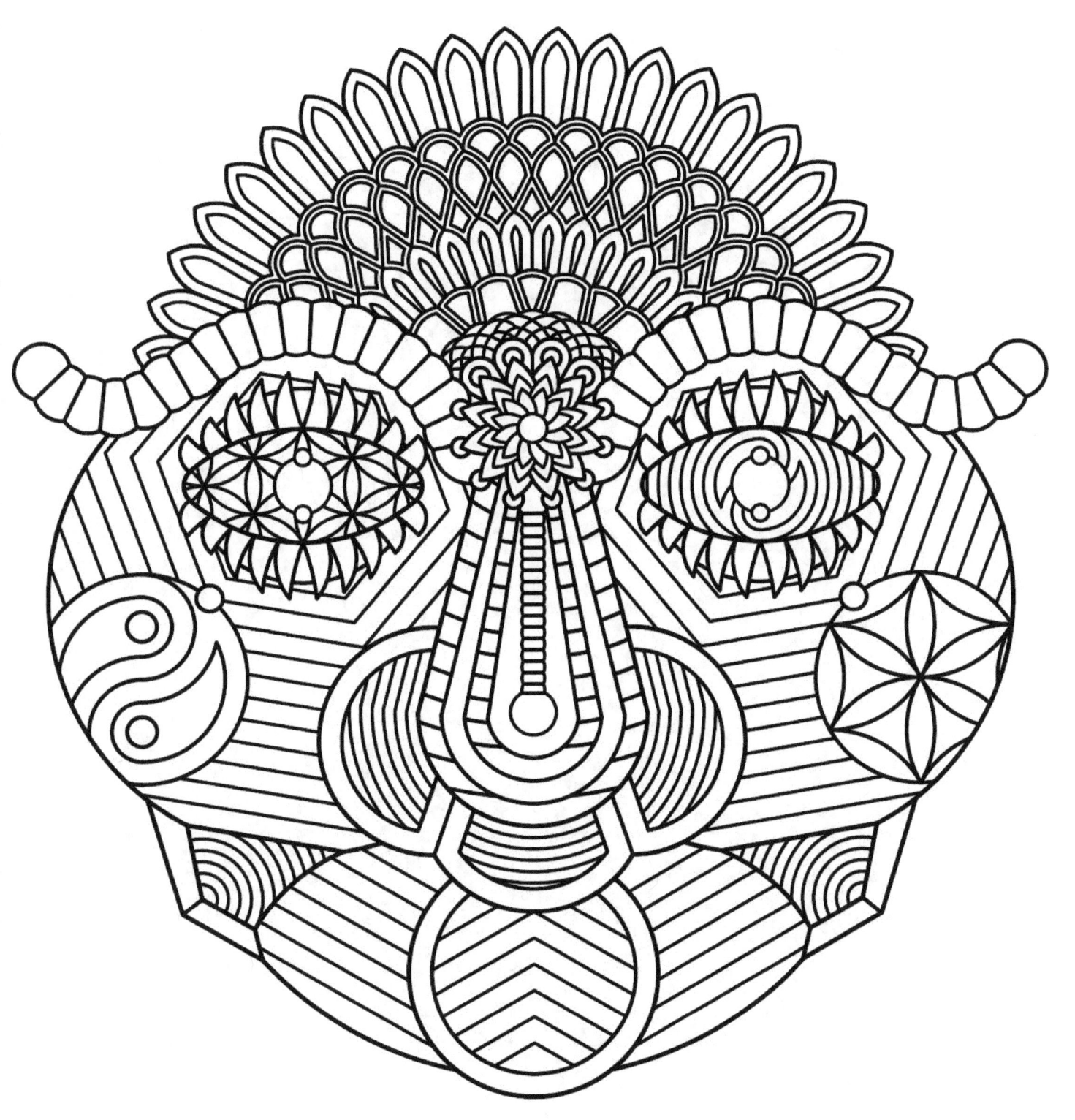

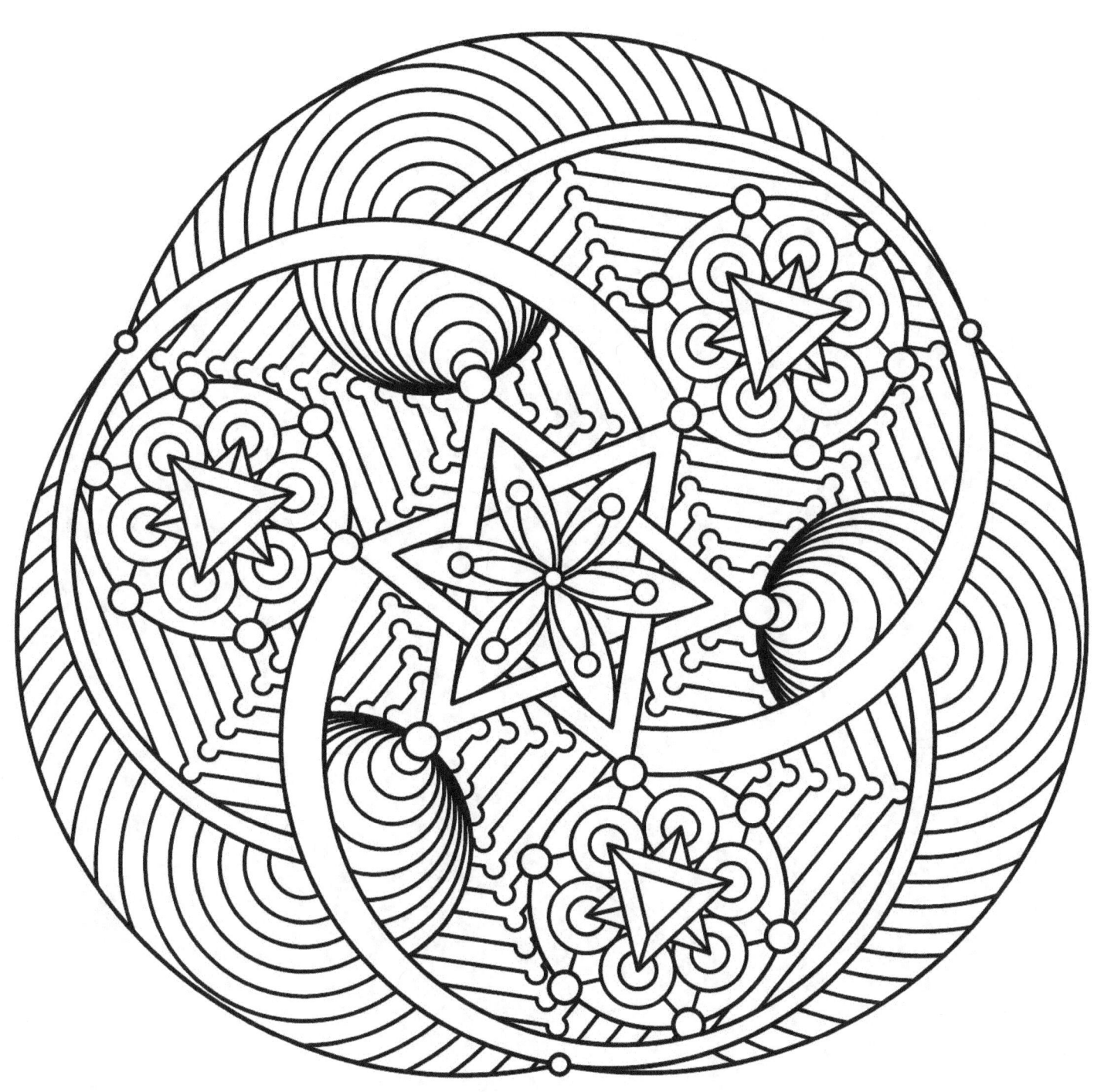

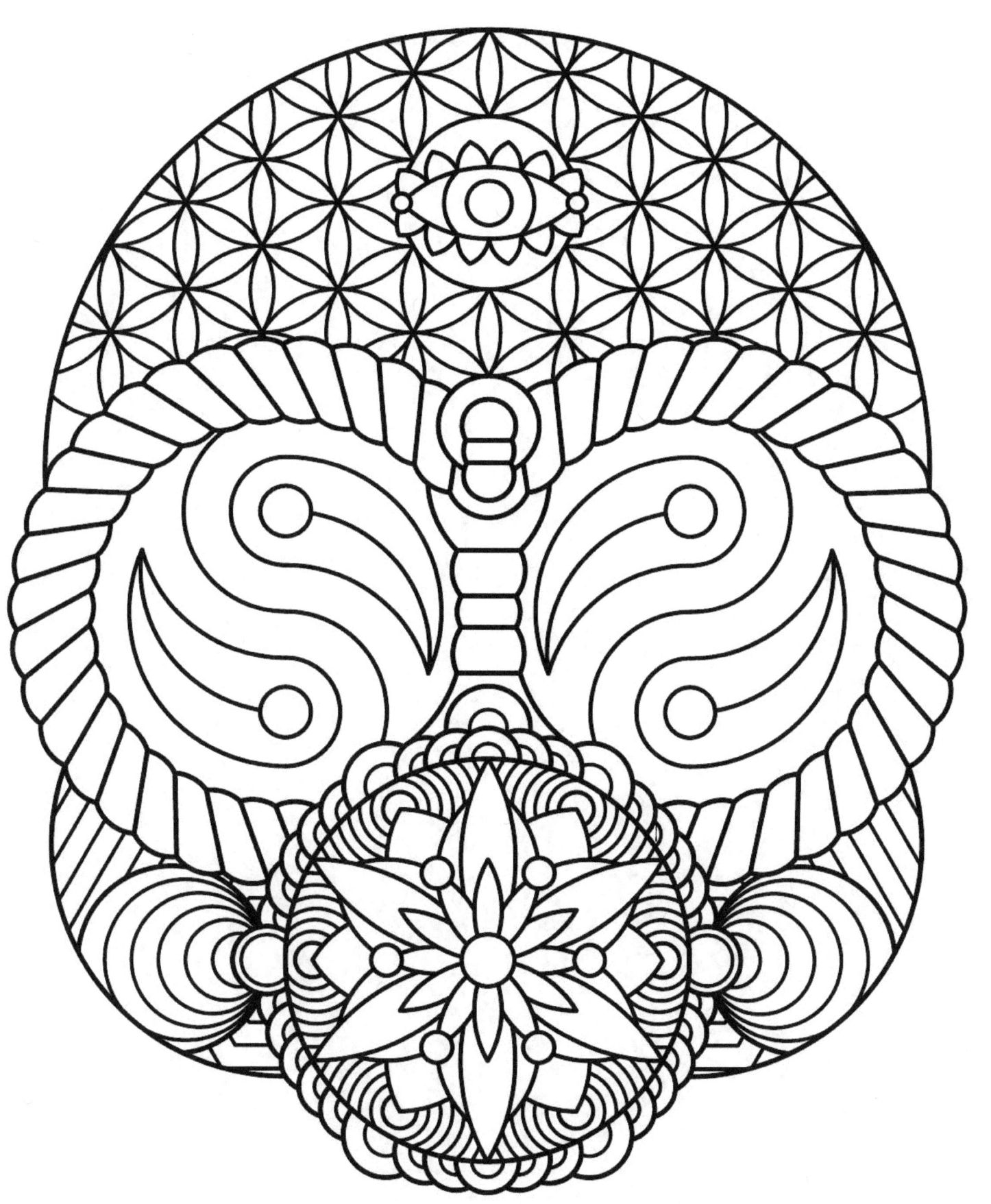

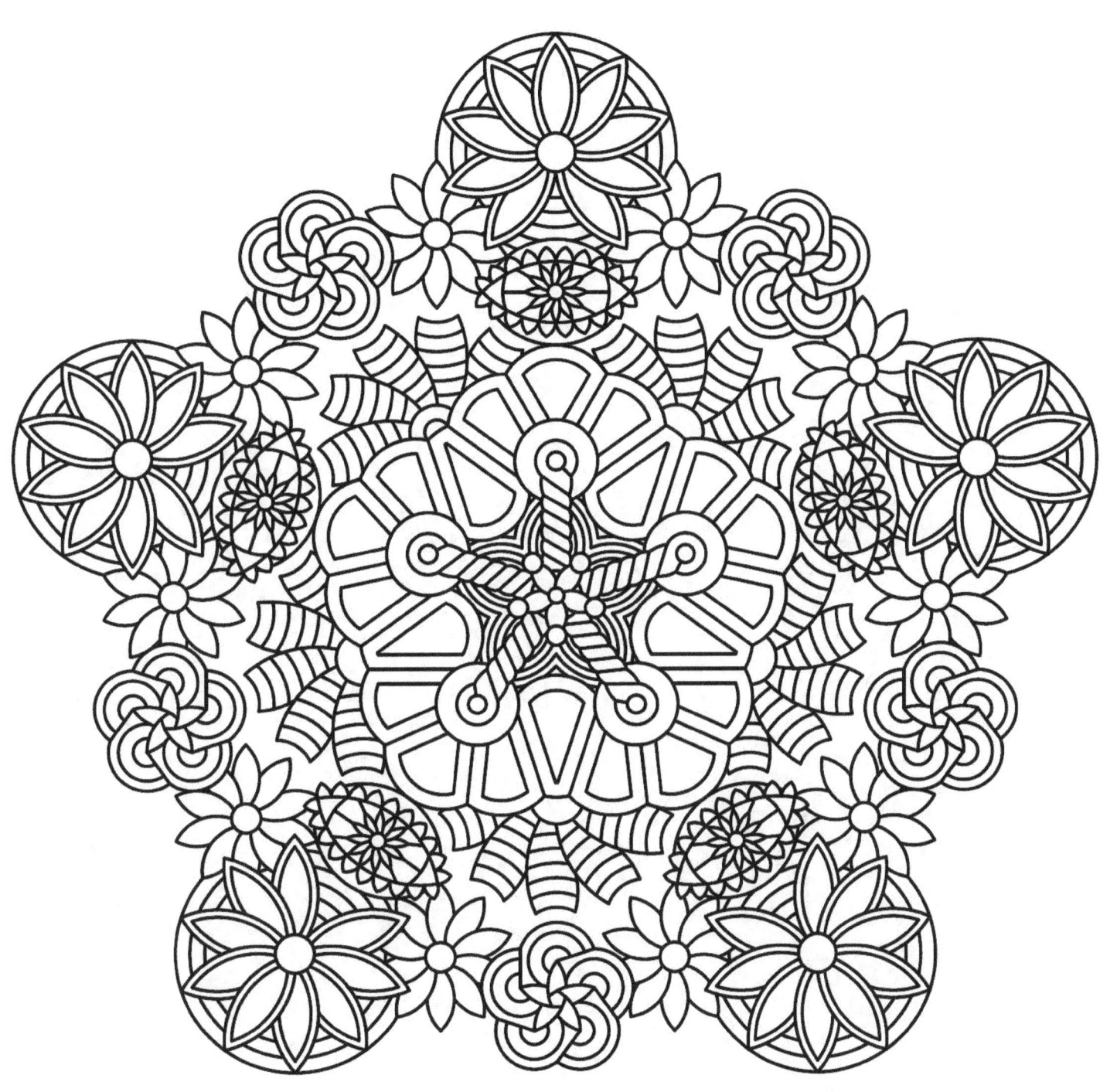

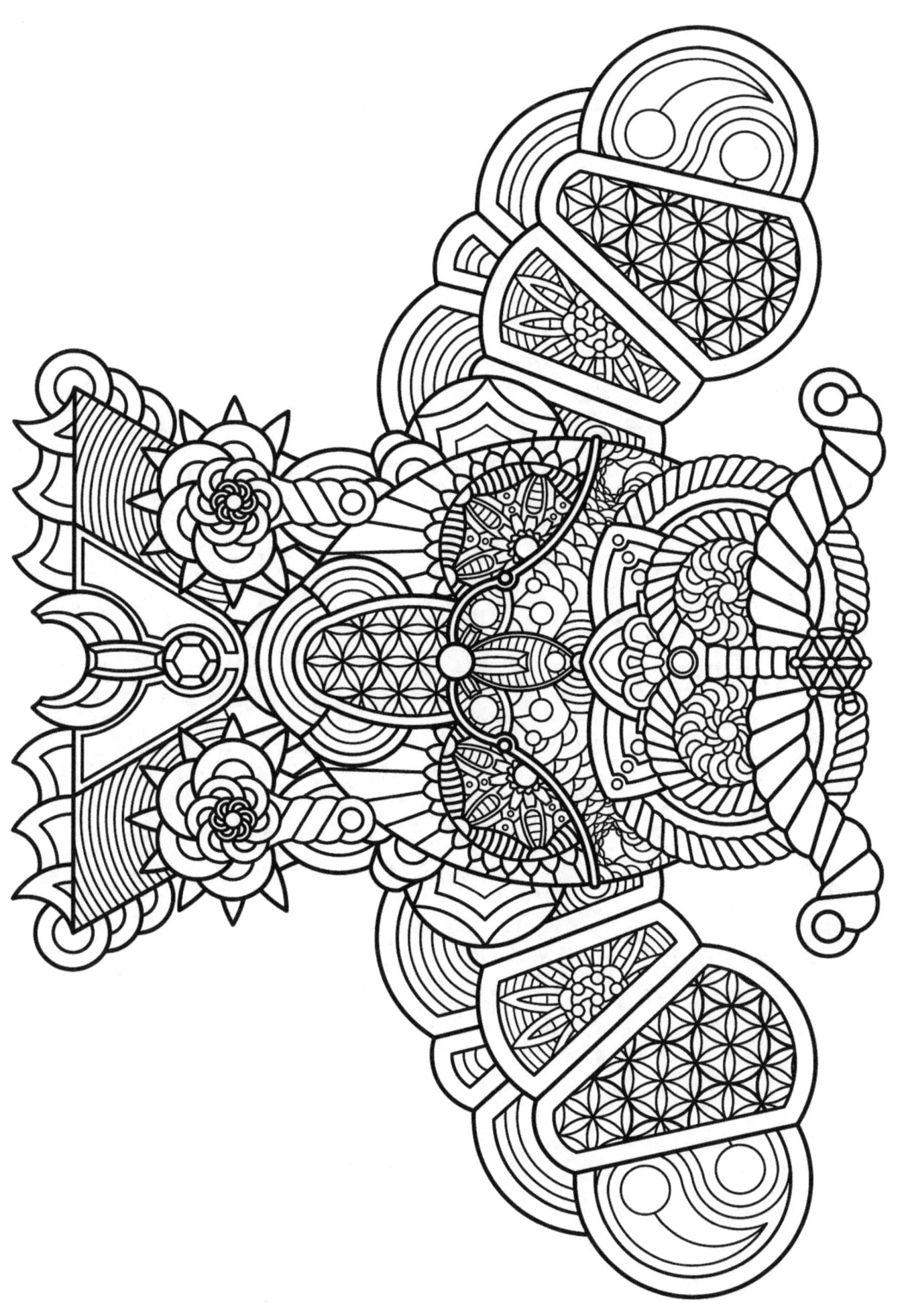

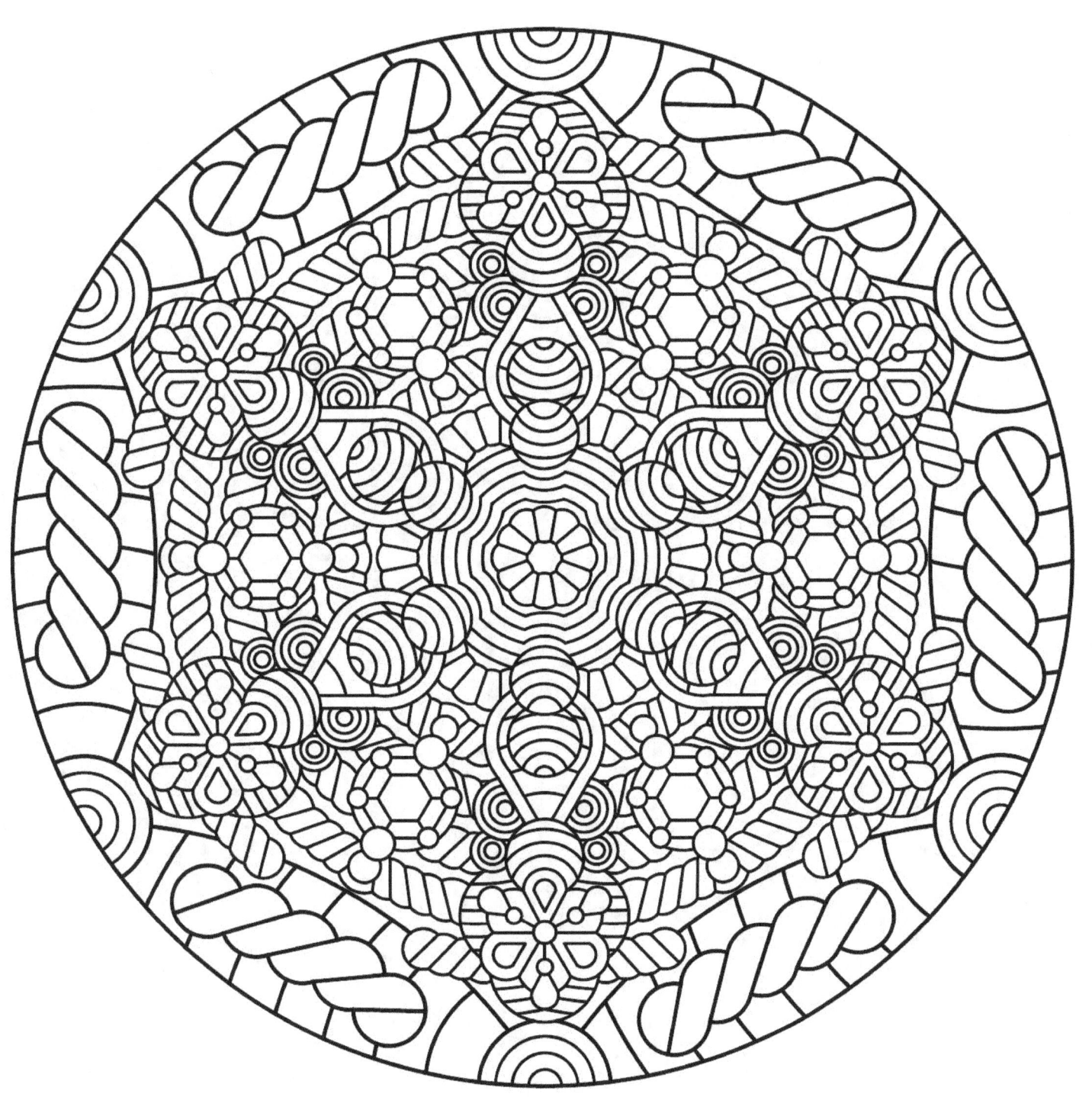

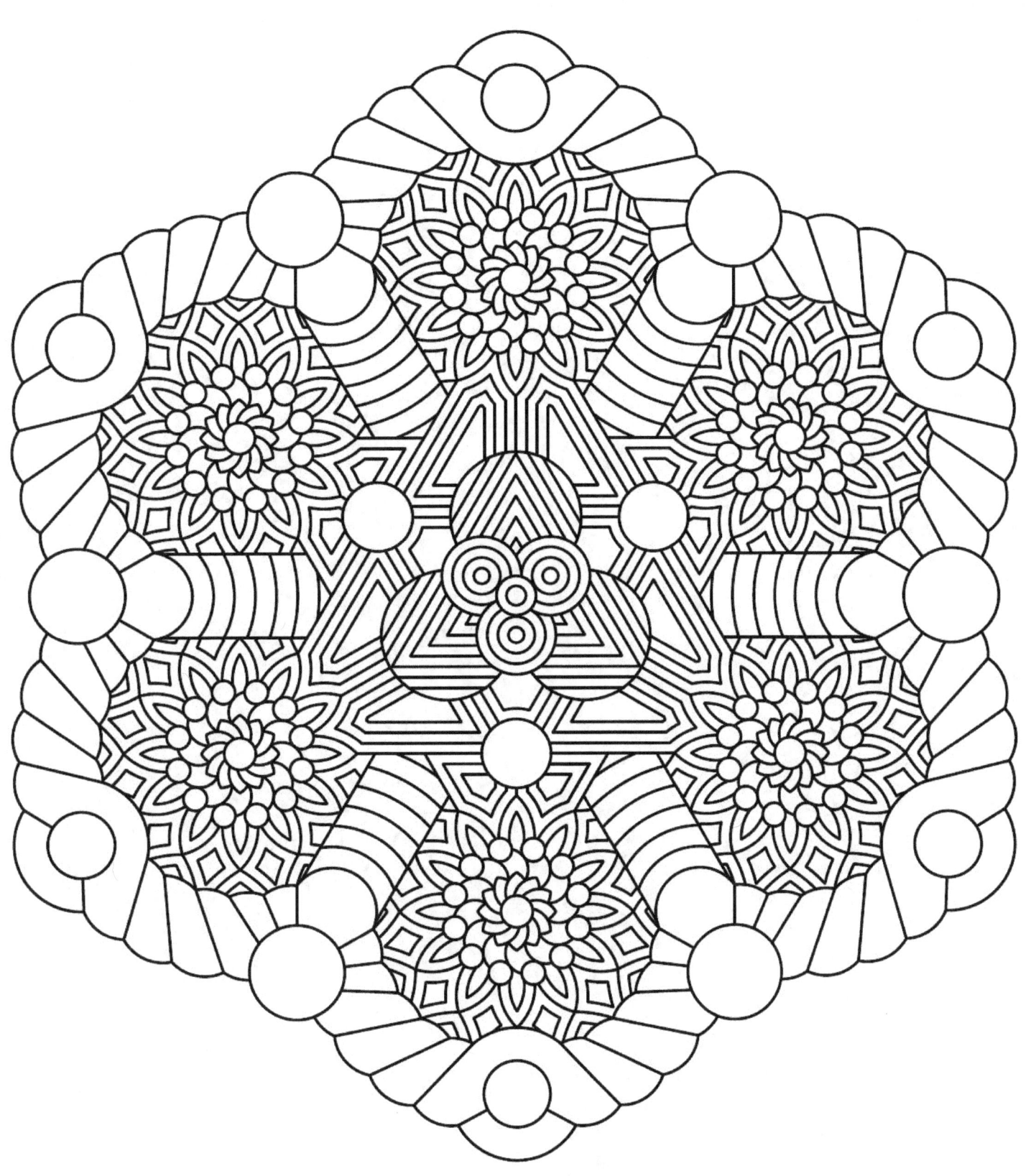

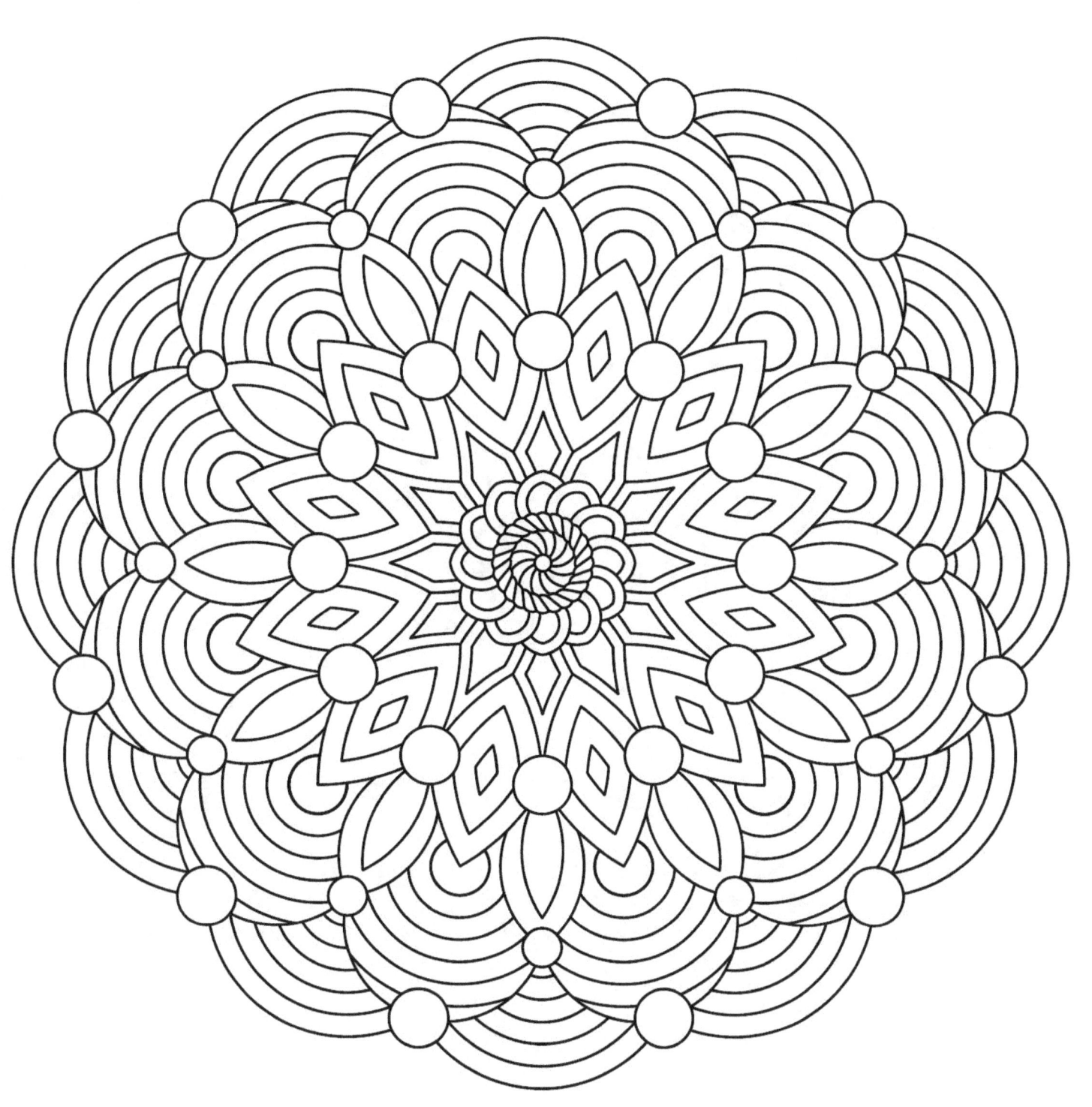

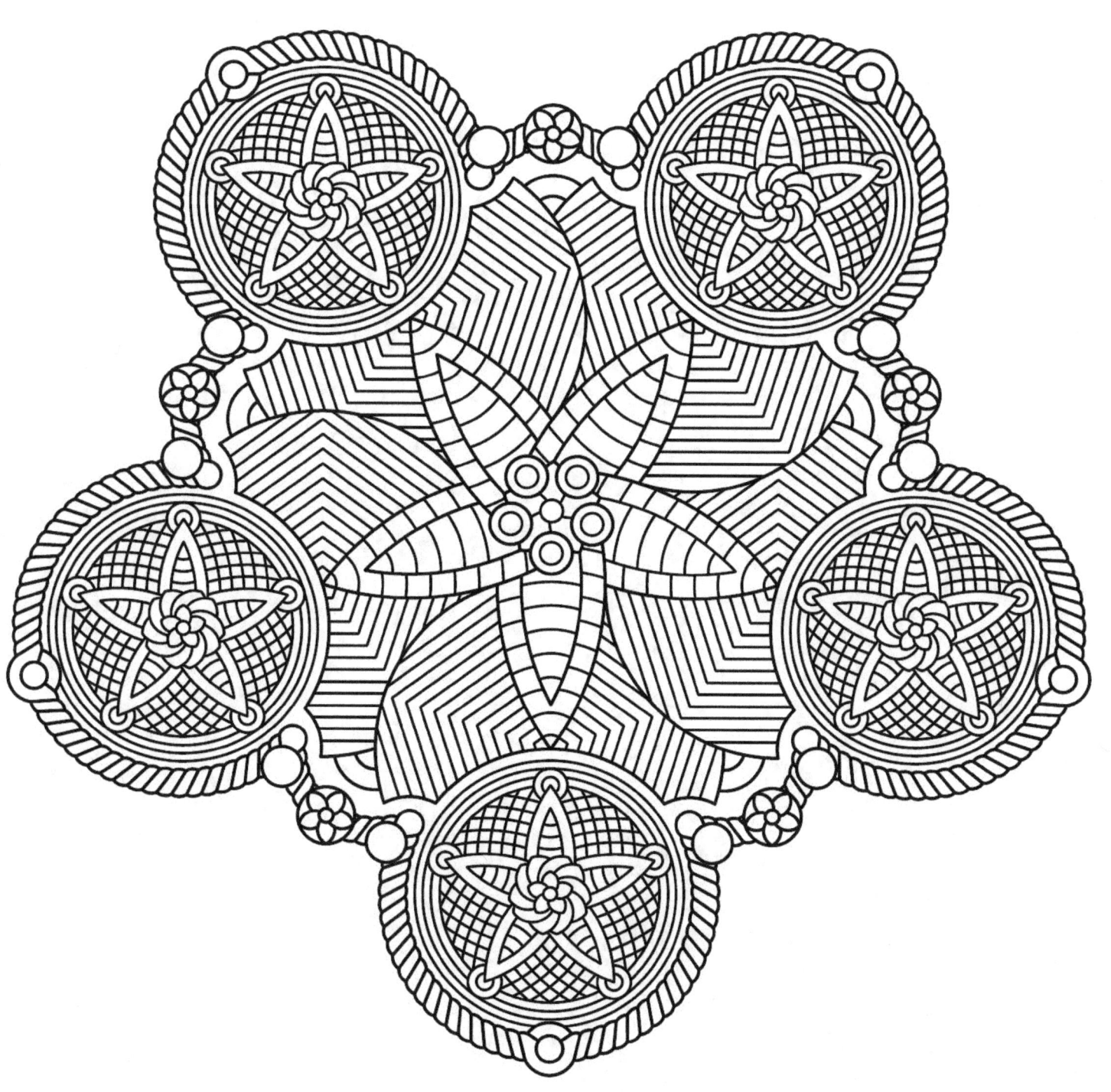

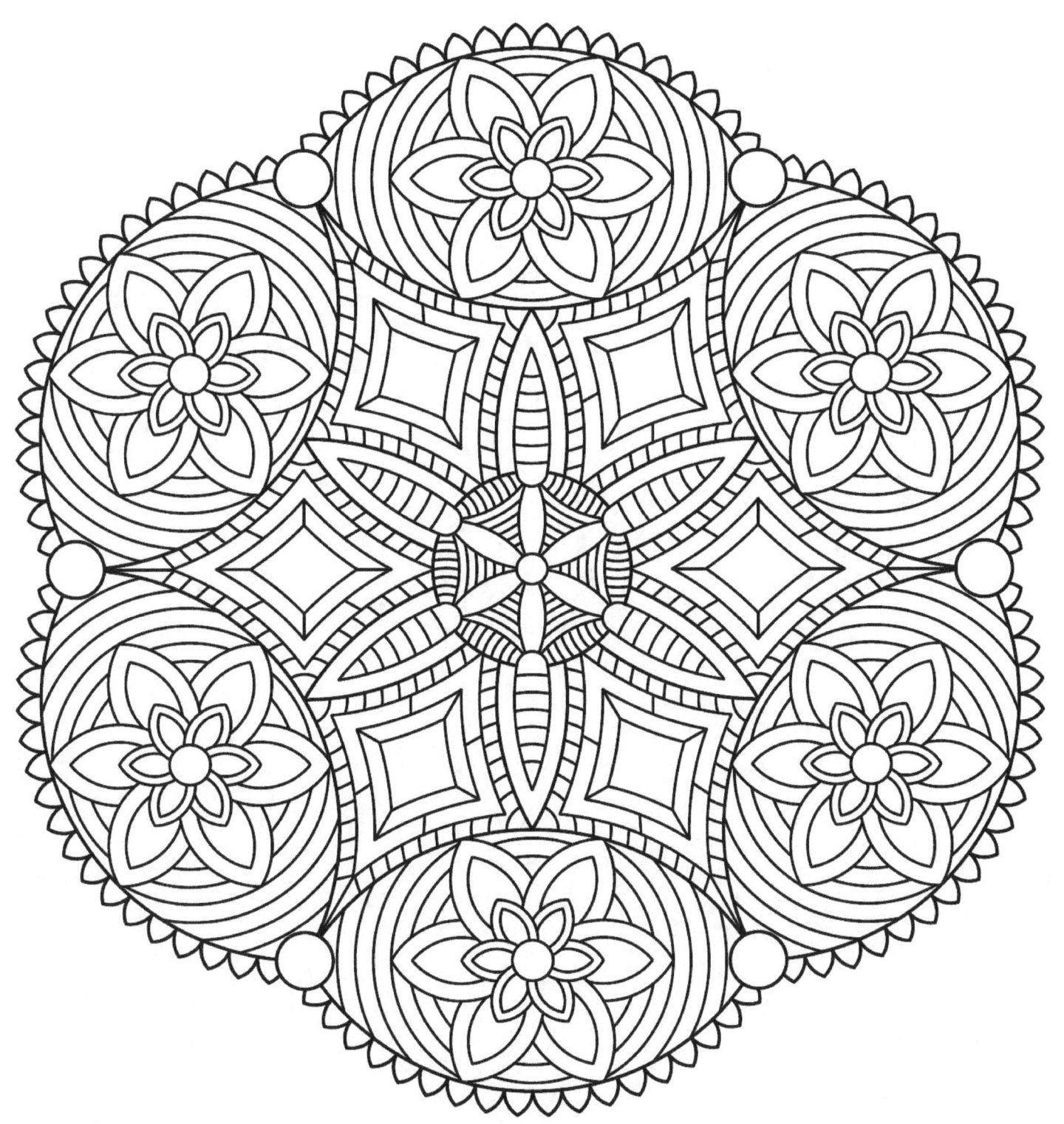

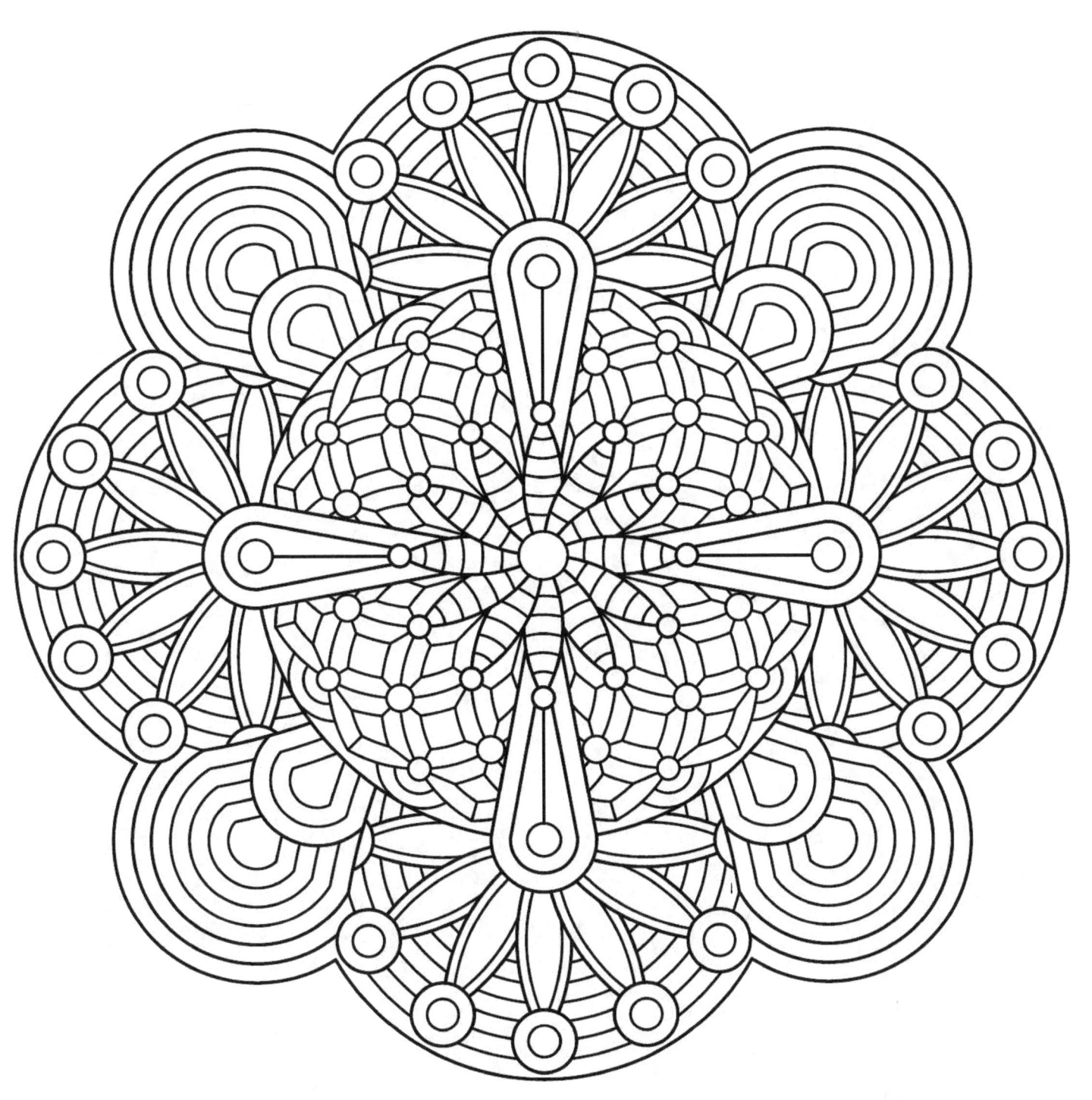

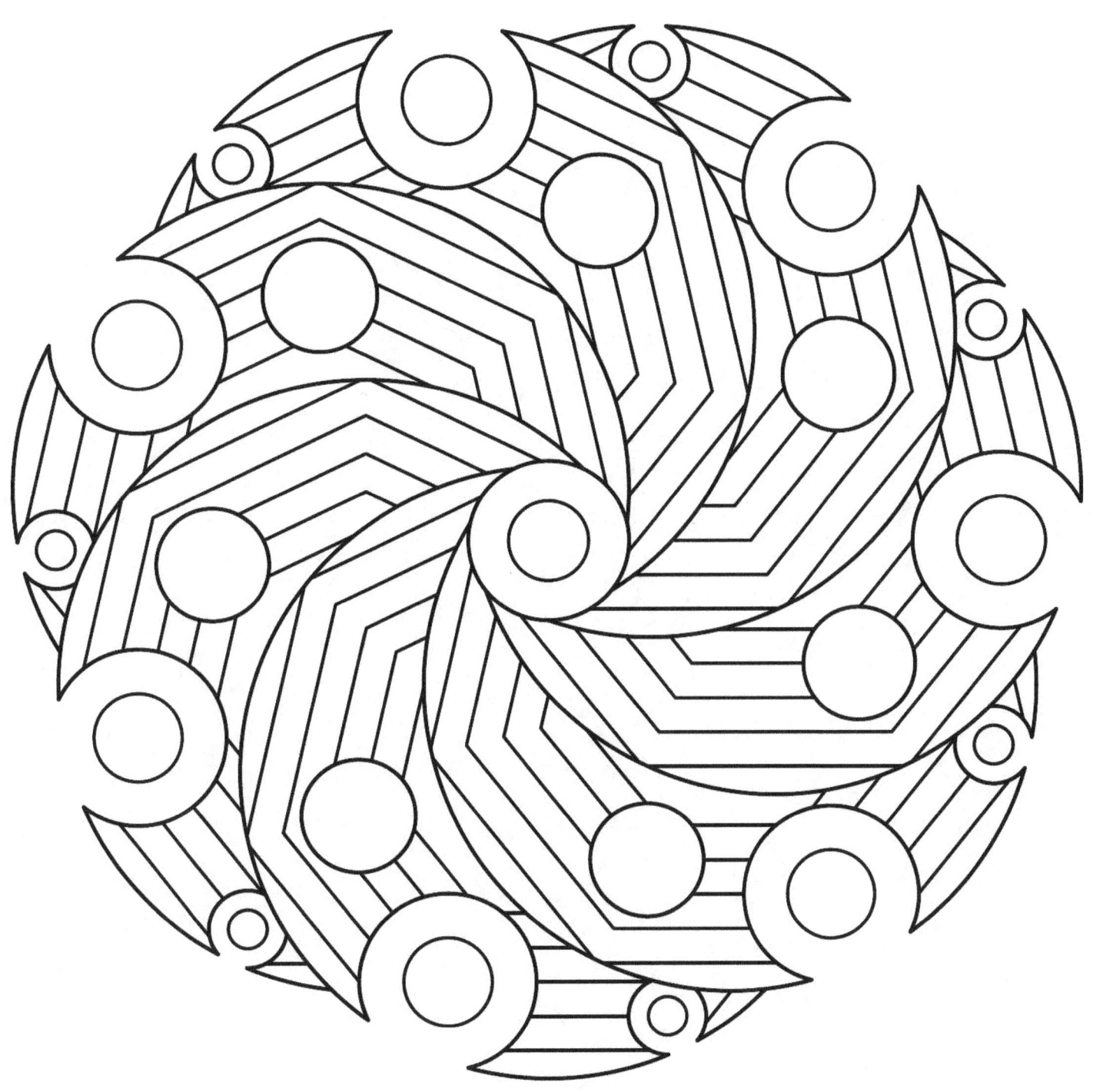

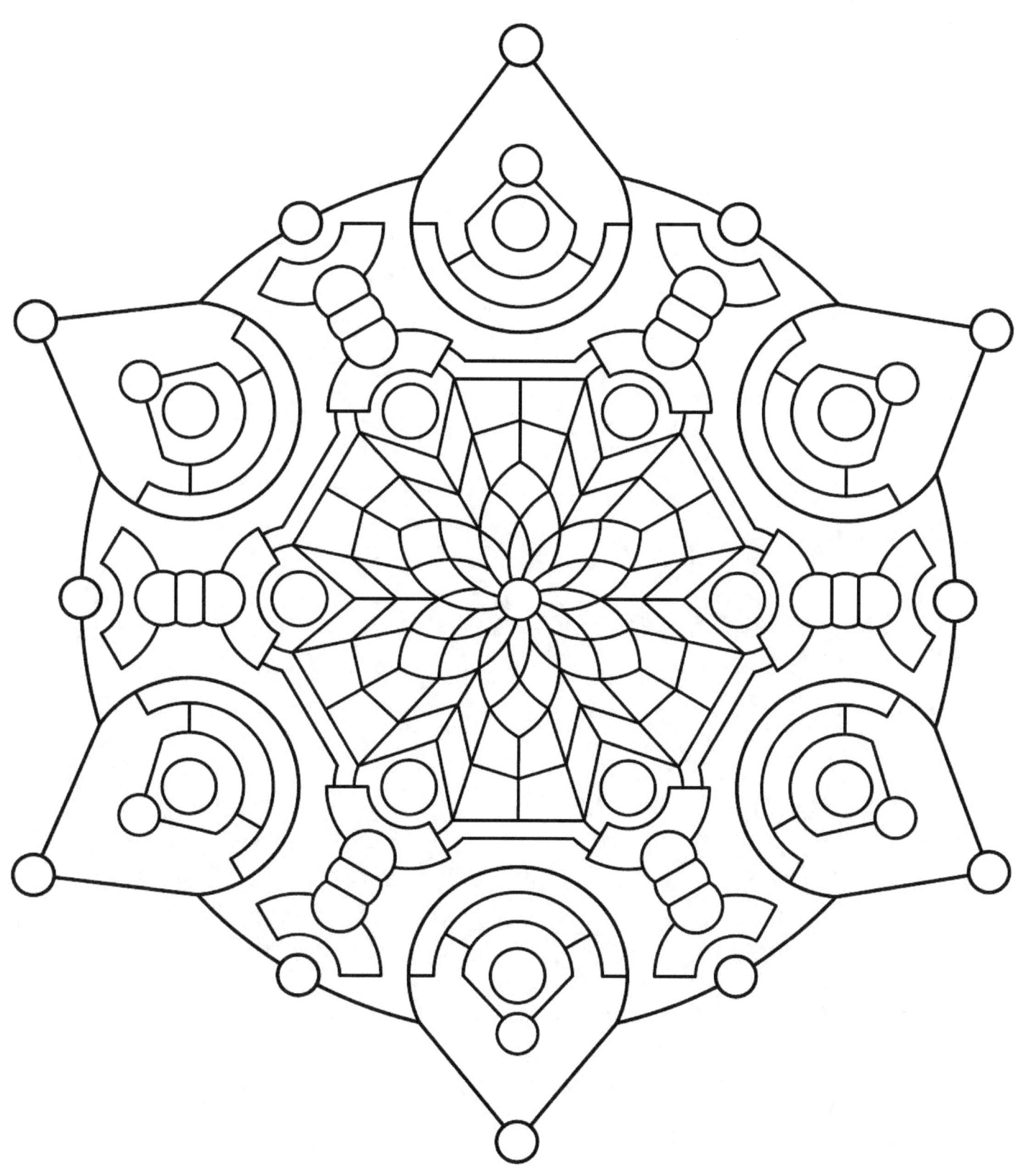

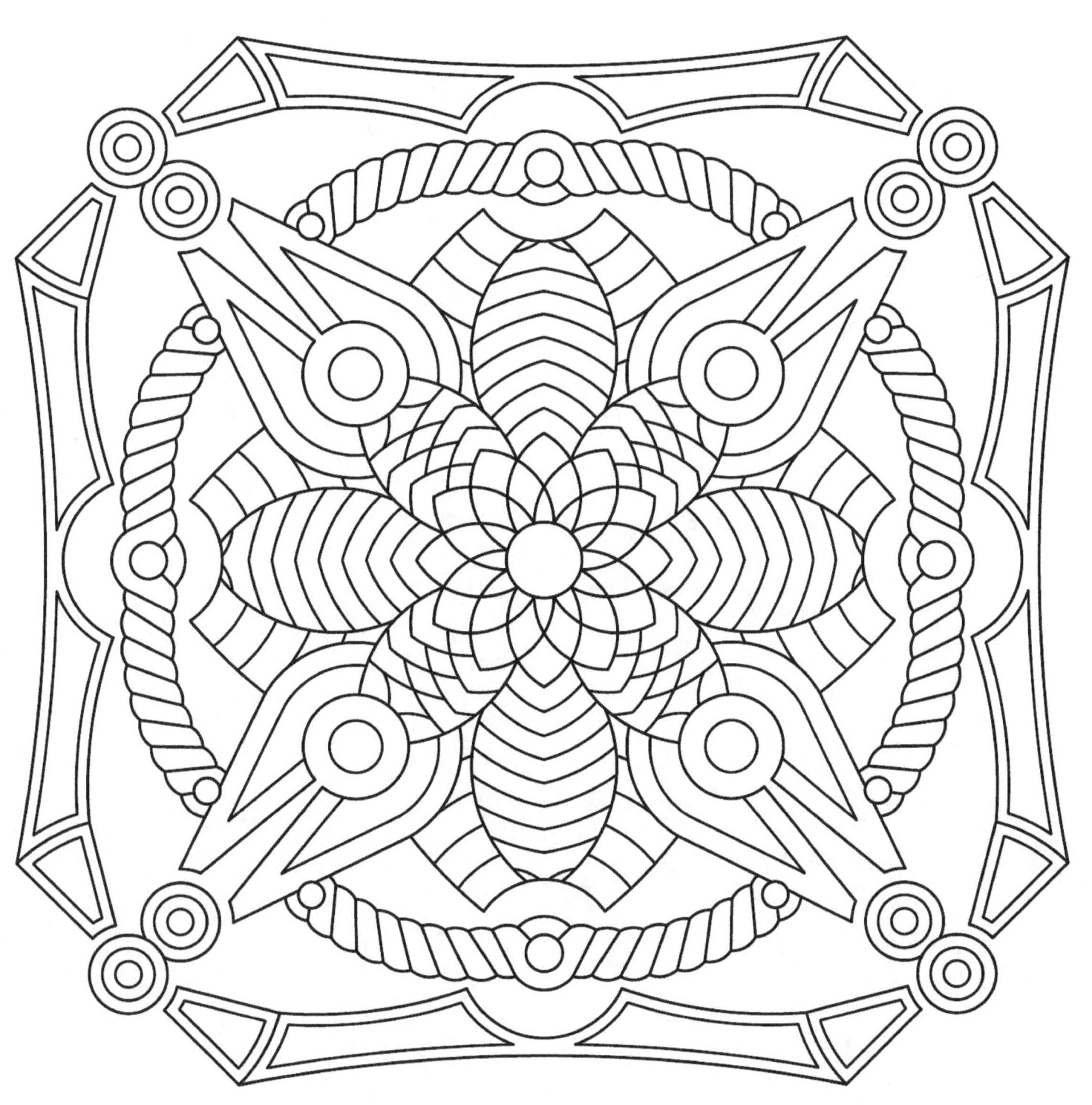

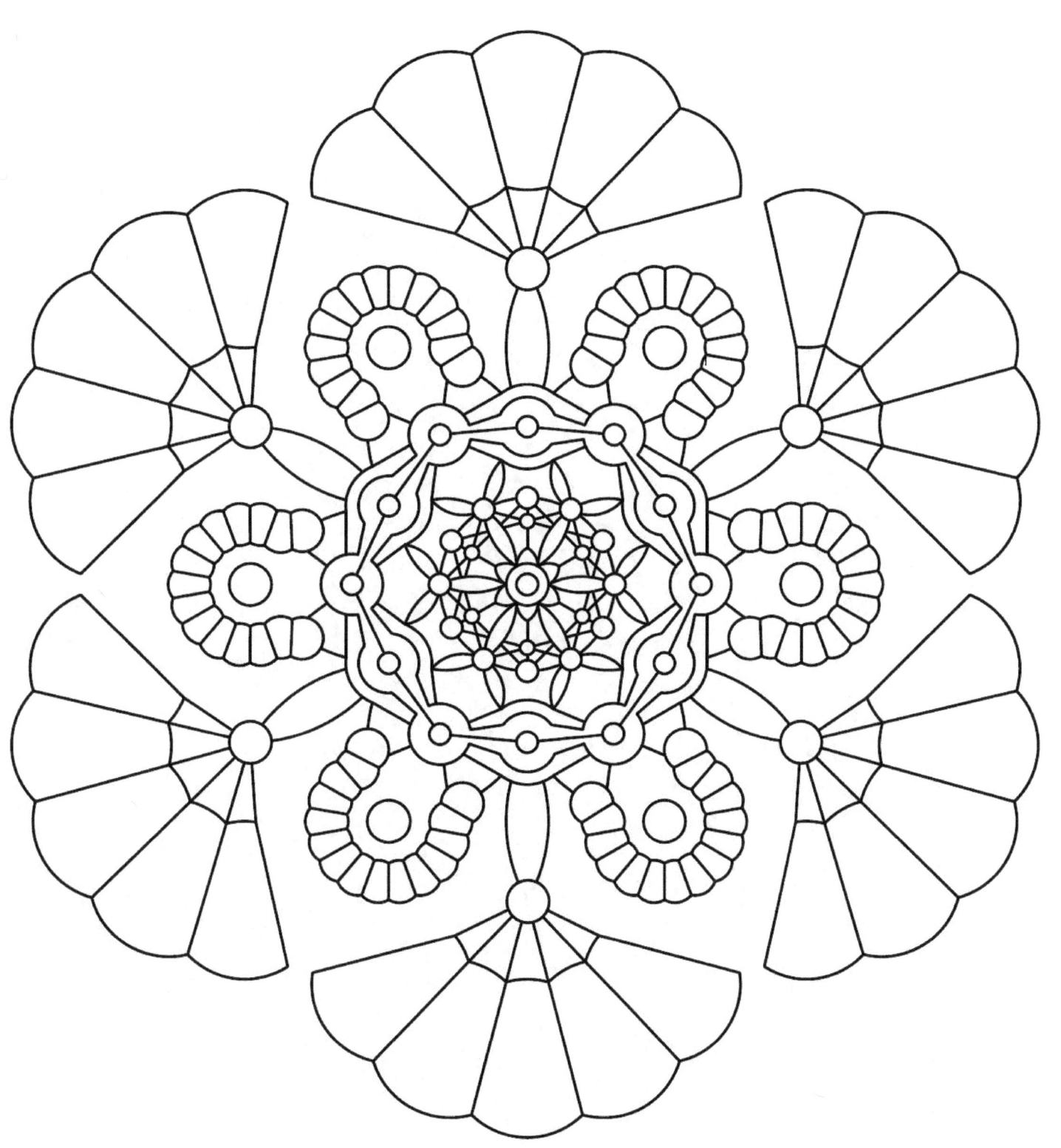

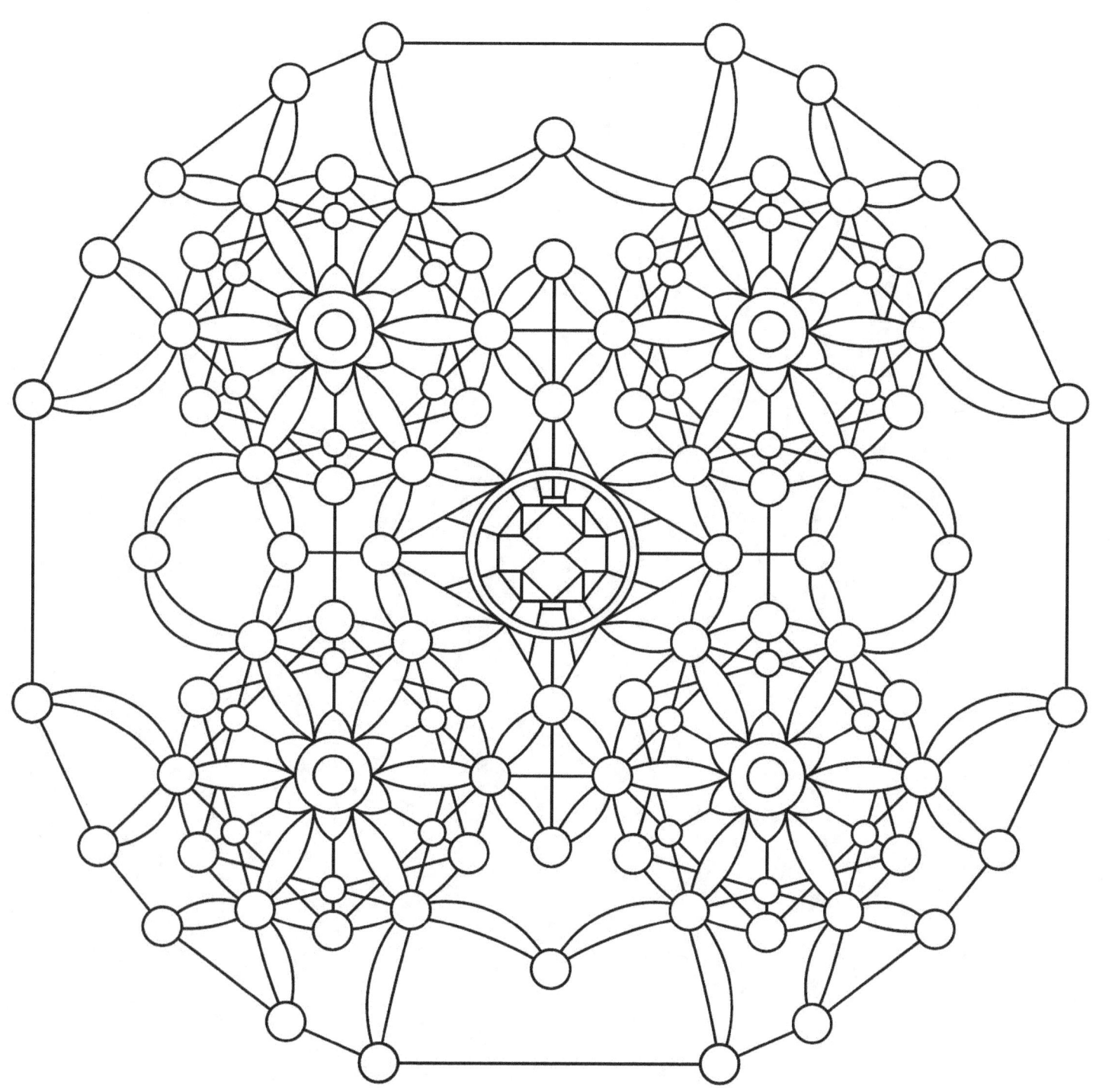

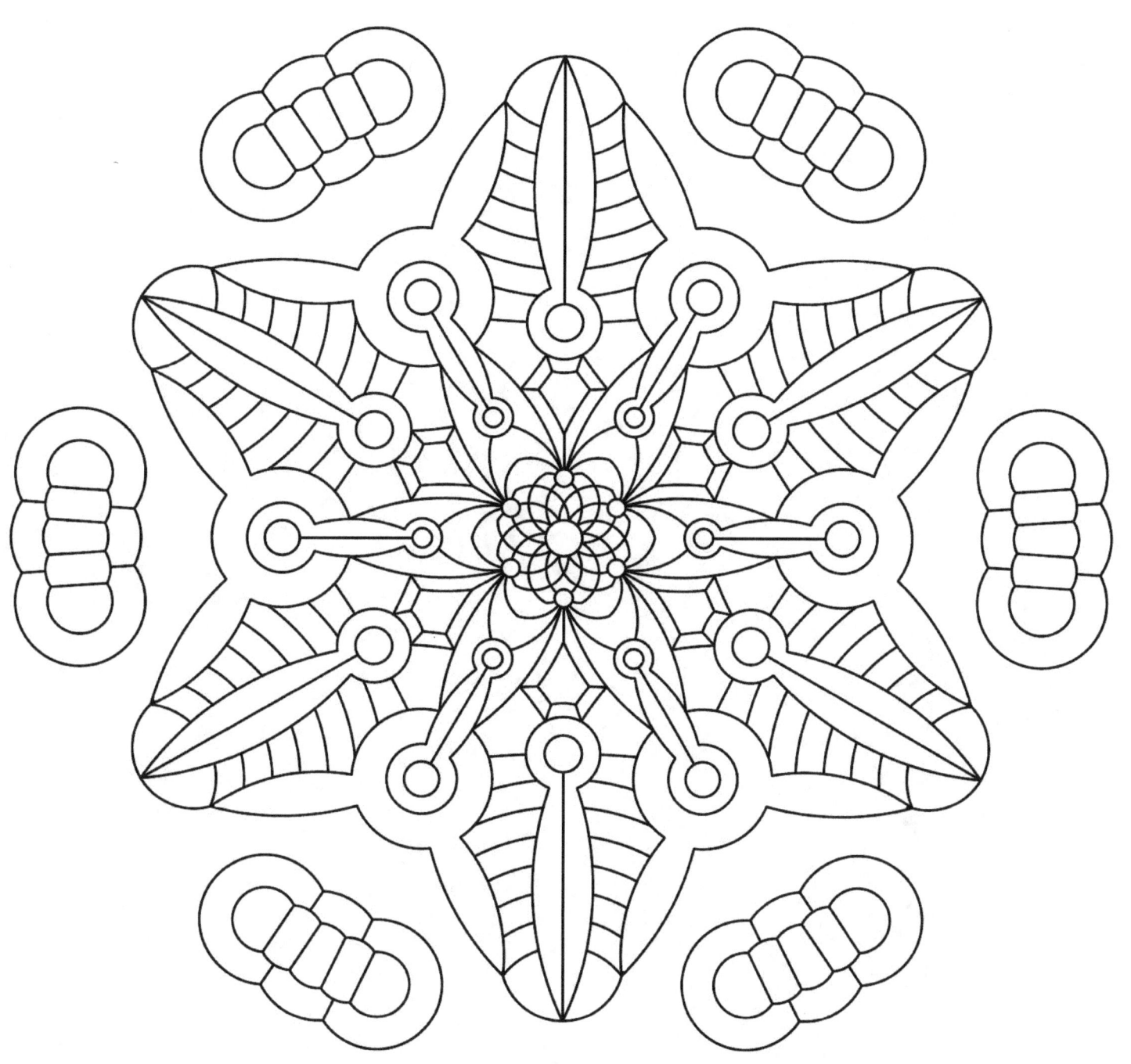

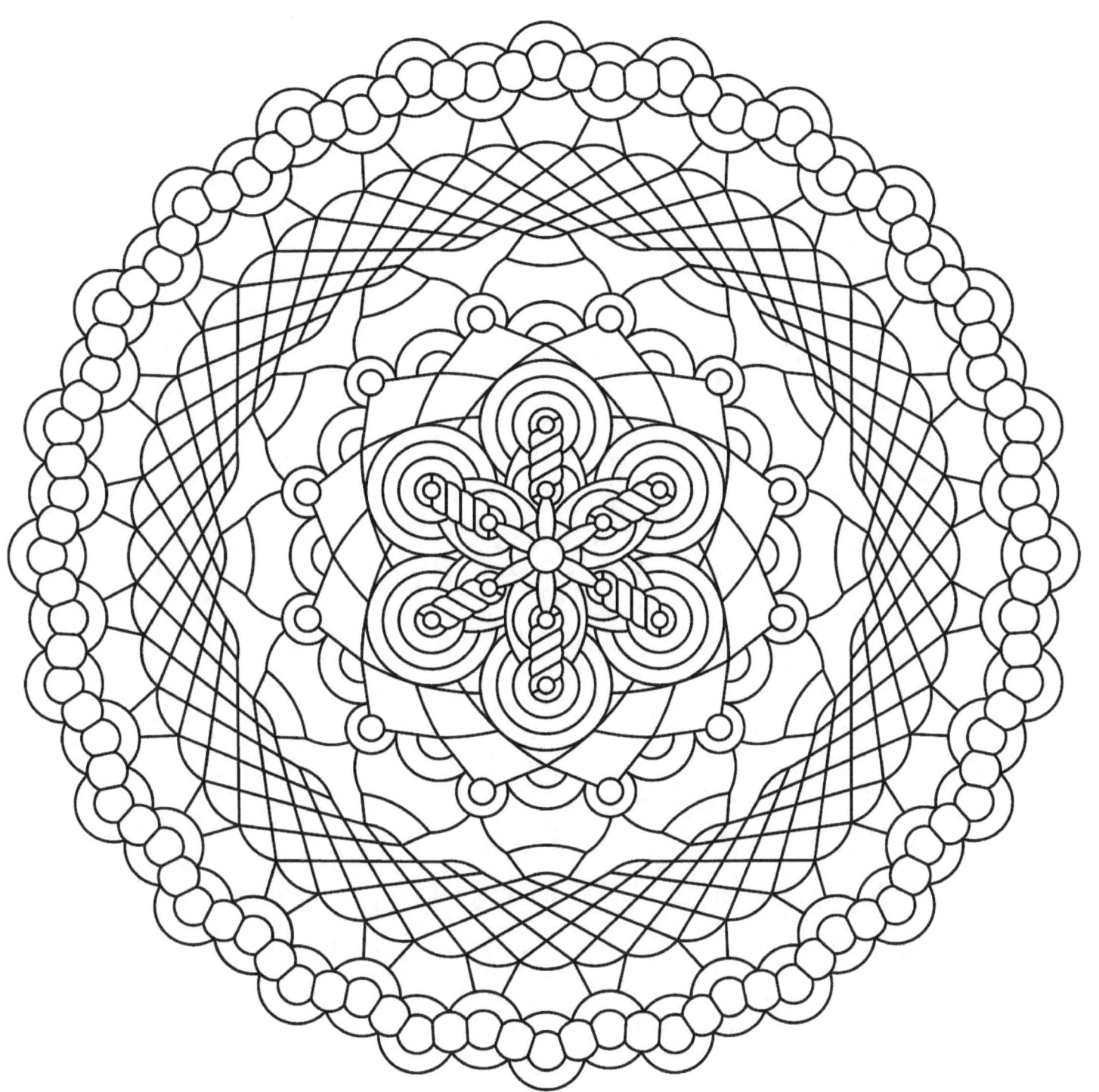

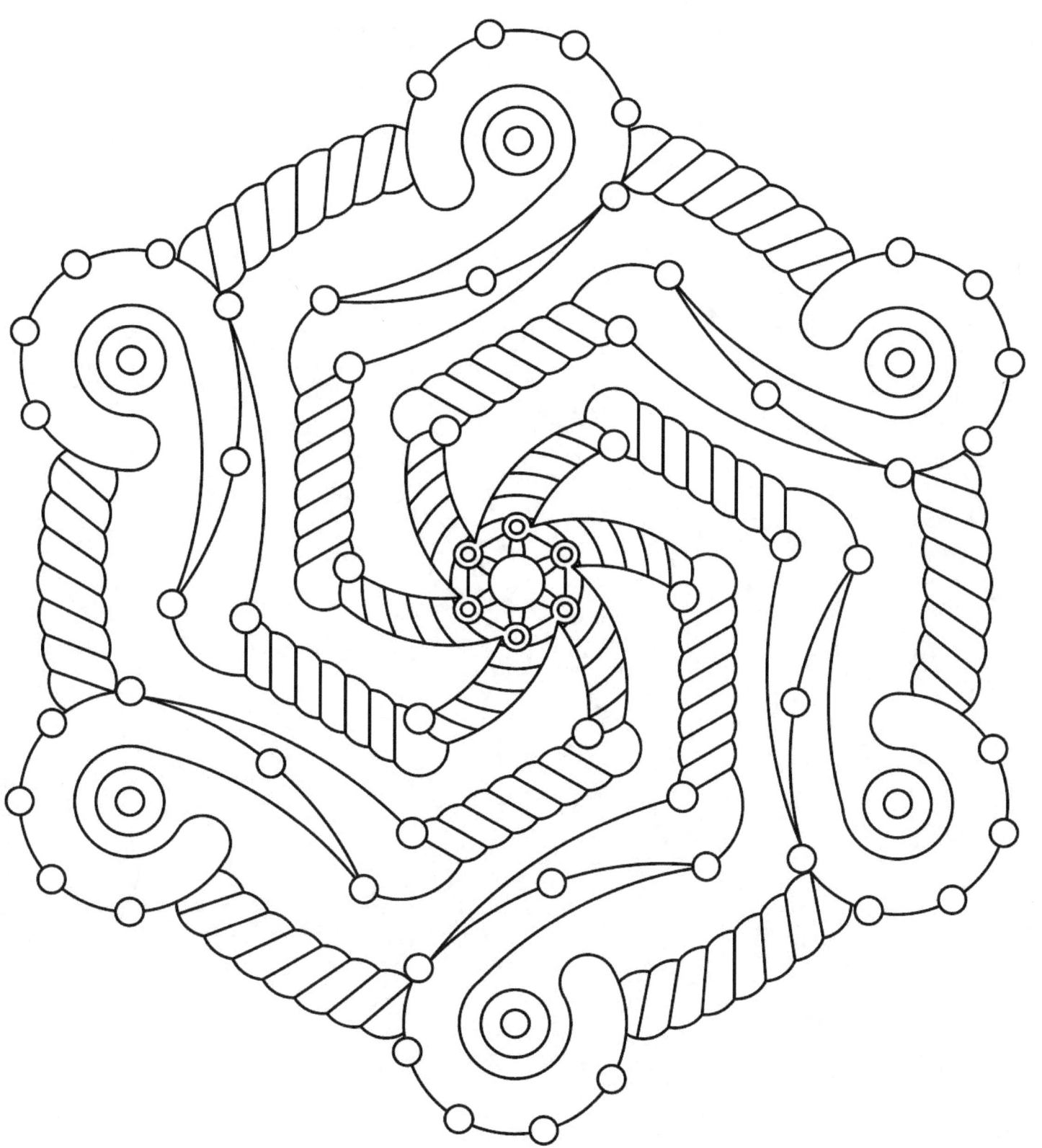

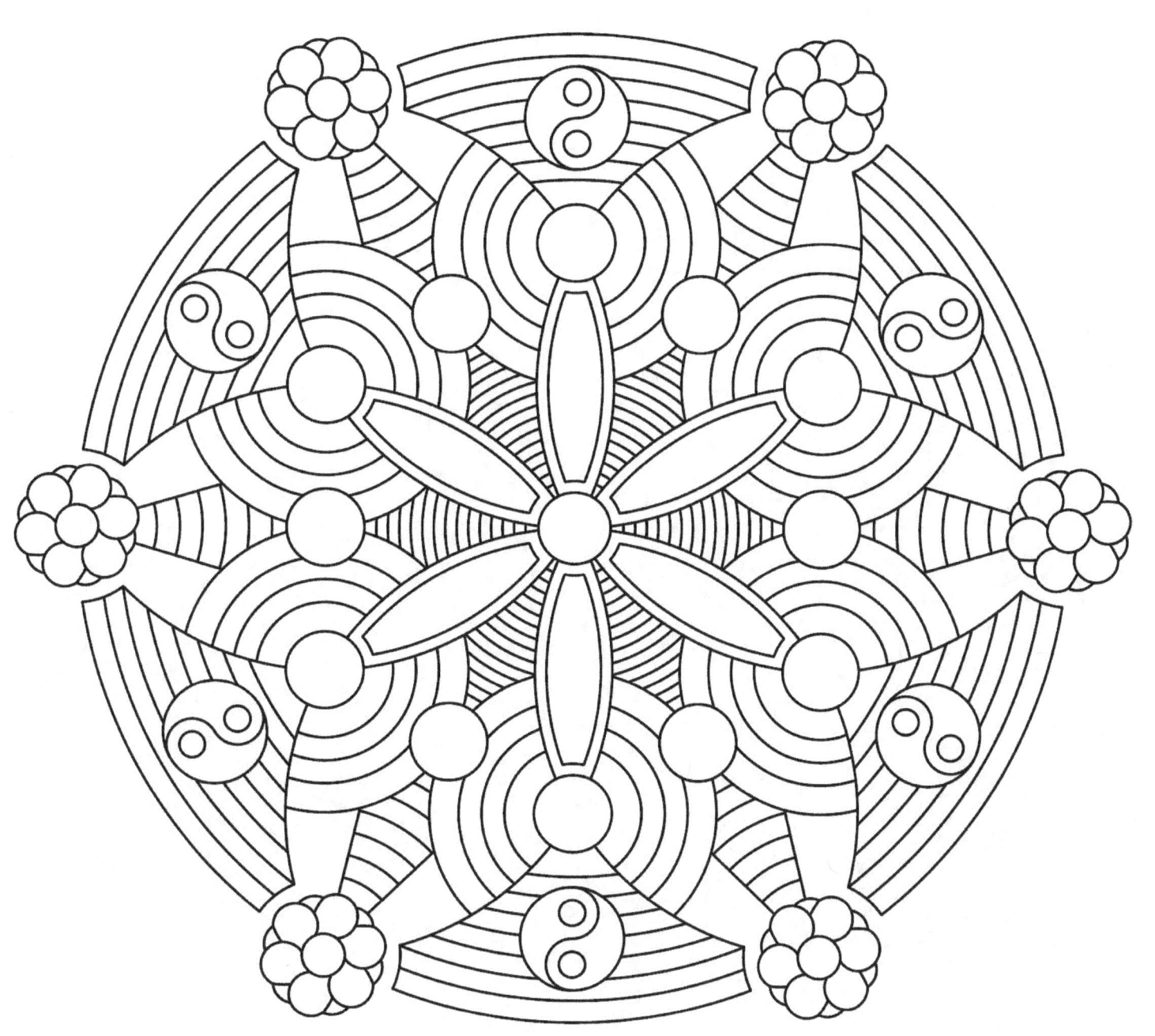

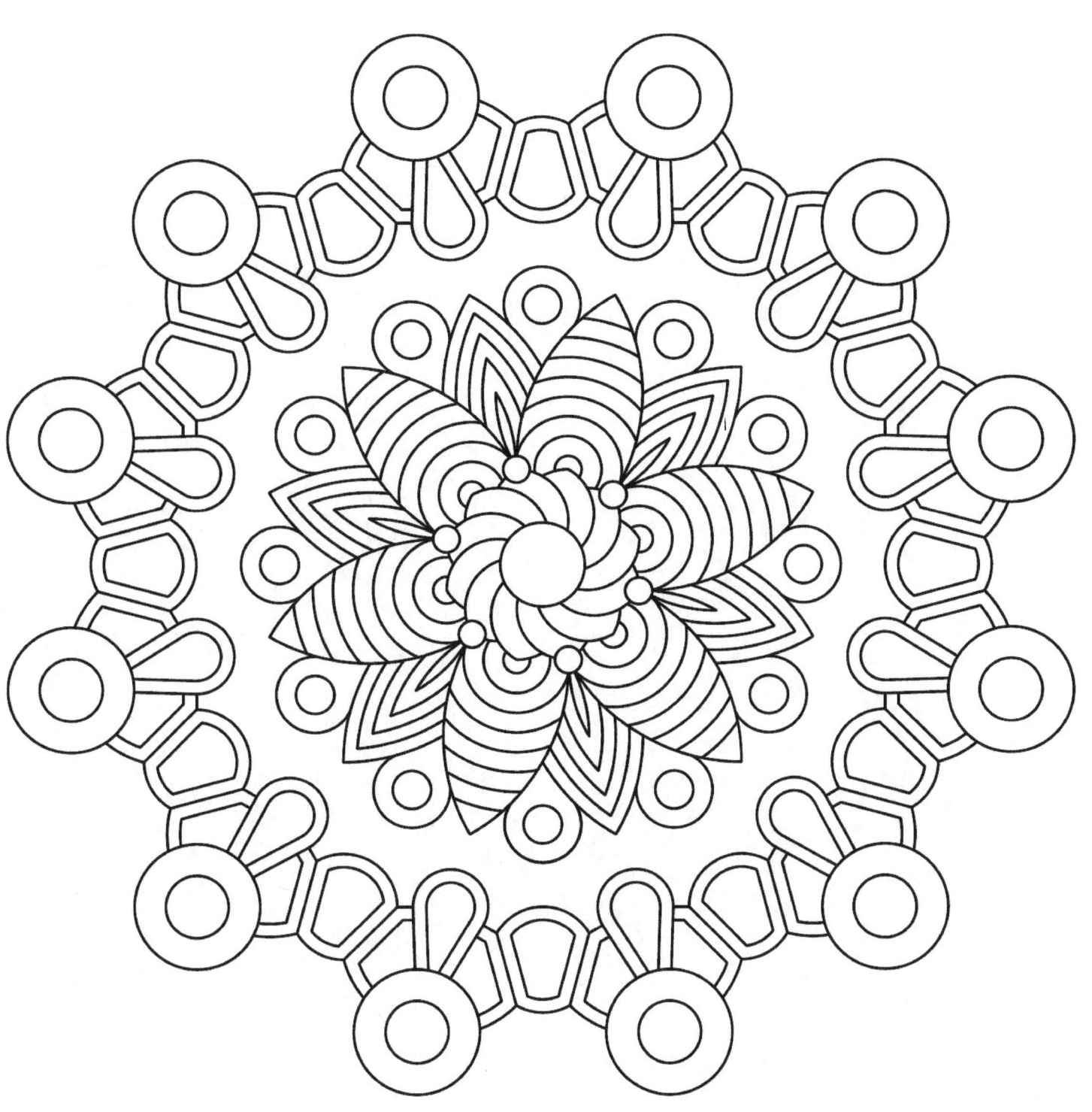

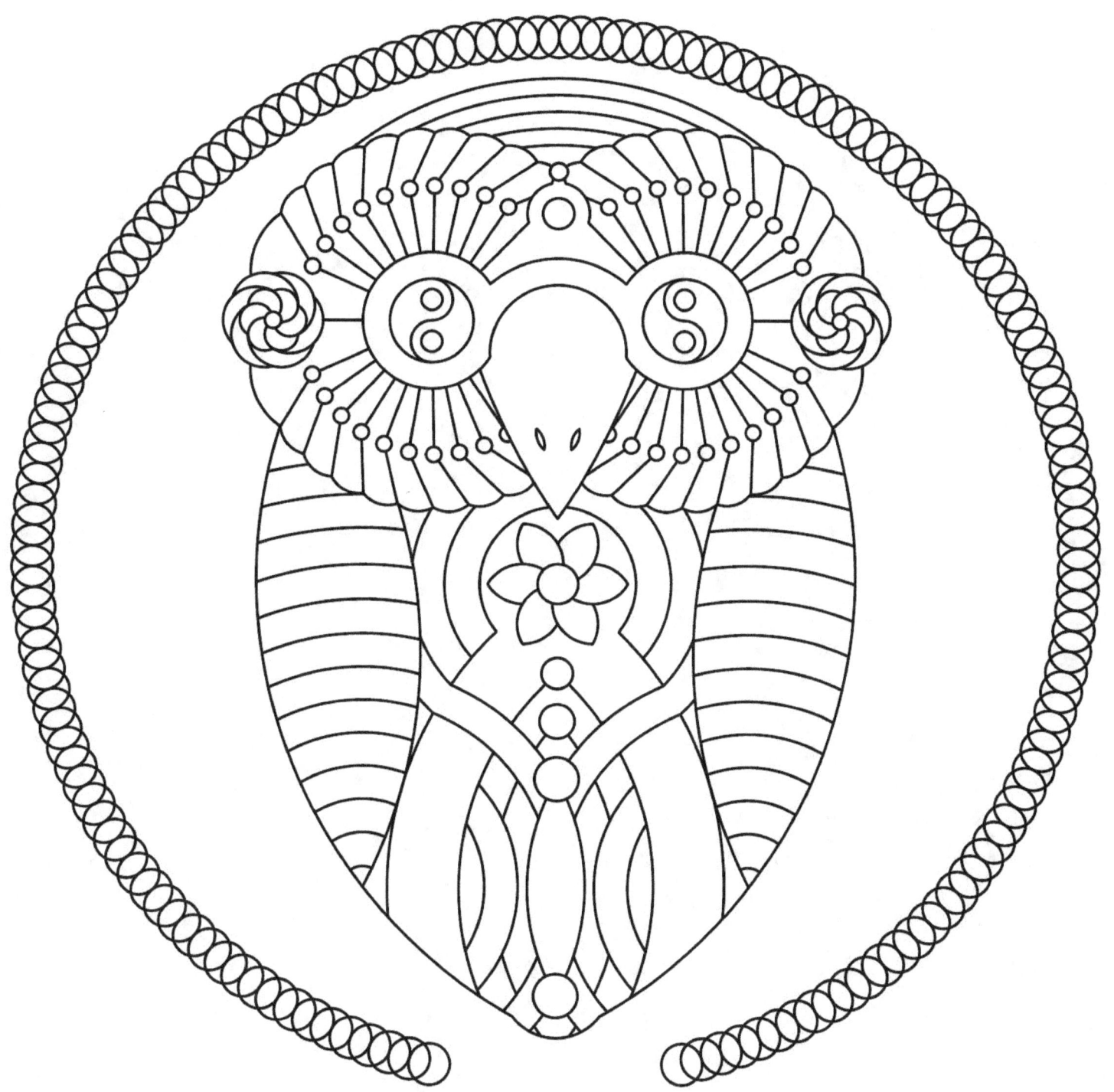

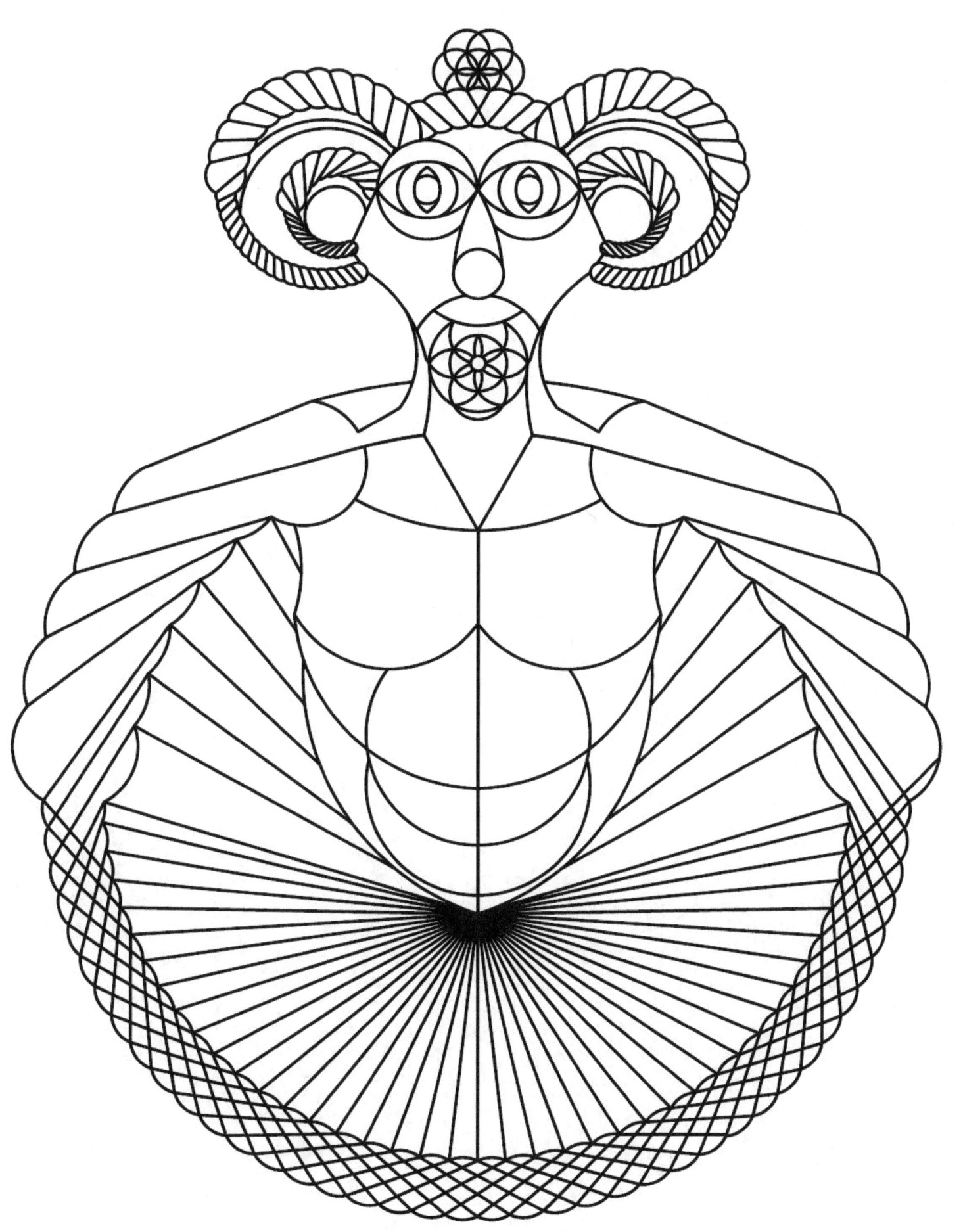

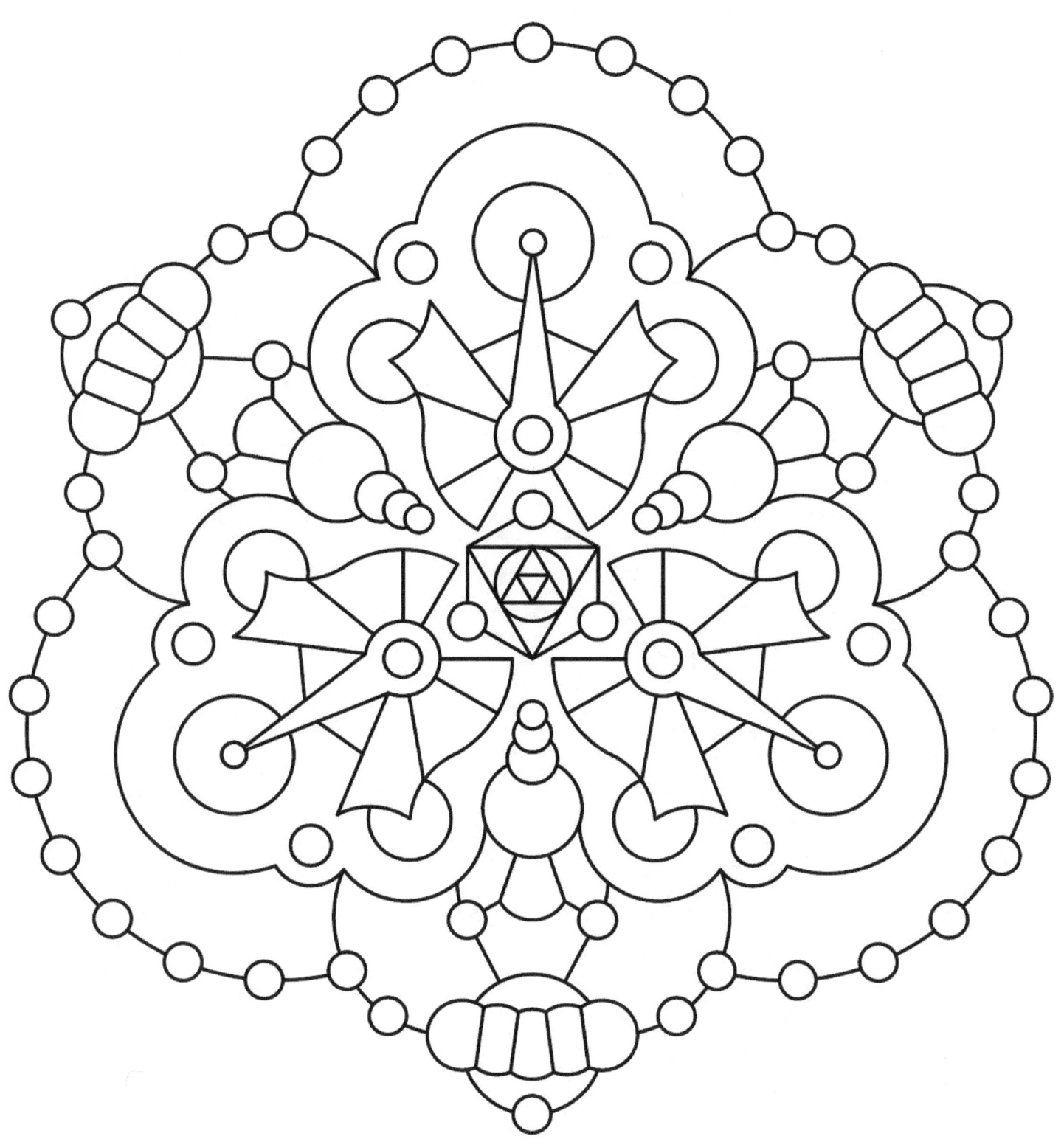

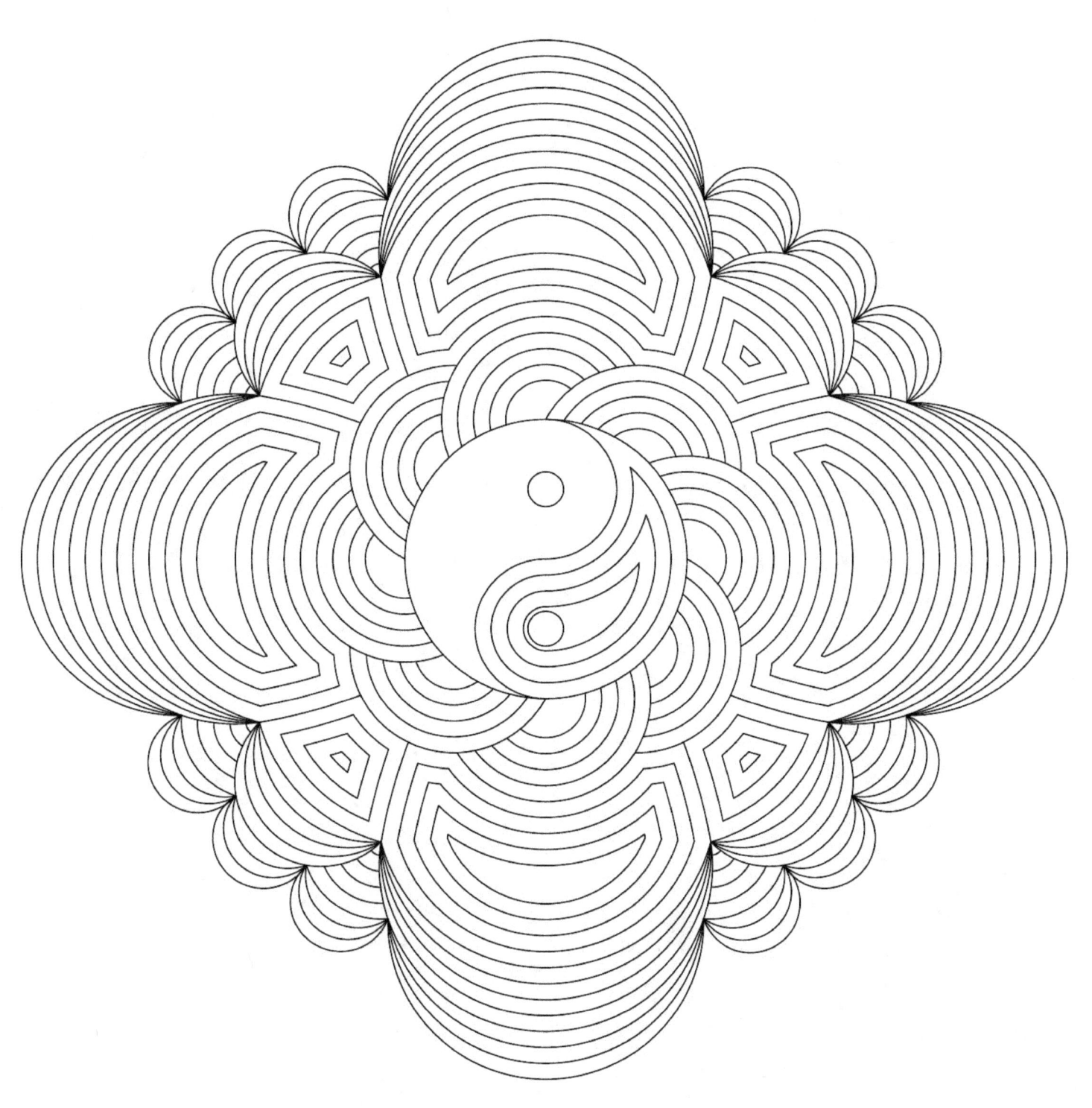

www.ingramcontent.com/pod-product-compliance
Lightning Source LLC
Chambersburg PA
CBHW081427220526
45466CB00008B/2291